Youth in Britain since 1945

Making Contemporary Britain Series

General Editor: Anthony Seldon
Consultant Editor: Peter Hennessy

Published

Northern Ireland since 1968
Paul Arthur and Keith Jeffery

The Prime Minister since 1945
James Barber

British General Elections since 1945
David Butler

The British Economy since 1945
Alec Cairncross

Britain and the Suez Crisis★
David Carlton

Town Planning in Britain since 1900
Gordon Cherry

The End of the British Empire
John Darwin

Religion in Britain since 1945
Grace Davie

British Defence since 1945
Michael Dockrill

British Politics since 1945
Peter Dorey

Britain and the Falklands War★
Lawrence Freedman

Britain and European Integration since 1945
Stephen George

British Social Policy since 1945
Howard Glennerster

Judicial Politics since 1920:
A Chronicle★
John Griffith

Consensus Politics from Attlee to Major
Dennis Kavanagh and Peter Morris

The Politics of Immigration
Zig Layton-Henry

Women in Britain since 1945★
Jane Lewis

Britain and the Korean War★
Callum Macdonald

Culture in Britain since 1945
Arthur Marwick

Crime and Criminal Justice since 1945★
Terence Morris

Electoral Change since 1945
Pippa Norris

Youth in Britain since 1945
Bill Osgerby

The British Press and Broadcasting since 1945
Colin Seymour-Ure

The Labour Party since 1945
Eric Shaw

Third Party Politics since 1945
John Stevenson

The Trade Union Question in British Politics
Robert Taylor

The Civil Service since 1945
Kevin Theakston

British Science and Politics since 1945*
Thomas Wilkie

British Public Opinion
Robert M. Worcester

Local Government since 1945
Ken Young and Nirmala Rao

* Indicates title now out of print.

The series *Making Contemporary Britain* is essential reading for students, as well as providing masterly overviews for the general reader. Each book in the series puts the central themes and problems of the specific topic into clear focus. The studies are written by leading authorities in their field, who integrate the latest research into the text but at the same time present the material in a clear, ordered fashion which can be read with value by those with no prior knowledge of the subject.

THE INSTITUTE OF CONTEMPORARY BRITISH HISTORY

Senate House
Malet Street
London WC1H 7HU

Managing Editor: Paul Nicholson

Youth in Britain since 1945

Bill Osgerby

BLACKWELL
Publishers

First published 1998

Blackwell Publishers Ltd
108 Cowley Road
Oxford OX4 1JF
UK

Blackwell Publishers Inc.
350 Main Street
Malden, Massachusetts 02148
USA

British Library Cataloguing in Publication Data

A CIP catalogue record for this book is available from the British Library.

Library of Congress Cataloging-in-Publication Data

Osgerby, Bill.
    Youth in Britain since 1945 / Bill Osgerby.
        p.   cm. – (Making contemporary Britain)
    Includes bibliographical references and index.
    ISBN 0–631–19476–2. – ISBN 0–631–19477–0
    1. Youth – Great Britain.   2. Great Britain – Social
conditions – 1945–   I. Title.   II. Series.
HQ799.G7083   1997   97–17855
305.235'0941 – dc21   CIP

Typeset in 10 on 12pt Ehrhardt
by Grahame & Grahame Editorial, Brighton
Printed and bound in Great Britain by MPG Books Ltd, Bodmin, Cornwall

This book is printed on acid-free paper

Contents

Figures

Tables

General Editor's Preface

The Institute of Contemporary British History's series *Making Contemporary Britain* is aimed directly at students and at others interested in learning more about topics in post-war British history. In the series, authors are less attempting to break new ground than presenting clear and balanced overviews of the state of knowledge on each of the topics.

The ICBH was founded in October 1986 with the objective of promoting the study of British history since 1945 at every level. To that end, it publishes books and a quarterly journal, *Contemporary Record*; it organizes seminars and conferences for school students, undergraduates, researchers and teachers of post-war history; and it runs a number of research programmes and other activities.

A central theme of the ICBH's work is that post-war history is too often neglected in British schools, institutes of higher education and beyond. The ICBH acknowledges the validity of the arguments against the study of recent history, notably the problems of bias, of overly subjective teaching and writing, and the difficulties of perspective. But it believes that the values of studying post-war history outweigh the drawbacks, and that the health and future of liberal democracy require that its citizens know more about the most recent past of their country than the limited knowledge possessed by British citizens, young and old, today. Indeed the ICBH believes that the dangers of political indoctrination are higher where the young are *not* informed of the recent past.

This volume by Bill Osgerby examines a subject, youth and youth culture, which has been a major omission in the series to date. The behaviour and identity of youth in post-war Britain, and the way they have been courted, or not, by changing governments, commercial organizations, the legal system, the media and cultural world, is a vast topic, of essential importance to an understanding of post-war Britain. The author presents the subject with admirable clarity, and his book deserves a wide audience.

Anthony Seldon

Preface and Acknowledgements

This book aims to serve as an introduction to the key transformations that have taken place in the lives of British youngsters since the Second World War. Specifically, it examines post-war changes in the social and cultural practices of young people, the way these changes have been interpreted and responded to by various social institutions and their significance within the broader development of British society. As such it is hoped that the book will be useful not only to readers interested in the history of British youth, but also to those with a more general interest in the social, economic and political development of contemporary Britain. The breadth of the book's scope and subject matter means that it is necessarily selective, though the notes and bibliography are intended to guide readers to texts that explore specific areas in more detail and depth. The book's structure is loosely chronological, though certain themes (for example the experience of young women, issues of race and the relationship between young people and the agencies of social control) warrant specific consideration and have been accorded chapters of their own.

Youth and youth culture are subjects that have come to straddle a range of academic disciplines. Therefore, although this book is essentially historical in orientation, it also draws on a range of work generated within the disciplines of sociology, cultural studies and women's studies. However, specialized 'jargon' is kept to a minimum and the more theoretical elements of the text are, I hope, elaborated with clarity and concision.

Space dictates that I am unable to thank individually all the friends and colleagues who gave me their kind help and support in the course of writing this book. However, a number of people deserve particular acknowledgement and gratitude. I am especially indebted to Tessa Harvey at Blackwell for all her patience and encouragement over the many months of writing and I hope the final results were worth waiting for. Although I must bear responsibility for any flaws and omissions this book may contain, I would also like to thank Andy Medhurst for reading through an earlier draft of the text – his consummate editorial skill and cogent guidance were invaluable, together with his encyclopaedic knowledge of British popular culture. The expert librarianship of Helen Davies of the West Midlands Probation Service was a blessing, while at Southampton Institute I am fortunate in having so many colleagues ready to proffer encouragement and helpful suggestions. In particular Pete Stanfield, Esther Sonnet and Chris Bullar were always on hand with stimulating ideas and enjoyable discussion. I am also grateful for the various contributions made by George Osgerby, Sean Gregory, Dave Quinn, John McIvor and Doug Colvin. Above all I owe special thanks to Liz Davies for her indefatigable support while the book was being written and completed.

The author and publishers gratefully acknowledge the following for permission to reproduce copyright material:

Cadbury Ltd for Figure 4.3; Freedom to Party Campaign for Figure 12.1; Imperial Tobacco Ltd for Figure 4.2; MGN Ltd for Figure 13.1; *Punch* Library and Archive for Figures 4.1 and 9.1 from *Punch*, 30 September 1953 and 10 September 1958.

Every effort has been made to trace copyright holders. The publishers apologize for any errors or omissions in the above list and would be grateful to be notified of any corrections that should be incorporated in the next edition or reprint of this book.

Bill Osgerby

1 Introduction: 'All the Young Dudes'

From the flick-knife wielding Teddy boy of the early fifties to the 'luv'd-up' raver of the early nineties, youth has been subject to more public scrutiny than any other social group since 1945. Young people's social, economic and cultural life has been the focus for a continuous stream of media investigations, government reports and academic literature. The source of this fascination lies in the way young people and their cultures have become symbolic of the scale and dynamics of wider patterns of social change. Throughout the post-war decades representations of youth and debates about young people have possessed a powerful metaphorical dimension. The youth debate has come to function as an important ideological vehicle that encapsulates more general hopes and fears about the state of the nation. As such, a survey of British youth and youth culture since 1945 is invaluable. It tells us not only about the social and economic experiences of young people, but also provides us with an insight into the broader climate of social and political opinion at specific historical moments.

The concept of youth is, itself, more problematic than might initially be supposed. Rather than being an immutably fixed and timeless stage in human physical and psychological development, the distinguishing features of youth as an identifiable phase in the life course have varied across time and between different cultures. Certainly, the physical transformations associated with puberty represent a tangible moment of transition from childhood to mature adulthood. Yet even these physical changes have been subject to social, economic and cultural influences. Since the Industrial Revolution, for example, improvements in diet and living conditions have lowered by several years the average age for the beginning of puberty among British youngsters. Historical context has wielded an even greater influence on the social characteristics ascribed to those who fall within the age category labelled 'youth'. According to John Gillis (1974), for example, modern concepts of youth only began to take shape during the late nineteenth century, the outcome of a growing apprehension among legislators and reformers that the teenage years were a life stage distinguished by social and psychological vulnerability. As a consequence there followed a torrent of protective legislation which, coupled with a new range of specialized welfare bodies and employment practices, marked out youth as an identifiably distinct social group associated with particular needs and social problems. Rather than an objective physiological stage in the process of human development, therefore, the concept of 'youth' is a social construct – a subjective set of cultural characteristics shaped by the social, economic and political conditions of a particular historical context.[1]

It may be inevitable that conceptions of 'youth' and chronological age will prominently figure in attempts to make sense of social change. At instances of profound transformation, however, youth's metaphorical capacity has become powerfully extended. The decades that followed 1945 marked just such a period – the 'youth question' functioning as a medium through which fundamental shifts in social boundaries and cultural relationships were explored, made sense of and interpreted.[2] The principal intentions of this book, therefore, are twofold. Firstly, it seeks to chart the major changes that have taken place in the lives and cultures of British youngsters since the Second World War. Secondly, and equally importantly, it aims to outline the key shifts in the ways that youth has been socially, economically and politically represented and responded to during the post-war period.

The book begins with a consideration of the development of discernible youth cultures in the century before 1939, the discussion then moving to the impact of the Second World War on youngsters' lives and the post-war stereotyping of young people as the embodiment of both the best and the worst facets of social and cultural change. Chapter 3 examines the way in which, after 1945, a range of factors combined to intensify the institutionalization and formalization of youth as a distinct age grade, a process which was augmented by economic trends that increased demand for young people's labour and delivered greater financial power to working youngsters. The next chapter explores the consequences of these changes – the considerable expansion of the commercial youth market and the rise of the 'teenager' as a social construct that epitomized the mythologies of classless affluence that were prominent in British political discourse during the fifties and early sixties. Chapter 5 concentrates on the significant changes that have taken place in the lives of young women during the post-war period, in particular the gradual emergence of more active and assertive versions of feminine identity. This is followed by a survey of developments in subcultural style in the late sixties and the rise of sociological approaches which highlighted social class as a key determinant of the lifestyles and fashions of British youth.

In chapter 7 the focus of analysis switches to middle-class youth and the various bohemian and anti-establishment movements that came to the fore during the 1960s, these developments being placed in the context of the wider transformation of British cultural and political life. The confrontational subcultural styles of the late seventies and early eighties are considered in chapter 8, while chapter 9 examines the history of black youth subcultures and the impact of issues of race and racism on the field of British youth culture. Chapter 10 traces the post-war history of the juvenile justice system and those agencies related to the social control of young people, discussion focusing on the way that a 'reformist' spirit of rehabilitation and welfare was displaced, during the seventies and eighties, by a more punitive set of responses as the post-war political consensus gave way to a more authoritarian form of political state. This is followed by a more detailed consideration of changes in the life experiences of British youngsters during the 1980s, particularly those changes related to the collapse of the youth labour market and the increasing incidence of urban disorder. Chapter 11 concentrates on the important changes in youth culture during the late eighties and early nineties, especially the impact of the 'acid house' and rave phenomena and the rise of the New Age traveller movement – developments which were met by the passage of the 1994 Criminal Justice Act, one of the most repressive pieces of legislation to be introduced by a modern British government. The book concludes with an overview of the social and economic conditions facing young people as Britain enters the new millennium. In particular attention is given to the idea that the forms and styles of contemporary youth culture have become characterized by new, 'post-modern' features of fluidity and hybridity. Consideration is also given to the marked elements of risk and uncertainty that have come to distinguish young people's position in the labour market – a status which stands in stark contrast to the notions of 'affluent youth' that predominated during the fifties and early sixties.

Notes

1   A more detailed discussion of the evolution of modern conceptions of youth in western Europe can be found in Michael Mitteraurer, 1992, *A History of Youth*, Oxford: Blackwell.

2   For further exploration of this 'metaphorical' facet to youth debates see A. C. H. Smith, Elizabeth Immirizi and Trevor Blackwell, 1975, *Paper Voices: The Popular Press and Social Change, 1935–65*, London: Chatto and Windus, p. 242; John Clarke, Stuart Hall, Tony Jefferson and Brian Roberts, 1976, 'Subcultures, cultures and class: a theoretical overview', in Stuart Hall and Tony Jefferson (eds), *Resistance Through Rituals: Youth Subcultures in Post-War Britain*, London: Hutchinson, pp. 9–74; John Davis, 1990, *Youth and the Condition of Britain: Images of Adolescent Conflict*, London: Athlone.

2 'All Shook Up': Continuity and Change in British Youth Culture

Youth Culture before 1945

In the writing of British history it is commonplace to take the Second World War as a watershed, a decisive turning point in the nation's social, economic and political life. Nowhere is this more evident than in the study of British youth, where 1945 often assumes the aspect of a gaping divide between two distinct and contrasting cultural worlds. From reading many accounts it is easy to get the impression that youth culture simply did not exist before the war, that it suddenly and spontaneously materialized in the 1950s amid a wave of rock'n'roll records, coffee bars and brothel-creeper shoes. One historian, for example, writes of the mid-fifties as witnessing a 'youthquake' that encompassed the 'explosive discovery of teenage identity' (Lewis, 1978, p. 118), while another contends that before the 1950s 'there was no such thing as youth' and that young people 'were not different but simply younger versions of their parents' (Cashmore, 1984, pp. 9, 23). Nor are such views entirely without foundation. The post-war era saw a range of developments in labour markets, earning power, cultural provision and marketing which, together, served to accentuate considerably the profile of 'youth' as an identifiable social category. However, consummate breaks in history are rare and claims to the 'novelty' of the post-war British youth experience distort and exaggerate the nature of change. Rather than representing a dramatic break with the past, the youth culture of the fifties and the social responses it elicited are more accurately seen as an extension of phenomena long a feature of British society. A faithful account of British youth culture after 1945, then, demands an appreciation of elements of continuity with earlier historical periods – a recognition of the way in which post-war social and economic trends had been prefigured by developments stretching back as far as the late nineteenth century.

Even in Victorian and Edwardian Britain it is possible to identify, in incipient form, the key facets to the area of social and cultural life that we now label 'youth culture'. From the middle of the nineteenth century, for example, something resembling a youth leisure market had begun to take shape. Generally, this period saw the emergence of a nascent entertainment industry catering for an urban working class whose disposable income and leisure time were gradually being extended. As part of the general development of a commercial leisure market there also arose a range of goods and entertainments geared to the recreation and interests of young people. By the late nineteenth and early twentieth centuries a clearly discernible youth leisure market had appeared, a response to the significant level of disposable income enjoyed by many working youngsters. In 1905, for example, a commentator in Manchester described how a nineteen-year-old, semi-skilled youth employed in an iron foundry could earn a pound a week and, after surrendering twelve shillings to his parents for board, was free to spend the remainder on clothes, gambling and the music halls.[1]

Patterns of youth employment occasioned a marked degree of public concern throughout the late nineteenth century. From the late 1880s policy-makers and social reformers became preoccupied with the propensity of working youngsters to take 'blind alley' jobs as errand boys or casual workers – employment that offered much higher immediate rewards than those available from an indentured apprenticeship, though which held limited long-term career prospects.[2] The 'boy labour' problem, as it became known, was cited as a cause of a plethora of social and economic ills that included adult unemployment, low adult wages and the decline of British economic competitiveness. In particular 'blind alley' employment was blamed as a prime cause of juvenile delinquency. The relatively high earnings available in casual jobs, it was felt, delivered undue economic independence to youngsters whose leisure and cultural preferences were viewed with mounting anxiety. Victorian concerns cohered especially around cheap literature and 'penny dreadfuls', gambling and the music hall – all of which were seen as having a pernicious influence on the young, exposing them to a harmful and 'indecent' atmosphere and offering opportunities for delinquent and immoral behaviour. Here, then, the fears and uncertainties of Victorian Britain anticipated and rehearsed many of the debates and controversies that were to become recurring features of social responses to youth throughout the following century.

Nor were the streets of nineteenth-century Britain immune to 'spectacular' subcultural styles among sections of working youth. Long before the Teddy boy or skinhead attracted the glare of media attention, groups of Victorian and Edwardian youths sporting distinctive styles of dress had attracted similar social comment and official opprobrium. By the end of the nineteenth century wide leather belts, bell-bottomed trousers and a 'donkey-fringe' haircut had become the favoured apparel of many working lads. Known in Manchester as 'scuttlers' or (later) 'ikey lads' and in Birmingham as 'peaky blinders', there were many local variants to the style, yet the subculture seems to have existed in some form in most major cities and towns.[3] For example, in his autobiographical account of a working-class boyhood at the turn of the century, Robert Roberts recalls 'the union shirt, bell-bottomed trousers, the heavy leather belt, picked out in fancy designs with the large steel buckle and the thick, iron-shod clogs' that were the trademark of groups of youngsters who gathered at the end of Salford's terraced streets (Roberts, 1973, p. 155). Contemporary social observers tended to fix their attention on the behaviour and attire of young men, yet there is sufficient evidence to suggest that girls also participated in the subcultural spectacle of the period. Roberts recollects that the scuttler's girlfriend had her own distinctive style – 'clogs and shawl and a skirt with vertical stripes' (1973, p. 155) – while in 1888 the *Oxford Times* entreated 'What would our grandmothers have thought of girls, sixteen or eighteen, parading the fair alone, dressed in jockey-caps . . . imitation open jackets and waistcoats and smoking cigars or cigarettes?' (cited in Thompson, 1975, p. 64).

In the decades after the First World War youngsters' spending power was constricted by the effects of the Depression and, rather than 'blind alley' jobs or irresponsible affluence, it was levels of youth unemployment that perplexed social commentators. Though relatively little research has been undertaken on rates of adolescent unemployment between the wars one contemporary survey estimated that throughout the early thirties unemployment among youths aged between fourteen and seventeen hovered around the 150,000 mark, still standing at about 100,000 towards the end of the decade.[4] More recent research suggests that boys aged between sixteen and seventeen were especially badly affected by unemployment during this period, the rate of unemployment for this group rising from 4.3 per cent in 1925 to 8.3 per cent by 1932 (Garside, 1977, p. 337). In urban areas hardest hit by inter-war unemployment the scale of young people's joblessness came to be seen as a pressing social problem. Youth unemployment was regarded as not simply a cause of social problems such as juvenile crime, but as the source of a more pervasive condition of demoralization among Britain's youngsters. Prompted by these concerns, the inter-war period saw the launch of initiatives such as the King George's Jubilee Trust, founded in 1935 with a brief to advance the physical, mental and spiritual welfare of the younger generation.

However, the traditional view of inter-war Britain as typified by mass unemployment and industrial decay has been modified in recent years.[5] Although heartlands of heavy industry such as South Wales, the North East and central Scotland certainly suffered, areas of the South and the Midlands fared much better, sustained by the growth of 'new' industries such as vehicle manufacture and electrical engineering. In aggregate terms the inter-war years were actually a period of economic growth, the period 1920–37 seeing an average annual growth rate of 3.1 per cent, and for a significant section of the population this meant a marked improvement in real wages and standards of living. For many people, then, access to leisure and amusement was considerably enhanced and the commercial leisure industry, in its embryonic stages before 1914, grew into a vast and diverse sector of the economy between the wars. Moreover, despite the high levels of youth unemployment, the demand for labour generated by the First World War and the cost-cutting encouraged by the Depression meant that throughout the twenties and thirties there always existed significant numbers of working youngsters with a margin of income available for personal consumption. Indeed, during the 1930s there blossomed a youth market for a range of consumer goods and entertainments – in particular the American-style dance music and new dance halls which burgeoned during the period.[6]

With the outbreak of the Second World War youth employment was considerably boosted and the stability of young people's earnings was maintained. Indeed, the growing demand for adolescent labour and the relatively high earnings possible from unskilled work through overtime revived concerns about young people's 'free and easy' attitude to employment and the detrimental influence of 'easy money'. In the early 1940s *The Times* featured a long correspondence on youngsters' 'excessive earnings' and the suggestion of upper limits on youngsters' pay was prompted by press stories of youths earning between £5 and £7 a week. The general feeling was encapsulated in 1942 by a memo sent to the Chairman of Clerkenwell Juvenile Court from a spokesperson for London Hospital. In the writer's opinion unskilled work had 'nothing to offer a boy except the inducement of high wages now. The joy of creative skilled work is lacking. The prospects of beneficial employment after the war are doubtful.'[7] Although the building trade replied to these anxieties by bringing youths' wages under stricter regulation, the general response was one of composure. Empirical investigation showed 'excessive' youth wages to be the exception rather than the norm and the Minister of Labour assured Parliament that the scale of youth earnings did not represent a major problem.

The Second World War also saw trends in young people's sartorial preferences come under scrutiny. Conventional wisdom holds that the 'Edwardian' style favoured by the fifties' Teddy boys was created in 1950 by Savile Row tailors catering for respectable young gentlemen, the fashion subsequently appropriated by working-class youngsters from south London. The Teds' style, however, can be more reasonably understood as a variant of the American-based fashions which had become popular among working youngsters during the 1940s, a look that was inspired by the iconography of the Chicago gangster and the zoot-suit styles imported with the arrival of GIs during the war. These styles were originally associated with the 'spivs', the cockney wide-boys who wheeled and dealed in the black market of the 1940s, but although it was used to denote any kind of 'flashy' petty villain, the term 'spiv' often bore specifically youthful connotations. For example, in 1946 the *News Chronicle* associated 'the spiv' with a particular section of working-class youth, the newspaper contending that 'Spivs, it may be seen, live easy – for a time. Spivs begin being spivs when other boys are joining in activities at their clubs; and they stop being spivs, rather suddenly, when they reach Borstal' (15 December 1946). In the late forties the equation between 'spivs' and a particular kind of working-class adolescent had become more firmly established. Describing the crowd gathered at a London dance hall in 1949, a Mass Observer focused on a group of youngsters of what he termed 'the "Dago" or "Spiv" type', the young men being 'dressed in their own, or rather the American singular style – i.e. cut back collar with large knotted tie; "Boston Slash Back" hair cut; and a "house coat" style of jacket' (Willcock, 1949, p. 49).

Wartime also saw growing anxiety at the apparent increase in levels of juvenile delinquency. Throughout the 1930s statistics had shown a relentless rise in juvenile crime, yet many contemporaries had been cautious in their interpretation of these figures, only too aware that the passage of the 1933 Children and Young Persons Act had formalized key aspects of the juvenile justice system so that many youngsters were coming before the courts when once they might have been dealt with through less formal strategies. The outbreak of war, however, saw a further leap in the number of juvenile convictions and its cause was hotly debated. Evacuation, shelter life, the effects of bombing, the interruption of schooling and high juvenile earnings were all routinely cited as being the root cause of increasing delinquency. Again, however, there is reason to suppose that this rise in rates of juvenile crime was a statistical phenomenon. Anticipated and watched for by expectant social agencies, the rise in rates of delinquency was duly identified – a classic case of a self-fulfilling prophecy. Indeed, after reaching a peak in 1941 the number of convictions of young offenders began to decline significantly as police policy shifted away from prosecutions to a greater use of cautioning.[8]

Youth in the Aftermath of War

Peacetime saw a renewed increase in the indices of juvenile crime, once again attended by apprehensions that society was witnessing a quantum leap in the scale of delinquency. Within both popular opinion and academic enquiry there arose the widely held belief that the destruction of the war, the absence of fathers and the long working hours of mothers had all contributed to a breakdown in processes of socialization, 'war babies' growing up to be post-war delinquents. Among the leading exponents of this perspective stood the writer and journalist T. R. Fyvel who, through a number of articles and his study *The Insecure Offenders*, helped popularize the notion that post-war increases in juvenile crime were, at least partly, 'the expression of a particularly disturbed generation, a delayed effect of the war' (Fyvel, 1963, p. 51). From this perspective juvenile delinquency was regarded as endemic to the post-war milieu, Fyvel going so far as to talk of a 'Teddy-boy international', the war having disrupted the lives of young people around the globe. His views were echoed by many journalists and academics who were quick to draw parallels between the behaviour of British youths and that of their peers abroad. *Picture Post*, for example, explained to its readers that 'Russia has her "Teddy boy" problem too', the periodical quoting Soviet reports of youngsters known as *Bikiniarz* who had adopted western styles of dress in their rebellion against the discipline of the school and the workplace (12 June 1956). *The Times*, meanwhile, reported on the *Tayozoku* youths of Japan who could be seen sporting 'a sort of shaggy crew-cut, sunglasses, aloha shirts, stovepipe trousers, drinking whisky, brawling, rough-housing and love-making with equally youthful and abandoned young women' (12 September 1956).

In retrospect the post-war rise in recorded levels of juvenile crime can be seen as largely the outcome of changes in the scope and organization of law enforcement and the greater formalization of police procedures.[9] During the late forties and fifties, however, the notion that the social disruptions of wartime had generated an unprecedented wave of juvenile delinquency was widely held, the violent young criminal becoming a stock figure in the popular culture of the period. For example, *Brighton Rock*, Graham Greene's 1938 novel based on the inter-war exploits of the race-track underworld, was released as a film in 1947 with Richard Attenborough taking the role of Pinky, the murderous young leader of a racetrack gang. In a similar vein 1949 saw Dirk Bogarde feature as a reck-less young killer in *The Blue Lamp* (dir. Basil Dearden), the film's sombre-toned voice-over warning audiences of a young generation who were showing 'the effects of a childhood spent in a home broken and demoralized by war':

> These restless and ill-adjusted youngsters have produced a type of delinquent which is partly responsible for the post-war increase in crime. Some are content with pilfering and petty theft. Others, with more bravado, graduate to serious offences. Youths with brain enough to plan and organize criminal adventures and yet who lack the code, experience and self-discipline of the professional thief – which sets them as a class apart. All the more dangerous because of their immaturity.

These popular representations of a young generation of unparalleled criminality found empirical support in research conducted for the Home Office by Leslie Wilkins and published as *Delinquent Generations* in 1960. Juggling with reams of statistics Wilkins claimed that children born between 1935 and 1942 were more prone to delinquency than those born in any other seven-year period and, he argued, the highest delinquency rates were to be found among those who had been aged between four and five years old during the war.[10] Wilkins, however, judged that wartime conditions alone could not account for subsequent rises in levels of juvenile crime. In addition to the destabilizing effects of the war Wilkins also cited the recent stylistic adaptations of the young as an important contributory factor, arguing that 'One of the most disturbing features of the pattern of post-war criminal statistics is the recent crime-wave among young adult males between seventeen and twenty-one years of age. The crime wave among young males has been associated with certain forms of dress and other social phenomena' (Wilkins, 1960, p. 9).

Nor was Wilkins alone in his speculation. Throughout the post-war period the new fashions of the young were a recurring theme in attempts to understand the apparent upsurge of juvenile crime. In the early 1950s the association of particular styles of dress with what was perceived to be a 'new wave' of vicious delinquency crystallized around two notorious murder cases. The first, in 1952, saw the controversial conviction and subsequent execution of nineteen-year-old Derek Bentley for the shooting of a police officer in Croydon. The second, in 1953, saw twenty-year-old Michael Davies convicted and sentenced to death (later commuted to life imprisonment) for the stabbing of a youth on Clapham Common.[11] In both cases the dress of the young defendants became symbolically significant. The press drew attention to their 'flashy', 'American-style' clothes and demeanour, the two accused being presented as the embodiment of a dissipation of traditional culture and values which was judged to be a growing feature of life in post-war Britain.

Antipathy toward the forms and institutions of a 'commercialized', 'mass' culture was nothing new. Similar fears and controversies had existed in the nineteenth century and during the 1930s notions of a cultural 'levelling-down' increasingly centred on the idea of 'Americanization'. America, the home of monopoly capitalism and commercial culture, came to epitomize the processes of debasement and deterioration which, many commentators argued, were coming to characterize popular cultural forms and practices in Britain. As Dick Hebdige shows, this use of America as a paradigm 'for the future threatening every advanced industrial democracy in the western world' (Hebdige, 1988a, pp. 52–3) intensified after 1945, the growth of working-class affluence prompting heightened anxieties that British culture was set to become a degraded and desocialized mass. The post-war period also saw a growing liberal/socialist inflection of these anxieties. This trend was epitomized, above all, in Richard Hoggart's (1958) *The Uses of Literacy* and its rejection of the 'candy-floss world' with its 'canned entertainment and packeted provision' which, Hoggart claimed, offered a culture that was shallow and insipid compared to that of his working-class boyhood between the wars. It was typical of the period that Hoggart should single out the younger generation as emblematic of the growing paucity of contemporary working-class life. Modern youth was, for Hoggart, a 'hedonistic but passive barbarian' and he deplored 'the juke box boys' with their 'drape suits, picture ties and American slouch' who spent their evenings in 'harshly lighted milk bars' putting 'copper after copper into the mechanical record player' (Hoggart, 1958, pp. 248–50).

Throughout the post-war decades it became commonplace to draw links between young people's sartorial preferences, growing levels of delin-quency and a general decline in cultural values and standards. During the early fifties these anxieties found coherence around the figure of the Teddy boy. First identified by the media in the working-class neighbourhoods of south London in 1954, the Ted was soon presented as a shockingly new apparition haunting street corners and dance halls all over the country. The Teddy boy's negative image was compounded by the cinema 'riots' that followed screenings of the film *Rock Around the Clock* in August 1956 and by the 1958 'race riots' in Nottingham and Notting Hill in which Teddy boys were implicated as principal aggressors (see chapter 9). By the late fifties the Ted's drape-suit had been superseded by the 'Italian' look of 'bum-freezer' jackets and 'slim Jim' ties, though dominant reactions to the mods of the early sixties replicated many of those that had earlier attended the Ted. Like the Teddy boys before them, the mods' style was often judged to represent not simply a mode of dress, but a symbol of national decline and cultural degradation. This negative stereotyping of young people, moreover, was maintained throughout the second half of the twen-tieth century in a demonology of deplorable youth stretching from the skinheads of the late sixties, through the punks of the late seventies, to the 'lager louts', 'New Age travellers' and 'acid house ravers' of the late eighties and early nineties.

To portray social reaction to post-war youth as entirely negative, however, would be a gross distortion. Indeed, since the late nineteenth century a spectrum of social and political interests have advanced a much more positive notion of youth as a national resource deserving encouragement and respect. During the Second World War this theme was given especially powerful articulation through a patriotic rhetoric in which the conflict became not simply a battle against the Third Reich but a 'People's War' fought for a future in which the dole queues and hardships of the inter-war Depression could never be repeated. In this vein newspaper series such as the *Daily Mirror*'s 'Youth Plans Its Tomorrow' gave stirring accounts of how British youngsters had risen to the challenges of wartime and had 'set foot on the path to a better world' (25 October 1940). Similar themes also underpinned many plans for post-war reconstruction, concern focusing on the need to make adequate social provision for the nation's young. The school-leaving age was due to be raised to fifteen in 1939 but this had been postponed with the outbreak of war. During wartime, however, the expansion of Britain's education system was perceived as a fundamental priority, youth increasingly being seen as a national resource whose potential had been regretfully wasted in the past through educational inadequacy. As a consequence the 1944 Education Act established the provision of free secondary education for all children 'according to ability', with the establishment of a tripartite system of grammar, modern and technical schools, while the school-leaving age was finally raised to fifteen in 1947.

Social and political responses to youth, therefore, were never entirely negative. Throughout the post-war period a recurring duality saw young people both vilified as the most deplorable evidence of cultural bankruptcy and, almost simultaneously, celebrated as the exciting precursor to a prosperous future. These contrasting representations of young people – which Dick Hebdige (1988b, p. 19) has termed 'youth-as-trouble' and 'youth-as-fun' – were obviously stereotypes which often bore tenuous relation to social reality. Yet their symbolic power was potent, images of youth serving as a key motif around which dominant interpretations of social change were constructed. During the 1950s, moreover, this motif was lent increased weight by a range of social and economic variables which combined to spotlight youth as an especially discrete and identifiably distinct section of the population.

Notes

1　C. E. B. Russell, 1905, 'Manchester boys: sketches of Manchester lads at work', cited in John Springhall, 1980, *Coming of Age: Adolescence in Britain, 1860–1960*, Dublin: Gill and Macmillan, p. 89.

2   Contemporaneous accounts and discussion of the 'boy labour' problem can be found in E. J. Urwick (ed.), 1904, *Studies of Boy Life in Our Cities*, London: Dent; Arnold Freeman, 1914, *Boy Life and Labour: The Manufacture of Inefficiency*, London: King. Historical analysis of the phenomenon is provided in Springhall, *Coming of Age*, pp. 84–5 and 100–3; H. Hendrick, 1990, *Images of Youth: Age, Class and the Male Youth Problem, 1880–1920*, Oxford: Clarendon Press.

3   The most authoritative account of working-class youth subcultures in Victorian and Edwardian Britain is provided in Geoffrey Pearson, 1983, *Hooligan: A History of Respectable Fears*, London: Macmillan.

4   John Gollan, 1937, *Youth in British Industry*, cited in John Davis, 1990, *Youth and the Condition of Britain: Images of Adolescent Conflict*, London: Athlone, p. 74.

5   The work of John Stevenson and Chris Cook has been especially influential on reappraisals of British social and economic life between the wars. See John Stevenson, 1976, 'Myth and reality: Britain in the 1930s', in Alan Sked and Chris Cook (eds), *Crisis and Controversy: Essays in Honour of A. J. P. Taylor*, London: Macmillan, pp. 90–109; John Stevenson and Chris Cook, 1994, *Britain During the Depression: Society and Politics, 1929–39*, 2nd edn, London: Longman.

6   The work of David Fowler offers a meticulous survey of British youngsters' life and culture between the wars. See David Fowler, 1992, 'Teenage consumers? Young wage-earners and leisure in Manchester, 1919–39', in Andrew Davies and Steven Fielding (eds), *Workers' Worlds: Cultures and Communities in Manchester and Salford, 1880–1939*, Manchester: Manchester University Press, pp. 133–55; David Fowler, 1995, *The First Teenagers: The Lifestyle of Young Wage-Earners in Interwar Britain*, London: Woburn.

7   Memo from D. Tait, F.A.U., London Hospital to J. F. Watson, Chairman of Clerkenwell Juvenile Court, 7 February 1942, Mass Observation Archive, 'Youth' Box 2, File C.

8   See Edward Smithies, 1982, *Crime in Wartime: A Social History of Crime in World War II*, London: Allen and Unwin, pp. 186–200.

9   See Pearson, *Hooligan*, pp. 213–19.

10   Wilkins's calculations and conclusions were, in fact, seriously flawed. Not only were his statistical inferences invalid but he failed to consider variations of delinquency rate between different types of offence and completely ignored non-indictable offences. Moreover, by the 1960s the generation of youngsters born in the years following the war had begun to register rates of delinquency even higher than their immediate predecessors.

11   In both cases serious doubt exists as to the guilt of the accused. It is possible that the authorities sought to make salutary examples of both Bentley and

Davies, demonstrating to the public that the juvenile 'crime-wave' was being firmly dealt with. For details of the Bentley and Davies cases see, respectively, David Yallop, 1990, *To Encourage the Others*, rev. edn, London: Corgi, and Tony Parker, 1965, *The Ploughboy*, London: Hutchinson.

3 'The Young Ones': The Growing 'Visibility' of Youth after 1945

The 'Institutionalization' of Youth after the Second World War

As the preceding chapter established, many features of young people's lives after the Second World War had been anticipated by earlier social, economic and cultural trends. Spectacular subcultural groups had existed among sections of working-class youth since the nineteenth century, while the degree of disposable income possessed by many working youngsters sowed the seeds of a commercial youth market which began to flourish between the wars. Concerns about the social behaviour and cultural preferences of the young, meanwhile, also possess a pedigree stretching back to at least the nineteenth century – with successive generations believing they faced a new breed of youngster characterized by unprecedented levels of delinquency and cultural impoverishment. Nevertheless, while points of continuity cannot be ignored, there remains justification for seeing the Second World War as marking a crucial turning-point in the development of British youth culture. In the decades that followed 1945 a range of factors combined to highlight the social 'visibility' of the young, giving British youngsters definition as a distinct cultural entity as never before and convincing many contemporary commentators that post-war youth was palpably different from previous generations of young people.

As we saw in the introduction, rather than being marked off by a set of objective and unchanging distinguishing features, the concept of 'youth' is a social construct. As such, its boundaries and characteristic qualities have varied between different societies and across different historical periods.

The modern notion of 'youth' as a particular stage in biological, psycho-logical and social development that begins with puberty and ends in mature adulthood first came to be fixed in the late Victorian and Edwardian eras. Central to this sedimentation were demographic shifts which, in the early twentieth century, saw ages for marriage reach their highest ever averages – twenty-five years for men and twenty-seven years for women – with the consequence that the period of pre-adulthood was extended, highlighting 'adolescence' as an age grade in its own right. A comparable 'peak' in the social and cultural 'visibility' of youth came in the mid-twentieth century and, once again, demographic factors played an important role. Although the post-1945 period saw a trend towards earlier marriage, the shorter 'life-span' of youth was compensated for by other factors. In the aftermath of the Second World War there was a significant, if temporary, 'baby boom' that saw the British youth population during the 1950s and 1960s grow, both in absolute numbers and as a percentage of the national total (see table 3.1). Additionally, scientific evidence suggested that with higher standards of living children were maturing at a much younger age, this further contributing to ideas of a qualitatively different younger generation.[1] These factors, sufficient in themselves to enhance youth's profile, were further reinforced by developments which formalized and institutional-ized notions of young people as an identifiable social group with a specific set of social requirements.

The reorganization of education that followed the implementation of the 1944 Education Act had a major impact on the structure of age relations in Britain. The expansion of educational provision, together with the raising of the school-leaving age to fifteen, increased the number of young people attending age-specific institutions and awaiting entry to the 'adult' world of full-time employment, thus helping to magnify and reinforce the

Table 3.1   Growth of UK youth population, 1951–1966

	Total UK population (in thousands)	Number of males and females under 20 (in thousands)	Males and females under 20 as % of total population
1951	37,908	3,066	8
1961	39,360	3,575	9
1966	40,041	4,088	10

Source: Department of Employment, 1971, *British Labour Statistics Historical Abstract 1886–1968*, London: HMSO, Table 109, pp. 206–7.

conceptualization of 'youth' as a discrete social entity with its own needs and problems. Subsequent years saw trends in the educational system further mark out youth as a discrete generational category, in 1959 the Crowther Report on secondary education recommending a further raising of the school-leaving age to sixteen, supported by both the Newsom and Robbins Reports of 1963 and finally implemented in 1973. This formalization of age categories within the field of education was complemented, moreover, by the simultaneous expansion of the youth service and the rise of myriad attempts to marshal the leisure time of young people.

In his analysis of juvenile delinquency in Oxford at the turn of the century, John Gillis (1975) found that the expansion of institutions seeking to organize young people's leisure actually helped crystallize concepts of youth as a distinct group associated with particular social problems. Much the same was true of the period after 1945, the expansion of the youth service helping to institutionalize 'youth' as a social category and 'fix' this categorization. Since 1918 Local Education Authorities had been empowered to give financial and other assistance to voluntary youth organizations, but statutory provision was piecemeal and disparate. It was only with the issue of Circular 1486, *The Service of Youth*, in November 1939, that the Board of Education recorded its decision to take direct responsibility for the welfare of youth within an integrated system of national education. (The post-war growth of the youth service is covered in more detail in chapter 10.) For the purposes of the youth service 'youth' was defined as the age range between fourteen (then the school-leaving age) and twenty-one, thereby encompassing the entire 'pre-adult' workforce. The existence of 'suitable' leisure provision for this group was regarded as a significant gap in the socialization of young people and following Circular 1486 a National Youth Committee (later the Youth Advisory Council) was established as a body to advise the Minister of Education and to administer grants to youth bodies and organizations. Under the 1944 Education Act it also became the statutory responsibility of Local Education Authorities (LEAs) to provide adequate recreational facilities for young people in their area, LEAs being encouraged to set up committees to discharge these responsibilities and to co-ordinate local voluntary groups.[2]

The post-war 'institutionalization' of youth through the expansion of education and the youth service was further augmented by a third, often overlooked, influence – the introduction of National Service. Following the National Service Act of 1948 compulsory military service became a fact of life for millions of young men in Britain who, on turning eighteen, had to register with the Ministry of Labour and National Service. Deferment was available to those completing apprenticeships or courses of education and about 16 per cent were exempted on medical grounds, but on average 160,000 young men were annually conscripted for two years' training in the Forces. Between 1945 and 1960 well over two million young men were 'called up', yet there is a surprising dearth of historical research dealing with National Service and its social impact.[3]

Socialization of the young was never itself an influence on the introduction of conscription. Rather, National Service was established as a cheap way of building up a large strategic reserve at a time when Britain was striving to maintain a global military presence that entailed a widespread and heavy commitment of the armed forces. Only after its cessation did claims emerge regarding conscription's possible contribution toward the 'character development' of the young. In contrast, while it existed, National Service was often regarded as a factor that actually contributed to the 'youth problem'.

From the state's point of view it would have been convenient if conscription had begun at school-leaving age, but the Forces refused to accept conscripts as young as fifteen and would have preferred them even older than eighteen. This meant that for most young men there existed an interregnum between leaving school and beginning National Service – a period which came to be regarded as an awkward and troublesome hiatus. Many employers were reluctant to offer jobs requiring training or tuition to young men who might quickly disappear to the Forces and never return, with the result that many school-leavers found difficulty in entering permanent jobs or careers during the 1950s. Moreover, there were many others who were unwilling to settle into routines which seemed prematurely onerous and constraining. As *Picture Post* found in 1957, among many British youths there existed 'a feeling of urgency' engendered by:

> the looming call-up which spreads a kind of smoke-screen over the long-term future. 'Well, there's no need to think too far ahead, is there? When I get in the Army I suppose most of my ideas will change anyway. There'll be time enough to think about a job when I come out' . . . 'Between now and the time I'm eighteen I've got to "do the lot". 'Ave a good time, I say, before I get called up, blown up or married'. (*Picture Post*, 8 April 1957)

Throughout the 1950s, therefore, dominant opinion was ambivalent about the social impact of National Service. Conscription was often seen as an unnecessarily disruptive and destabilizing episode in the lives of young men – one local newspaper even going so far as to venture that National Service had contributed to the rise of the Teddy boy, an editorial suggesting that:

> conscription may have a great deal to do with this new cult of gangsterism. The period prior to National Service is unsettling even for the best behaved youth. Too many lads, especially those from indifferent homes, adopt a don't-care attitude. Why should they not do as they like in civilian life when they are faced with two years of military discipline? . . . there is no question that conscription temporarily disrupts a lad in his civilian life and job. The year or so preceding service is a dangerous and frustrating period. (*Evening Argus*, 4 May 1954)

The impact of National Service aroused marked disquiet among those who feared a disruption in the socialization of a disciplined workforce. Probation officers and youth workers, for example, warned of a restlessness and unsettled state of mind among lads who had lost the stimulus to settle down to a permanent job because they knew that within two or three years they would have to uproot themselves. Anxiety further extended to the employment attitudes of young men after leaving the Services. In the mid-fifties researchers at Glasgow University claimed that former conscripts experienced difficulty in settling into the rhythms of civilian work. As a consequence they were prone to frequent changes of job which was, the researchers argued, 'a bad thing for the lads concerned and, in the long run, for the country' (Fergusson and Cunnison, 1956, p. 101).[4]

It also seems likely that conscription had a range of other important social and cultural consequences. The experience of National Service, for example, probably engendered a feeling of generational consciousness among young men detached from the ties of their domestic environment and gathered together with thousands of others undergoing the same experience. It was, furthermore, likely that the posting of young National Servicemen to bases in the heart of the British countryside brought the subcultural styles of urban youth to rural communities which otherwise would have been touched much less by rock'n'roll, winkle-pickers and other post-war shifts in youth style and culture.

'Well, It's Saturday Night an' I Just Got Paid': The Economics of Post-War Youth Culture

Undoubtedly, demographic shifts, the expansion of secondary education and the youth service and the introduction of National Service all combined to enhance the 'visibility' of young people as a distinct social category throughout the 1950s and 1960s. However, the factor that most profoundly accentuated British youth's social profile during this period was the intensification of long-term economic trends. As we saw in chapter 2, a section of working-class youth had possessed a degree of disposable income since the nineteenth century. After 1945, however, changes in Britain's economic structure markedly increased demand for youngsters' labour, with the consequence that their earning power was also significantly augmented.

The decline of heavy industries, the movement of capital into lighter forms of production (especially the manufacture of consumer durables), the expansion of labour processes based on production-line technologies, trends towards 'de-skilling' and the movement of labour out of direct production and into distribution were not unique to the post-war period. Nevertheless, after 1945 these trends intensified, registering an impact on the working class as a whole but holding their greatest consequences for

Table 3.2   Proportion of young people within the British workforce, 1950–1968

	Numbers of persons aged 15–17 years entering employment (in thousands)			Persons aged 18–20 years as % of UK employees		
	Male	*Female*	*Total*	*Male*	*Female*	*Total*
1950	273.2	263.5	536.7	3.0	3.9	6.9
1952	266.9	256.1	523.0	2.4	3.7	6.1
1954	258.4	246.6	505.0	2.4	3.8	6.2
1956	246.9	235.5	482.4	2.7	3.7	6.4
1958	269.8	253.8	523.6	3.1	3.6	6.7
1960	286.3	261.5	547.8	3.6	3.5	7.1
1962	336.0	321.3	657.3	4.2	3.5	7.7
1964	314.8	293.5	608.3	4.3	3.8	8.1
1966	270.2	251.7	521.9	4.8	4.2	9.0
1968	255.8	232.4	488.2	4.6	4.0	8.6

Source: Department of Employment, 1971, *British Labour Statistics Historical Abstract 1886–1968*, London: HMSO, Table 151, p. 297; Table 158, p. 304.

young workers. During the 1950s and 1960s demand for youngsters' unskilled and semi-skilled labour grew noticeably, leading to an increase in young people as a proportion of the national workforce (see table 3.2) and reviving wartime anxieties that trends in youth employment were having a deleterious impact on the national economy.

As demand for youth labour began to outstrip supply young people experienced few problems in finding employment. With a buoyant job market many youngsters were free to move quickly from job to job in search of the highest immediate rewards, giving rise to fears that Britain would soon face a serious shortage of skilled industrial workers. Statistics, in fact, suggest the opposite, showing that during the fifties and sixties numbers of boys entering apprenticeships rose steadily, while those of girls fluctuated but did not decline significantly (see table 3.3). These figures, however, should be treated with caution. 'Apprenticeship' was often a vague term, covering employment that could entail only a limited amount of skill development and instruction. Many youngsters, meanwhile, might begin an apprenticeship after leaving school but this was no guarantee they would remain in the position for the duration of the training. Indeed, the period saw large numbers of apprenticeships discontinued prematurely as conscription inducted youngsters into the services.

The decline of the apprenticeship system, however, did not have the disastrous economic effects that many had predicted. Changes in the labour market and shifts in production processes had made an

Table 3.3   Percentage of young people aged 15–17 entering apprenticeship to skilled occupation in the UK, 1950–1968

	Males	*Females*
1950	33.8	8.0
1952	34.8	5.9
1954	34.2	6.0
1956	37.8	6.8
1958	34.5	6.9
1960	36.0	7.6
1962	36.2	6.6
1964	36.4	5.8
1966	42.3	6.7
1968	43.0	7.4

Source: Department of Employment, 1971, *British Labour Statistics Historical Abstract 1886–1968*, London: HMSO, Table 153, p. 304.

anachronism of traditional employment structures and British industry simply had much less use for a highly skilled workforce. De-skilling and production-line technologies had, to a large part, displaced artisan trades and created instead a demand for flexible, though not especially skilled, workers. Cheaper to employ than adults, young people were an ideal source for this labour and were often only too willing to enter such positions. Indeed, rather than undertaking a period of relatively poorly paid training or apprenticeship, many youngsters much preferred the relatively high immediate rewards offered by unskilled or semi-skilled work.

The enhancement of youth's economic muscle through greater demand for their labour made a profound impression on social commentators after the Second World War. As early as 1947 the Clarke Report had drawn attention to the financial power accruing to the young worker, observing that 'when juvenile workers are scarce, as they are now, and are likely to continue to be, he [sic] quickly realises that he may not be so unimportant as he seemed at first; and after two or three years his income may be larger compared with his needs and with his contribution to his maintenance than at any other period of his life' (Ministry of Education, 1947, p. 47). This equation of 'youth' with 'affluence' became a prevalent theme throughout the post-war decades. A recurring motif of the fifties and sixties, the image of young workers with plenty of disposable income owed a considerable debt to Mark Abrams's research, conducted for the London Press Exchange, on the spending patterns of young people in the late 1950s. According to Abrams, the post-war period had seen youth, more than any other social group, materially prosper. Compared to pre-war levels Abrams calculated that young people's real earnings had risen by 50 per cent (roughly double that of adults) with male teenagers earning, on average, £8 per week and their female peers about £6 (Abrams, 1959, p. 9). Moreover, Abrams estimated that youth's 'discretionary' spending had risen by as much as 100 per cent, with the average boy spending 71s 6d a week and the average girl 54s, collectively representing an annual expenditure of around £830 million. Further, this spending was concentrated in particular consumer markets (for instance constituting 44 per cent of total spending on records and record players and 39 per cent of spending on bicycles and motorcycles) which, according to Abrams, represented the rise of 'distinctive teenage spending for distinctive teenage ends in a distinctive teenage world' (Abrams, 1959, p. 10).

Recited almost verbatim in a multitude of contemporaneous books, newspapers and articles, Abrams's figures went a long way toward sedimenting notions of a newly affluent body of young people patronizing a youth market of unprecedented scale. It is, perhaps, unfair to subject Abrams's data to rigorous scrutiny since it was never produced with the intention of being a thoroughgoing piece of academic investigation. However, given the regularity with which his figures were, and continue to be,[5] uncritically cited it is essential that the accuracy of Abrams's work be seriously assessed. Indeed, room exists to question and qualify many of his points. In the first place, Abrams's rather strange definition of teenagers as 'those young people who have reached the age of fifteen but are not yet twenty-five years of age and are unmarried' (Abrams, 1961, p. 3) would undoubtedly have disguised considerable differences of earnings and expenditure within the group, while his discussion of *total* expenditure and *average* earnings would, again, have concealed major differences and disparities. Abrams, furthermore, took no account of marked regional variations – less widely publicized, locally based research painting a picture in stark contrast to his own. Unlike Abrams's 'affluent teenagers', Pearl Jephcott (1967) found that 59 per cent of fifteen- to seventeen-and-a-half-year-olds in Scotland had less than £1 a week spending money, while 81 per cent of those aged between seventeen-and-a-half and nineteen had less than £3. Along similar lines Cyril Smith's (1966) study of youth in Bury

Table 3.4   Average weekly earnings of young manual workers, 1948–1968

	Youths and boys (under 21 years)			Girls (under 18 years)		
	(£)	(s)	(d)	(£)	(s)	(d)
1948	2	18	0	2	8	11
1950	3	2	6	2	12	8
1952	3	13	4	2	19	4
1954	4	3	10	3	7	8
1956	5	1	5	3	19	10
1958	5	10	10	4	6	2
1960	6	6	7	4	15	0
1962	7	1	6	5	4	4
1964	8	1	6	5	18	1
1966	9	12	4	6	15	5
1968	10	14	11	7	11	0

Source: Calculated from Department of Employment, 1971, *British Labour Statistics Historical Abstract 1886–1968*, London: HMSO, Table 49, pp. 116–17.

found that only 5.5 per cent of fifteen-to eighteen-year-olds spent over £2 per week, while 61.5 per cent spent less than 15s. 'The popular picture of affluent teenagers', Smith concluded, 'grossly simplifies the very real differences in income among them.'

Nevertheless, while Abrams's figures clearly distorted and exaggerated the scale of young people's economic power, the broad sweep of his claims should not be dismissed out of hand. Alternative statistics, produced by the Department of Employment, are certainly lower than those recorded by Abrams, yet they still confirm that young people's weekly earnings *did* rise steadily in the post-war era (see table 3.4). Furthermore, data from the same source indicates that, whereas male manual workers under the age of twenty-one received only 36 per cent of their older workmates' weekly earnings in 1935, by 1959 this had risen to 43 per cent. Over the same period, meanwhile, the weekly earnings of female manual workers under eighteen rose from 52 per cent to 64 per cent of older women's earnings.[6] The notion of a more affluent younger generation, then, was not entirely mythological. In the 1950s and 1960s the wage packets of young workers were not bulging. Yet, compared to those of their predecessors, they were proportionally more replete and many young people *did* enjoy a degree of *relative* prosperity on entering the world of work.

'A Distinctive Teenage World'? The Rise of Notions of Youth Culture

While post-war demand for young people's labour increased the earning capacity of many youngsters, it is important to recognize that these gains did not take place across the social scale. During the fifties and early sixties it was working-class youngsters who flexed the greatest economic muscle, Abrams concluding from his research that 'teenage demand' was 'typical only of working class teenagers' and 'largely without appeal for middle class boys and girls' (Abrams, 1961, p. 10). Abrams's announcement of a 'distinctive teenage world' had seemed to suggest the development of a youth market cutting across traditional class boundaries, yet upon closer scrutiny Abrams observed that the 'teenage market' was 'almost entirely working class' and that 'not far short of 90 per cent of all teenage spending is conditioned by working-class taste and values' (Abrams, 1959, p. 13).

It is possible to overstate the degree to which middle-class youngsters were excluded from the youth culture of the post-war decades. As we shall see in chapter 7, middle-class youngsters participated in the period's youth 'spectacle' to an extent that is seldom acknowledged. Nevertheless, during the fifties and early sixties this participation was circumscribed by the tendency for middle-class youngsters to remain in secondary education for a longer period than their working-class peers, combined with the fact that middle-class career structures delayed high reward until much later in life. A significant middle-class presence was not felt within British youth culture until the mid-1960s, when the expansion of higher education afforded a growing section of middle-class youth the relative freedoms of living away from home on a student grant. In contrast, throughout the fifties and early sixties middle-class youngsters were, for the most part, external to (and often alienated from) a youth culture which was, in essence, a working-class experience – the product of shifting labour markets and a rise in working youths' spending power. Peter Lewis, for example, in recalling his youth at a Dorset public school in the 1950s, underlines the gulf that separated him from his working-class peers:

> Teenagers, viewed from the shelter of this middle-class enclave, were a working-class phenomenon . . . Boys like me tried to dress (tweed jackets, grey flannel trousers) and talk like men . . . There was no space in between being a boy and becoming a man for any distinctive style or assertion of identity. (Lewis, 1991, pp. 179–80)

Within much academic discourse, however, there was a tendency to evacuate class division from the analysis of youth, instead presenting young people as a unified social entity. Notions of young people as representing a relatively homogeneous social group distinct from wider 'adult' society first developed in the late nineteenth and early twentieth centuries. The work of psychologists such as G. Stanley Hall (1904) and his followers popularized the concept of a developmental phase beginning with puberty and ending in mature adulthood. This bio-psychological approach conceived adolescence as a transitional period of adjustment which, almost inevitably, encompassed elements of psychological unbalance coming close to 'symptom formation of the neurotic, psychotic or dissocial order' (Freud, cited in Rutter et al., 1976, p. 35). After the Second World War this perspective retained influence in branches of psychology but, more generally, fell from favour as empirical investigation pointed to the conventionality of most young people and the degree of correspondence between the norms, values and behaviour of various generations.[7] In place of innate bio-psychological characteristics, therefore, theorists increasingly focused on the social and economic conditions which were believed to set youth apart as a discrete social group. As early as 1942 the American sociologist Talcott Parsons had coined the term 'youth culture' to denote a distinct set of social structures inhabited by the young, stressing the positive contribution this system made to the equilibrium of the social structure as a whole. During the fifties and sixties many researchers, on both sides of the Atlantic, followed in his footsteps, giving generational divisions precedence over those of social class.[8] In these terms young people were presented as being drawn together in a new 'culture of youth' – youngsters sharing a homogenous cultural universe separate and distinct from that of their parents.

We have already seen, however, that this 'youth culture' perspective did not accord with the realities of young people's lives in post-war Britain. Rather than transcending class barriers, the post-war youth 'experience' continued to be mediated by structural divisions, social class remaining a crucial determinant of youngsters' employment opportunities and leisure preferences. The question, therefore, arises as to *why* post-war social commentators should have been so willing to depict young people as uniquely separate from wider, 'adult' society. Part of the answer lies in the fact that, as we have seen, some real changes *did* take place in the lives and culture of young people which, taken together, tended to accentuate their social profile in the post-war period. Additionally, though, these changes were inextricably bound up with broader transformations taking place in Britain, transformations which the burgeoning youth market came to epitomize – the 'teenager' emerging as an ideological axis around which cohered debates about these more fundamental shifts in social and cultural relations. It is to these issues that we turn our attention in the following chapter.

Notes

1   For an example of this perspective see Alex Comfort, 1960, 'Growing up faster', *The Listener*, vol. LXIV, no. 1632, 7 July.
2   The inevitable consequence of this 'localized' approach to youth provision was that there emerged a very varied pattern of organization across the country – a characteristic which dogged the youth service for years to come.
3   For the best available accounts of National Service, its history and the

experiences of National Servicemen themselves see P. Chambers and A. Landreth, 1955, *Called Up: The Personal Experiences of Sixteen National Servicemen*, London: Allan Wingate; B. S. Johnson (ed.), 1973, *All Bull: The National Servicemen*, London: Quartet; Trevor Royale, 1988, *The Best Years of Their Lives: The National Service Experience 1943–63*, London: Cornet.

4   For similar concerns regarding the impact of National Service on youngsters' attitude to employment see 'Impact of National Service on youth', *Nature*, vol. 179, no. 4559, 16 March 1957; T. Fergusson and J. Cunnison, 1959, 'The impact of National Service', *British Journal of Sociology*, vol. 10, no. 4, pp. 283–90.

5   The validity of Abrams's figures continues to be uncritically accepted by many otherwise excellent studies. See, for example, Iain Chambers, 1985, *Urban Rhythms: Pop Music and Popular Culture*, Basingstoke: Macmillan, pp. 26–7; Eric Dunning, Patrick Murphy and John Williams, 1988, *The Roots of Football Hooliganism*, London: Routledge and Kegan Paul, p. 160; Jeffrey Weeks, 1989, *Sex, Politics and Society*, London: Longman, p. 252; Jane Pilcher, 1995, *Age and Generation in Modern Britain*, Oxford: Oxford University Press, p. 67.

6   These figures are calculated from Department of Employment, 1971, *British Labour Statistics Historical Abstract 1886–1968*, London: HMSO, Table 38, p. 96; Table 41, pp. 100–1; Table 49, pp. 116–17.

7   In Britain during the fifties and sixties the work of the Eppels was especially influential. See E. M and M. Eppel, 1953, 'Young workers at a county college', Parts 1 and 2, *British Journal of Educational Psychology*, vol. 23, pp. 29–44 and pp. 87–96; E. M and M. Eppel, 1963, 'Teenage values', *New Society*, vol. 2, no. 59, 14 Nov.; E. M and M. Eppel, 1966, *Adolescents and Morality: A Study of Some Moral Values and Dilemmas of Working Adolescents in the Context of a Changing Climate of Opinion*, London: Routledge. More recent sociological research continues to show the degree of continuity between the norms and values of adolescents and those of adults. See, for example, Tom Kitwood, 1980, *Disclosures to a Stranger: Adolescent Values in an Advanced Industrial Society*, London: Routledge; John C. Coleman and Leo Hendy, 1989, *The Nature of Adolescence*, 2nd edn, London: Routledge; Adrian Furnham and Barrie Gunter, 1989, *The Anatomy of Adolescence*, London: Routledge.

8   In America the most well-known study to develop these themes was J. S. Coleman, 1961, *The Adolescent Society: The Social Life of the Teenager and its Impact on Education*, New York: Glencoe. For British studies that elaborate a similar account of a homogeneous 'culture of youth' see J. and M. Rowntree, 1968, 'Youth as social class', *International Socialist Journal*, no. 25, pp. 25–58; Ralph H. Turner, 1969, 'The theme of contemporary social movements', *British Journal of Sociology*, vol. 20, no. 4, pp. 390–405.

4 'Teenage Kicks': Youth and Consumption in Post-War Britain

'You've Never Had It So Good': Consumption and Consensus in Post-War Britain

It is impossible to understand the post-war saliency of youth as a cultural category without placing it in the context of the wider social, economic and political changes that took place in Britain during the period. The Labour Party's landslide general election victory of 1945 has often been taken as heralding a new era of consensus in British political life. Recently, however, the idea that the dole queues of the 1930s and the 'blood, toil, sweat and tears' of wartime engendered a convergence toward the political centre has been questioned.[1] Certainly, any consensus bequeathed by the Second World War was much less than complete. Key ideological differences always existed between the main political parties, elections were often bitterly contested and parliamentary debate was frequently acrimonious. Nevertheless, while the degree of political accord should not be overestimated, both Labour and Conservative governments of the fifties and early sixties operated within a framework of shared assumptions – the provision of the welfare state, the maintenance of high levels of employment and an acknowledgement of the state's general responsibility for the management of a mixed economy. In such an atmosphere it certainly seemed as though a new era was dawning, particularly during the 1950s when a series of Conservative election victories seemed to be part of a more wholesale social transformation wrought by economic prosperity and a marked growth in living standards.

Full employment and demand for labour sustained rises in real earnings throughout the fifties and early sixties and laid the basis for a steady growth in consumer spending. Moreover, the three Conservative terms of office saw reductions in interest rates and taxes and the relaxation of hire purchase controls – promoting high street sales and prompting, in 1957, Prime Minister Harold Macmillan's famous remark that the British people had 'never had it so good'. It is difficult to measure precisely the degree to which this new spending lay in the hands of the working class, though they clearly benefited, with a growing number of working-class households boasting televisions, motor cars, washing machines and an ever-spiralling range of domestic appliances and consumer durables.

In retrospect the prosperity of the post-war decades can be seen as insecure and transient, the ephemeral trappings of an 'age of illusion' (Bogdanor and Skidelsky, 1970, p. 7). Much of the consumer 'boom' was, for example, based on the vulnerable economic foundation of short-term credit, Britain's hire purchase debt rising faster between 1956 and 1959 than at any other time either before or since. Moreover, post-war 'affluence' depended on a level of growth that the British economic infrastructure was simply not in a position to maintain and by the late sixties the scale of these problems had become apparent. Nevertheless, however fleeting, the growth in living standards during the period was tangible and of a scale sufficient to underpin one of the most profound phases of transition in working-class life and culture.

During the fifties and early sixties enhanced incomes, shifting patterns of work and leisure and the redevelopment of traditional neighbourhoods combined to thoroughly reorganize and recast the forms and practices of working-class culture.[2] Though the British working class did not, in any sense, decompose or disappear, the dominant imagery of the period was one of a dawning 'classlessness', the pace of economic growth perceived as steadily ameliorating social divisions, neutralizing traditional class conflicts and ushering in a new epoch of 'post-capitalism'. Mark Abrams, once again, epitomized these sentiments in his arguments that since the war class barriers had 'tended to lose their clarity', with some working-class families having 'incomes as high as some white collar families and there [being] little to choose between their styles of living' (Abrams, 1964, p. 57).

Associated with this mythology of affluence there emerged a trinity of constructed social types that seemed to embody the new cultural order – 'the bourgeois worker', 'the housewife' and, above all, 'the teenager'. Home-centred, instrumentally oriented and materially prosperous, 'the bourgeois worker' was prominent in popular discussion, was courted by Conservative Party electioneering and was given academic recognition by sociological research claiming to have detected a 'bourgeoisification' of working-class lifestyles.[3] In a similar vein, the growth of high street spending, coupled with the growing battery of domestic appliances designed to relieve the drudgery of housework, promoted 'the housewife' as the natural heroine of 'People's Capitalism' (Hopkins, 1963, p. 324).[4] More than either 'the bourgeois worker' or 'the housewife', however, it was 'the teenager' that most fully encapsulated perceptions of social transformation after 1945.

'The Truth about Teenagers': Youth and the Mythologies of Post-War Affluence

As we saw in chapter 1, notions and representations of 'youth' have the capacity to play a metaphorical role in the ways sense is made of more general social developments, especially at times of dramatic social transformation. This was particularly so in the post-1945 era, young people becoming an important (possibly the *most* important) ideological vehicle for the discussion of wider shifts in social relations and changes in British cultural life.

From the mid-fifties a wealth of official research, both nationally and locally based, presented youth as a category integral to wider social changes. Published in 1960, the Albermarle Report on the condition of the youth service was indicative of the rising tide of official interest in young people. The report was especially notable for the explicit connection it drew between 'the youth question' and the broader pattern of social development, the report expressly stating that 'the "problems of youth" are deeply rooted in the soil of a disturbed modern world' (Ministry of Education, 1960, p. 2). Throughout the period this theme was mirrored by the work of innumerable agencies and organizations. For example, 1959 saw the publication of both the report of the Labour Party's Youth Commission and the British Medical Association's choice of 'The Adolescent' as its 'Subject of the Year'. The tone of much of this work was reassuring, presenting youth in a favourable and almost celebratory light. This positive view of young people as 'responsible' and 'mature' was further underlined by the publication of the Latey Report on the age of majority in 1967 and the subsequent extension of the electoral franchise (previously only held by those over twenty-one) to eighteen-year-olds in 1971.

The media could also present youth in glowing terms. Newspapers and magazines, especially, helped popularize notions of 'youth' as an excitingly new social force, a vigorous and uplifting contrast to the tired, old, traditional order. The field was led by the *Daily Mirror* where the theme of 'youth', along with an explicit appeal to a young readership, became a recurring feature as the paper sought to maintain its share of market sales as well as offering a meaningful response to the rapid pace of social change. The fifties saw the *Mirror* increasingly jump on the youth 'bandwagon', with the paper publishing several books on the quickly developing world of pop music and, in 1957, sponsoring a 'Rock'n'Roll Express' to take American rock'n'rollers Bill Haley and the Comets to London after they had arrived at Southampton for their first British tour. Sharing this enthusiastic interest in youth culture was *Picture Post*. Despite its share of histrionic articles on 'Boy Gangsters', the tone of *Picture Post*'s coverage was generally positive, culminating in 1957 with a four-part series entitled 'The Truth About Teenagers', which revealed 'what teenagers are, what they hate and what they hope for' (*Picture Post*, 18 March – 8 April, 1957).

As we saw in chapter 2, there was always a degree of ambiguity to notions and representations of youth during the post-war period. Throughout the fifties and early sixties, for example, a sense of uncertainty and apprehension always attended young people's patterns of consumption, youth culture invariably being taken as the nadir of post-war cultural change, a malignant presence lurking in the shadows of the 'affluent society' (see figure 4.1). Overall, however, the most striking feature of the imagery of youth in this period was its deployment as a shorthand signifier for unbridled pleasure in what seemed to be a new age of hedonistic consumption. Young people seemed to embody all that the consumer dream stood for and throughout the fifties and early sixties advertisers habitually used images of youth to associate their products with dynamic modernity and 'swinging' enjoyment (see figures 4.2 and 4.3). This equation of youth with consumption was exemplified, above all, by the addition of the term 'teenager' to everyday vocabulary. First coined by American market researchers during the mid-1940s, the term was formalized in the early fifties through the research of organizations such as the Student Marketing Institute, Teenage Survey Incorporated and Eugene Gilbert

A BOY

God who created me
Nimble and light of limb,
In three elements free,
To run, to ride, to swim:

Not when the sense is dim,
But now from the heart of joy,
I would remember Him:
Take the thanks of a boy.

"Prayers." Henry Charles Beeching

Figure 4.1 'A boy' – youth as the embodiment of the uncertainties lurking in the shadows of the 'affluent society', *Punch*, 30 September 1953

and Company which, in conjunction with an avalanche of books, magazine and newspaper articles, revealed to the US public what appeared to be a new social caste with its own culture and lifestyle. By the late forties the word 'teenager' had been imported into Britain and was rapidly integrated into popular discourse, the press making liberal use of the term by the early fifties.

In the image of the 'teenager' post-war mythologies of affluence found their purest manifestation. Taken as the quintessence of social transformation, 'teenagers' were perceived as being at the sharp end of the new consumer culture, distinguished not simply by their youth but by a particular style of conspicuous, leisure-oriented consumption. As Peter Laurie

Whatever the pleasure
Player's complete it

Because they are
so perfectly packed,
so swiftly sold,
the reputation of Player's
for freshness and
value is unexcelled.

Figure 4.2 'Whatever the pleasure . . .', advertisement for Player's Cigarettes, 1957

Figure 4.3   'Invitation to a world of pleasure ...', advertisement for Cadbury's Drinking Chocolate, 1955

contended in his anatomy of *The Teenage Revolution*, published in 1965, 'The distinctive fact about teenagers' behaviour is economic: they spend a lot of money on clothes, records, concerts, make-up, magazines: all things that give immediate pleasure and little lasting use' (Laurie, 1965, p. 9). The 'teenager', then, was far more than a simple descriptive term. Rather, the 'teenager' was an ideological terrain upon which a particular definition of post-war change was constructed. Central to notions of the 'teenager' was the idea that traditional class boundaries were being eroded by the fashions and lifestyles of newly affluent 'gilded youth' (*The Economist*, 11 January 1958). 'Teenagers' were presented as a class in themselves, what Laurie (1965, p. 11) termed a 'solidly integrated social bloc', whose vibrant, hedonistic culture seemed to be a symbolic foretaste of good times waiting around the corner for everyone. Indeed, in these terms, Harold Wilson's presentation of Variety Club awards to the Beatles in 1964 and his award of MBEs to the Fab Four in 1965 seem less the good-natured gestures of a 'man of the people' than a calculated appropriation of the 'language' of youth and modernity.

Of course, just as the more general notions of 'classless prosperity' distorted the real contours of post-war social change, the idea of 'teenage affluence' and a new 'culture of youth' misrepresented the true nature of changes in the lives of British youngsters. Social class did not disappear but continued, as it still continues, to mediate young people's cultural practices and experiences. Moreover, the scale of the 'explosion' of the post-war youth market should not be exaggerated. After visiting Britain in 1954, and again in 1956, Eugene Gilbert (who had made his name as 'the George Gallup of teenagers' through his market research on American youth's consumer preferences) concluded that no potential existed for his company to establish a permanent office in London. Even in the early sixties the Managing Director of Thomson Newspapers averred that 'As far as advertising goes the teenage market does not exist. As far as we are concerned, as magazine publishers, there *are* no teenagers' (Laurie, 1965, p. 62). Nevertheless, although its scale needs to be kept in proportion, it remains the case that consumer spending by British youngsters increased in the post-war decades, laying the basis for a youth market which surpassed by far its antecedents.

'Whole Lotta Shakin' Goin' On': The Expansion of the Commercial Youth Market

Though the 1950s and 1960s witnessed growing levels of consumer spending within the working class as a whole, it was young workers – unfettered by family responsibilities – who were most able to enjoy the fruits of a higher disposable income. Moreover, the spending patterns of young people were especially conspicuous. Unlike the home-centred consumption of their parents, youth's expenditure on commercial goods and entertainments primarily took place in public realms, this exposure contributing to impressions of a new, discrete and affluent 'young generation'. As Derek Hawes observed in his report published in consultation with the Standing Conference of National Youth Organisations during the mid-sixties:

> The quality of life lived by the average young person in Britain today is much affected by the realisation by commercial interests that the age group fourteen to twenty-five represents, in economic terms, a vast multi-million pound market; a well-defined consumer group, affluent and innocent, to be attracted and exploited and pandered to; second only to the housewife in potential spending power. (Hawes, 1966, p. 25)

The range of products geared to the post-war youth market was literally boundless, consumer industries interacting with and reinforcing one another in their efforts to cash in on youth spending. This expansion of the youth market had its greatest impact, of course, in the field of popular music. Symbolic of youth's growing importance to the music industry was the rise of the 7 inch, 45 r.p.m. single (introduced in 1952 and accounting for 80 per cent of British record sales by 1963), as well as the introduction of sales-based singles' charts (the first British singles' chart appearing in *New Musical Express* in 1952, followed by *Record Mirror*'s 'Top Fifty' in 1954) and the emergence of the pop star as a cultural phenomenon – most strikingly manifested in 1956 with the arrival from America of rock'n'roll. The initial wave of American stars such as Bill Haley, Little Richard, Chuck Berry and Elvis Presley was soon supplemented by home-grown talent such as Tommy Steele, Billy Fury, Adam Faith and Marty Wilde and, with the rise of British beat and rhythm and blues in the early sixties, British performers came to dominate the pop market.

As adult audiences declined, the film industry also began to focus more explicitly on the youth market. In America producers such as Roger Corman and Sam Katzman pioneered the 'teenpic' – low-budget, quickly released films geared to a young audience, especially the drive-in market.[5] The British film industry, too, attempted to exploit youth demand. Although Britain had nothing to match the scale and prolificity of the American 'teenpic' industry, the fifties and sixties saw the release of a host of British films that courted a young audience by featuring pop idols such as Cliff Richard, Tommy Steele and, later, the Beatles.[6] Many of these films were exemplary of the way in which youth emerged as a motif for post-war ideologies of confidence and growth. For example, Cliff Richard's films of the early sixties, *The Young Ones* (dir. Sidney Furie, 1961) and *Summer Holiday* (dir. Peter Yates, 1963), are both tales of ebullient youngsters liberating themselves from the dull conformity of their workaday lives. The young people here are not rebels but responsible and enterprising citizens, the films' unquestioning sense of freedom and optimism epitomizing the notions of prosperity and dawning social harmony that lay at the heart of dominant political ideologies during the early sixties.

In contrast to the cinema, British radio was much less willing to associate itself with post-war changes in popular music and youth culture. During the late fifties rock'n'roll could be heard by tuning in to American Forces Network or Radio Luxembourg but was largely ignored by the BBC as a consequence of restrictions on 'needle time'[7] and official antipathy toward the music's 'Americanizing' influences. It was not, therefore, until the appearance of pirate stations such as Radio Caroline in the early sixties and the subsequent launch of BBC Radio One in 1967 that Britain saw radio programmes specifically geared to the 'youth' audience.[8] British television, on the other hand, responded swiftly to the post-war 'youth scene' and both the BBC and ITV made many forays into the field during the fifties and sixties. Initially programmes such as *Hit Parade* (1952), *Music Shop* (1955) and *Off the Record* (1956) were rather muted in the directness of their appeal to youth. By the later fifties, however, a more fully formed youth-oriented genre had begun to emerge with shows such as *Six-Five Special* (1957), *Oh Boy!* (1958) and *Juke Box Jury* (1959).[9] It was, though, a lesser-known series entitled *Dad You're a Square* which went furthest in condensing notions of youth as a group with its own, unique, tastes and interests. Broadcast on Southern TV in 1963, *Dad You're a Square* used a format similar to the BBC's *Juke Box Jury*, with a panel reviewing recent record releases. In this case, however, the panel was composed of parents and their teenage children who argued over the relative merits of different discs – the programme crystallizing the idea of a popular culture beset by virtually insurmountable generational divisions.

While the cinema was able, indeed was economically forced, to seek out age-specific audiences in the fifties, early television programmes always had to allow for the domestic environment of their audiences. As John Hill (1991) shows, programmes made an appeal to adolescent viewers but this was tempered by their additional embrace of a heterogeneous, 'family' audience through the inclusion of either 'magazine' features (as in the case of *Six-Five Special*) or celebrities from the wider world of entertainment (as in the case of *Juke Box Jury*). By the early sixties, however, this emphasis on a general appeal had diminished. *Ready, Steady, Go!* (1963), for example, made few concessions to an adult audience, revelling in a preoccupation with the music, fashions and tastes of the youth scene, especially the developing mod subculture of the early sixties. As Ken and Sylvia Ferguson observed in their 1965 guide to British television:

> 'Ready, Steady Go!' is not . . . so much a programme – more a way of life.
> It is a mirror of teenage tastes, the stars they worship, the way they dress,
> all reflected in one huge television series that unfolds to a vast viewing audi-
> ence every Friday night. (Ferguson and Ferguson, 1965, p. 24)

Indeed, television became crucial in promoting and propagating all aspects of post-war British youth culture, George Melly describing how *Ready, Steady, Go!* 'plugged in direct to the centre of the scene and only a week later transmitted information as to clothes, dances, gestures, even slang to the whole British teenage Isles . . . *RSG* made pop work on a truly national scale' (Melly, 1972, p. 72). Overall, the media's growing intercession in the field of youth style marked a fundamental shift in the traditions of British youth culture. During the nineteenth and first half of the twentieth centuries youth style and culture had been largely locally based, with limited national cohesion or sense of a nationwide stylistic identity. During the fifties and sixties, however, as media industries responded more eagerly to the youth market, changes in style and fashion were promoted and popularized with much greater speed and vigour. In fact, without the definition and dissemination that the media and other commercial institutions afforded, it is probable that the Teddy boy, mod and skinhead would all have remained locally confined and vaguely defined subcultural variants –

much as 'scuttlers' and 'peaky blinders' had been in the nineteenth century.

The explosion of British pop music in the mid-fifties was a shot in the arm to many traditional entertainment venues whose adult patrons had begun to drift away. Instead, a younger generation of customers packed into dance halls, clubs and variety theatres, audiences flocking to see concert tour 'packages' of pop stars organized by impresarios such as Larry Parnes and, later, appearances by headline bands such as the Beatles and the Rolling Stones. Other businesses also thrived on youngsters' custom. The brewing industry did not seriously attempt to penetrate younger sections of the market until the late sixties and as a consequence pubs continued to have a dull, dingy, even rather boring image. Coffee bars, on the other hand, blossomed. The pre-eminent focal point to British teenage life, the coffee bar was a place where youngsters could gather and freely chat amongst themselves or dance to their favourite records on the juke box (itself appearing in much greater numbers from the mid-fifties), all for the price of a cup of foamy espresso or a bottle of Coca-Cola. The most famous coffee bars were in London – the 'Gyre and Gymble' near Charing Cross, the 'Breadbasket' near Middlesex Hospital and the 'Two I's' (reputedly the site of Tommy Steele's 'discovery') in Old Compton Street – but most provincial towns also developed their own network of espresso bars and 'dives'. Often furnished in a pseudo-exotic style (with bullfight posters, bamboo fixtures, tropical plants, an occasional shell or Mexican mask) coffee bars generated an excitingly cosmopolitan aura and stand as one of the most enduring images of not only fifties' youth style but British culture more generally during the period.

'This Is the Modern World': Developments in Subcultural Style

The continental air of the coffee bar was indicative of a broader popular cultural shift in the late fifties. American influences, so prominent at the beginning of the decade, remained important but became increasingly fused with styles derived from Europe. Italian design aesthetics in particular bewitched British style consciousness. Popularized by films such as *Roman Holiday* (dir. William Wyler, 1953) and *La Dolce Vita* (dir. Frederico Fellini, 1960) the chic, smoothly tailored lines of Italian fashion mods.

were first sported in Britain in about 1958 by the 'modernists' – fashion-obsessed youngsters who frequented the clubs and back streets of West London. Immortalized in Colin MacInnes's novel *Absolute Beginners* (1959), the modernists cultivated a sharp line in sartorial flair. With a preference for light, expensive yet understated suits with short jackets and tapered trousers, they set a pace for subcultural style at the beginning of the sixties.[10]

Though their 'look' quickly diffused outwards to the provinces, the original mods were a subculture centred on London. Their quest for exquisitely cut clothes took them to Soho tailors and shops like John Stephen on Carnaby Street – itself transformed from a fairly mundane London back street into the centre of the mod universe and, subsequently, into a bazaar of fashion and style at the hub of 'Swinging London'. Other centres of mod culture included London clubs such as the Scene and the Flamingo where young, white mods came into contact with black, American soul music (on the Motown, Stax and Volt labels), soul tightening its grip on popular musical tastes in the early sixties with the growing number of discotheques and the advent of pirate radio. Mod musical preferences also embraced black American rhythm and blues (emulated by 'mod' groups such as the Who and the Small Faces), together with Afro-Caribbean ska and bluebeat which was brought into the country by West Indians, settling in Britain in greater numbers from the late 1940s. Indeed, the exchange between mod and Afro-Caribbean styles marked a crucial stage in the developing intersection between black and white popular culture which became a central feature of British youth subcultures in the decades after 1945 (see chapter 9).

The mods, many of whom came from the housing estates of East and South London, were emblematic of a working class in transition. The mods' neat image of cool sophistication reflected the upwardly mobile character of post-war working-class life and contrasted sharply with the more class-bound qualities of their contemporary adversaries, the rockers. The media played an important role in consolidating the mod/rocker polarity, but the distinction was not pure invention. Tending to have lower paid, less skilled occupations, the rockers represented an affirmation of 'traditional' working-class lifestyles. With their motorbikes, leather jackets, jeans and boots the rockers rejected the 'effeminacy' of conspicuous consumption and instead cultivated an image of sturdy masculinity.[11] The mods, on the other hand, were often employed in lower white-collar jobs and their scooters and pristine dress made them the standard-bearers of the working class in 'the age of affluence'.

An additional (and frequently underestimated) influence on the development of British youth style during the early sixties was the transformations and shifts taking place within gay subculture. Since the early fifties many of the 'movers and shakers' of the English pop industry have been gay impresarios and promoters, possibly finding the 'marginal' world of entertainment more tolerant and accessible than the traditional world of business. More than this, however, the whole history of British youth subcultural fashion can be viewed as a series of interactions with gay styles and sensibilities.[12] In their various attempts to transgress everyday norms and boundaries gay and youth subcultures have mutually informed one another. Each has drawn styles of dress, music and posture from the other. The flamboyant 'Edwardian' look of the Teds, for example, had been anticipated by the appearance of similar styles within the gay underground during the late forties, while elements of cross-fertilization were especially evident in the mod and gay subcultures of the early sixties. Though most mods were avowedly heterosexual, they shared a set of musical and sartorial preferences which had first begun to cohere as an identifiable style within the gay clubs of the capital.[13] The beginning of the seventies saw mod narcissism further amplified in the rise of the glitter and glam rock cults which, once again, plundered gay subcultural music and apparel. Seventies' glam rock performers such as the Sweet and Slade were traditional masculine rock bands who drew on camp and androgynous imagery simply for their shock value but others, in particular David Bowie (himself a former mod), used their performance to explore notions of gender and identity in a way that was entirely new to most mainstream heterosexual audiences.

'We Will Fight Them on the Beaches . . .': Youth and Moral Panic in the 1960s

Superficially clean-cut and well-dressed, the mod's appearance was amenable to co-option within notions of post-war dynamism and modernity. The mods were treated as the trend-setters of sixties' stylishness and mobility and the press eagerly charted changes in the minutiae of mod dress and music. In media coverage of the mod phenomenon, however, the

media

duality of the imagery of youth continued. While mods were celebrated as classless consumers *par excellence* they were also reviled as the *bête noire* of the affluent society. This negative response to the mods was represented, above all, in the anxieties that surrounded the mod 'invasions' of several seaside towns in 1964. Working-class youngsters had traditionally visited seaside resorts at holiday times, but Easter 1964 was cold and wet and facilities for youngsters in such places were limited. In Clacton scuffles broke out between local youths and visiting Londoners, a few beach huts were vandalized and the odd window was broken. The total amount of violence and vandalism was not great, but the events were given front-page prominence by an outraged national press. Newspapers such as the *Daily Mirror* and the *Daily Express* were especially voluble in their fury, reporters regaling their readers with stories of a 'day of terror' in which a whole town had been overrun by a marauding mob 'hell-bent on destruction'. Reflecting wider unease about the 'irresponsible affluence' of post-war youth, the media found the apparent wealth of the youngsters especially galling – newspapers drawing attention to the effrontery of one young mod who had offered to pay his £75 fine for affray with a cheque (though the subsequent revelation that the youth had never in his life held a bank account let alone a cheque book attracted much less comment). The rest of the year saw extensive and sensational press coverage of Bank Holiday 'disturbances' at a range of British seaside resorts, including Brighton and Hastings, concerns that continued sporadically throughout the remainder of the sixties.

The spectacular reportage that surrounded the mod 'invasions' was, therefore, exaggerated and overwrought. The initial acts of violence and vandalism were slight and it is likely that the melodramatic press coverage actually served to engender and amplify subsequent disturbances. In his analysis of the events of 1964 Stanley Cohen termed such occasions of sensationalized media alarm 'moral panics', a situation in which:

> A condition, episode, person or group of persons emerges to become defined as a threat to societal values and interests; its nature presented in a stylized and stereotypical fashion by the mass media, the moral barricades are manned by editors, bishops, politicians and other right-thinking people; socially accredited experts pronounce their diagnoses and solutions; ways of coping are evolved or (more often) resorted to; the condition then disappears, submerges or deteriorates and becomes more visible. (Cohen, 1973, p. 9)

In these terms distorted media coverage plays an active role in shaping events. Media attention fans the sparks of an initially trivial incident, creating a self-perpetuating 'amplification spiral' which generates phenomena of much greater significance and magnitude.

Cohen's case study focused on media representations of the sixties' 'battles' between mods and rockers, charting how media intervention gave shape to these groups and crafted them into threatening 'folk devils'. However, his arguments could easily be applied to media treatment of the procession of subcultural groups that have appeared since.[14] From the skinheads of the late sixties, through the punks of the seventies, to the 'New Age travellers' and 'acid house ravers' of the late eighties and early nineties, youth subcultures have been subject to processes of stigmatiz-ation and stereotyping which, paradoxically, have worked to popularize and lend substance to styles that were initially indistinct and ill-defined. Media intervention, therefore, not only gives youth subcultures national exposure but also a degree of stylistic cohesion, uniformity and definition.

Paralleling Cohen's work on mods and rockers, Jock Young's (1971) study of young cannabis smokers also found that intervention by agencies of social control could play a key role in 'amplifying' deviance. According to Young, condemnation and stigmatization by the police and the media worked to confirm youngsters' self-conception as drug-takers and ulti-mately pushed them towards greater acts of deviance. The relation between youth and illicit drugs, in fact, represents one of the most enduring moral panics of the post-war period. The abuse of various drugs has a long history in Britain, but after 1945 the phenomenon gained par-ticular prominence as it became more specifically linked to trends in youth culture. Marijuana, amphetamines and heroin had all been used within British jazz subculture since before the war and the 'beatniks' of the fifties had dabbled with various substances (see chapter 7), but it was only in the 1960s that a state of 'moral panic' began to characterize social reaction to drug-taking among young people. Alarm first intensified around the mods' penchant for 'purple hearts', the *Sunday Mirror* (31 May 1964) reporting that Scotland Yard's Drug Squad had estimated that thousands of teenagers were regularly buying amphetamines on the black market. Additional press exposés led to questions in the House of Commons and ultimately to the passage of the Drugs (Prevention of Misuse) Act, which made unlicensed possession and importation of amphetamine a criminal offence. Similar concerns continued throughout the sixties, culminating with the introduction of the 1971 Misuse of Drugs Act, which represented the key piece of legislation governing the manufacture, supply and possession of illicit drugs throughout the following decades.

During the late fifties and early sixties concern also began to intensify in relation to the moral conduct of British youngsters. Coffee bars provoked particular disapproval as many girls began to spend their evenings away from parental control and outside the influence of official agencies. Indeed, while young women were marginal to moral panics about public order, their sexual behaviour occasioned considerable unease. Fears primarily cohered around a perceived rise in illegitimate pregnancies among teenage girls, but rises in recorded levels of venereal disease among young people also figured in calls for a greater surveillance of young women's sexuality and prompted the development of sex education in British schools.[15] As early as 1943 the Board of Education had advocated the provision of sex education in schools and during the 1950s and 1960s these ideas were increasingly implemented. Sex education in schools was delivered in generally conservative, moralistic tones, yet hostility to it remained pronounced in some quarters, the Longford Report on Pornography in 1972, for example, arguing that sex education should be confined to a familial context.

Moral panics about the activities and culture of young people punctuated the fifties and sixties with astonishing regularity. Such episodes certainly reveal a great deal about the wider preoccupations and anxieties of the period but they tell us little about the realities of life as experienced by young people themselves. In media coverage, especially, the behaviour and lifestyles of the young were consistently caricatured and overstated. For example, there were undoubtedly major shifts in the sexual attitudes and behaviour of young people after 1945 but empirical evidence suggests that, even in contemporary society, sex mostly takes place in the context of 'serious', monogamous relationships.[16] During the fifties and sixties youngsters obviously did have sexual experiences outside marriage but, even in the 'swinging sixties', young people's sexual activity was restrained and even furtive. We must remember, too, that the accessibility and acceptability of contraception came about very slowly, particularly for young people – and especially for young women. While the oral contraceptive pill was first marketed in 1963, it was not made available to single women until 1967, and the Family Planning Association did not officially give advice to unmarried women until 1966. Changes in sexual attitudes and behaviour, then, have always been piecemeal and never approached the scale of a permissive 'revolution'. However, as the following chapter makes clear, the post-war decades still marked a period of considerable change in the lives and culture of young women.

Notes

1   For studies which critically appraise the notion of a post-war political consensus see Roger Eatwell, 1979, *The 1945–1951 Labour Governments*, London: Batsford; Peter Jenkins, 1987, *Mrs. Thatcher's Revolution: The Ending of the Socialist Era*, London: Cape; David Marquand, 1988, *The Unprincipled Society*, London: Cape; Ben Pimlott, 1988, 'The myth of consensus', in L. M. Smith (ed.), *The Making of Britain: Echoes of Greatness*, London: Macmillan.

2   An insightful analysis of the main contours of change in British working-class life and culture during the fifties and sixties is provided in John Clarke, 1979, 'Capital and culture: the post-war working class revisited', in John Clarke, Chas Critcher and Richard Johnson (eds), *Working Class Culture: Studies in History and Theory*, London: Hutchinson, pp. 238–53.

3   One of the key studies to announce the 'bourgeoisification' of the post-war working class was Ferdynand Zweig, 1961, *The Worker in Affluent Society*, London: Heinemann. For a detailed survey of the weight of research and commentary suggesting the erosion of class distinctions during this period see Stuart Laing, 1986, *Representations of Working Class Life: 1957–64*, London: Macmillan, especially ch. 1, 'This new England', pp. 3–30.

4   Elizabeth Wilson goes so far as to argue that during the post-war era women were perceived as 'the touchstone for the social revolution', their situation seen as '*the* paradigm of Britain's successful experiment in non-revolutionary democracy and the gradualist approach to equality – of class as well as sex'. 'The woman wielding the hoover', Wilson concludes, 'could become the symbol of the social revolution that had obliterated inequality; for women were above all *classless*'. See Elizabeth Wilson, 1980, *Only Half Way To Paradise: Women in Postwar Britain: 1945–69*, London: Tavistock, p. 12.

5   The history of the American 'teenpic' industry is documented in John Doherty, 1988, *Teenagers and Teenpics: The Juvenilization of American Movies in the 1950s*, London: Unwin Hyman.

6   The rise and fall of the British pop film is meticulously charted in Andy Medhurst, 1995, 'It sort of happened here: the strange, brief life of the British pop film', in Jonathan Romney and Adrian Wootton (eds), *Celluloid Jukebox: Popular Music and the Movies Since the 1950s*, London: BFI, pp. 60–71.

7   Since the 1930s an agreement between the BBC and representatives of the

record industry and the Musicians Union had placed time limits on the radio broadcast of commercially produced records. This had originally been intended as a measure to protect both the profits of British record companies (who blamed falling record sales on the broadcast of recorded music) and the interests of musicians (who were anxious that records should not be used as a cheap alternative to live performance).

8   Accounts of the development of pop radio during this period are provided in Paul Harris, 1968, *When Pirates Ruled the Waves*, London: Impulse; Richard Nichols, 1983, *Radio Luxembourg: The Station of the Stars*, London: Comet; John Hind and Stephen Mosco, 1985, *Rebel Radio: The Full Story of British Pirate Radio*, London: Pluto Press, pp. 7–18; Stephen Barnard, 1989, *On the Radio: Music Radio in Britain*, Milton Keynes: Open University Press, pp. 32–49.

9   A history of British television's early forays into the field of pop music can be found in John Hill, 1991, 'Television and pop: the case of the 1950s', in John Corner (ed.), *Popular Television in Britain: Studies in Cultural History*, London: BFI.

10   Mod styles of the early sixties are vividly documented in Richard Barnes, 1979, *Mods!*, London: Eel Pie.

11   An excellent photographic history of rocker culture in the fifties and sixties has been compiled in Johnny Stuart, 1987, *Rockers!*, London: Plexus.

12   A perceptive overview of the influence of gay style on the universe of British youth culture is provided in Jon Savage, 1990, 'Tainted love: the influence of male homosexuality and sexual divergence on pop music and culture since the war', in Alan Tomlinson (ed.), *Consumption, Identity and Style: Marketing, Meanings and the Packaging of Pleasure*, London: Routledge, pp. 153–71. See also Richard Smith, 1995, *Seduced and Abandoned: Essays on Gay Men in Popular Music*, London: Cassell. An informed and insightful account of skin-head style as a meeting-ground between gay and heterosexual masculine styles is provided in Murray Healy, 1996, *Gay Skins: Class, Masculinity and Queer Appropriation*, London: Cassell. Though gay male style has exerted significant influence on youth subcultural phenomena, the influence of lesbian culture has been considerably less. This possibly reflects the greater degree to which lesbians have been marginalized and disempowered within mainstream culture.

13   An excellent account of the stylistic exchanges that took place between gay and mod subcultures can be found in Peter Burton's autobiographical account of life on the gay club scene during the early sixties. See Peter Burton, 1985, *Parallel Lives*, London: GMP.

14   A critical survey of the nature and process of moral panic in relation to post-war youth culture is provided in Ulf Boëthius, 1995, 'Youth, the media and

moral panics', in Johan Fornäs and Göran Bolin (eds), *Youth Culture in Late Modernity*, London: Sage, pp. 39–57.
15 For an overview and discussion of the history of sex education in British schools see AnnMarie Wolpe, 1987, 'Sex in schools: back to the future', *Feminist Review*, no. 27, pp. 37–47.
16 Empirical studies of young people's sexual behaviour can be found in Michael Schofield, 1965, *The Sexual Behaviour of Young People*, London: Longman; Michael Schofield, 1973, *The Sexual Behaviour of Young Adults*, London: Allen Lane; D. Leonard, 1980, *Sex and Generation*, London: Tavistock.

5 'Walkin' Back to Happiness'? The Cultures of Young Women since 1945

'Don't Treat Me Like a Child': Young Women and Post-War Socio-Economic Change

One of the most striking features of many accounts of youth in post-war Britain is the way that young women have invariably been 'hidden from history'. It is almost as though a process of 'masculinization' has taken place. The period has been cast largely in male terms, the history of post-war youth culture being reconstructed as chiefly a tale of spectacular male subcultures and masculine activity. This oversight is especially lamentable given that the trends which enhanced youth's general social profile after 1945 held particular significance for young women. Shifts in traditional labour markets had a profound impact on young women's employment structures, while many of the 'teenage' commercial industries were actually targeted at a specifically female market. Issues of gender relations, of course, cut across all areas of social and economic life and it would be erroneous to ghettoize the discussion of young women solely within a single chapter. The scale of change in the lives of young women, however, together with the centrality of the image of the teenage girl within post-war ideologies of classless prosperity, are issues deserving specific coverage.

Women were central to the post-war consumer 'boom' as both producers and consumers. After 1945 decreases in family size and a growing demand for women's labour combined to boost the proportion of married women in paid employment. As controllers of high-street spending, meanwhile, women were also pivotal within the emergence of a consumption-based economy, signified by the massive growth of advertising aimed at 'the housewife'. This did not, however, mark an era of dawning sexual equality. At home and in the workplace traditional divisions of labour remained essentially undisturbed and, since their employment was seen as subsidiary to their role as housewife and mother, women were often expected to do work that was low skilled and poorly paid. Nevertheless, the rise of a consumer society had a contradictory impact on women's lives. Gender inequalities were certainly confirmed and reinforced, but at the same time we should not lose sight of gains made in terms of economic and cultural enfranchisement, particularly in relation to young women.

Until the mid-sixties few contemporary researchers gave specific consideration to changes in young women's social and economic status. T. R. Fyvel's study of post-war youth, for example, dealt almost exclusively with young men and relegated girls to the position of 'dumb' and 'passive' 'camp-followers' (Fyvel, 1963, p. 96). Compared with those of their male peers, however, post-war shifts in the culture of young women were probably more pronounced. The transformation of traditional labour markets, for example, offered girls particular gains. Though domestic service is often thought of as largely a Victorian and Edwardian phenomenon, between 1920 and 1931 numbers of servants actually grew by 16 per cent, domestic service remaining a central experience for working-class women, especially girls, throughout the inter-war period.[1] This experience, moreover, could often be stifling and oppressive. Girls 'living-in' were especially constricted – subject to strict rules and rituals, with little free time and often having to send money home to help support the families they had left behind. After 1945, however, domestic service contracted into insignificance as an area of employment. In place of the constraints of domestic service girls took advantage of opportunities opened up by the expansion of consumer industries, business services, retailing and especially the growing clerical sector (see table 5.1). Whether they were secretaries or production-line workers, therefore, many girls' economic and cultural horizons were broader than might have been the case before the war, as they were increasingly able to leave behind the disciplines of the workplace in the evenings and at weekends.

Table 5.1   Percentage of young people aged 15–17 entering clerical employment, 1950–1968

	Males	Females
1950	9.8	24.9
1952	9.0	31.4
1954	8.7	32.1
1956	8.0	34.7
1958	10.6	35.0
1960	9.0	38.2
1962	9.0	35.3
1964	10.8	39.2
1966	9.1	40.1
1968	8.3	38.9

Source: Calculated from Department of Employment, 1971, *British Labour Statistics Historical Abstract 1886–1968*, London: HMSO, Table 158, p. 304.

Throughout the fifties and sixties high demand for their labour meant that most young women had little difficulty in finding work after leaving school. Wider gender inequalities, nevertheless, were reflected in the levels of young women's earnings, which grew at a slower rate (and were always significantly less) than their male equivalents (see table 3.4). Even so, throughout the fifties and sixties most working girls still possessed a margin of disposable income available for personal consumption. Indeed, in many respects young women represented a lucrative post-war market. Many of the new 'teenage' products were, in fact, specifically targeted at girls, while many 'traditional' products and brands (especially cosmetics and toiletries) also began to relocate their sales-drives to capture teenage girls' spending power – to the extent that in 1965 Peter Laurie could confidently assert: 'The real dynamo behind the teenage revolution is the anonymous teenage girl . . . Although girls spend less than boys, the dominant sales efforts for clothes, records, and cosmetics is aimed at girls' (Laurie, 1965, p. 151).

During the 1920s and 1930s many products and entertainments were already aimed at young female wage-earners. For instance, magazines such as *Girls' Cinema* (1920), *Secrets* (1932), *Oracle* (1933) and *Miracle* (1935) were targeted primarily at young working women. Nevertheless, the scale of this inter-war market and the cultural specificity of its products did not match that of the fifties and sixties. The shelves of post-war newsagents, for example, saw a plethora of new comics and magazines based on a diet of romance and pop music and geared specifically to young women. In the 1950s Amalgamated Press launched both *Marilyn* ('The Great All-Picture Love Story Weekly', 1955) and *Valentine* ('Brings You Love Stories in Pictures', 1957), while competitors City Magazines responded with *Boyfriend* (1959) and D. C. Thomson struck out with *Romeo* (1957), *Cherie* ('Exciting Love Stories in Pictures', 1960) and *Jackie* ('For Go-Ahead Teens', 1964).

Teenage girls' greatest post-war cultural influence, however, was in the world of clothes design, 'youth' coming to dominate British women's fashions as not only a market for retail sales but also as a predominant source of design imagery.[2] Developments reached their apotheosis in the mid-sixties – with the *Daily Express* promoting sixteen-year-old Lesley Hornby, under her pseudonym 'Twiggy', as 'The Face of 66' – though the roots of this trend lie a decade earlier. Dramatic change in the field of women's fashion was unlikely in the immediate aftermath of the Second World War given the constraints of clothes rationing and utility design. Yet even in the late forties and early fifties the established traditions of British couture were reasserted in the nostalgic sophistication of the New Look's swirling skirts and flouncing curves. By the mid-fifties, however, this mature elegance looked increasingly dated alongside the youthful chic pioneered by designers such as Mary Quant. In 1955 Quant, backed by her husband Alexander Plunkett Greene, opened her first boutique, 'Bazaar', in Chelsea and by the early sixties the influence of their fresh, 'young' look was pre-eminent. Quant's role as a trail-blazer in the frontiers of women's fashion was confirmed in 1962 when the cover of the first edition of the *Sunday Times Magazine* featured Jean Shrimpton modelling a sleeveless Quant dress, the same newspaper later awarding Quant for 'jolting England out of its conventional attitude towards clothes'.

Even when she went into mass production with her 'Ginger Group' label in 1963, Quant's designs were expensive. More affordable were clothes produced by Barbara Hulanicki and her husband John Fitz Simon under the 'Biba' logo. Launching a mail order fashion business in 1963, Hulanicki and Fitz Simon used its profits to open their first shop in Kensington the following year. Biba outlets were mainly confined to London (though there were also several branches in the provinces), but the Biba 'look' became a leading influence and the Biba strategy of combining intimate interior design with a constantly changing stock inspired the emergence of a new cultural institution – the 'fashion boutique'. Established department stores also adapted to the growing 'youthfulness' of women's fashion, opening sales areas specifically geared towards a younger market. In 1962, for example, Hanningtons' department store in Brighton opened a department 'for teenagers and the just-overs', the store management claiming it to be 'the first boutique outside London to cater for the developing shape of Miss Teenage Britain'. By the late sixties and early seventies this trend reached fruition with the ascendancy of Top Shop and Miss Selfridge – chain stores dealing exclusively in mass-produced clothes geared to a market of young women.

As a social construct, then, the 'teenager' was not gender specific. Whereas the categories of 'youth' and 'adolescent' generated during the late nineteenth and early twentieth centuries had been largely male in their connotations and associated imagery, the post-war 'teenager' was as often a girl as a boy. In fact, more than any other image, it was possibly the 'teenage girl' that most fully encapsulated the ideologies of energetic hedonism characteristic of Britain during the fifties and sixties. In the rhetoric of classlessness and affluence the figure of the teenage girl was especially prominent. Typical was *Picture Post*'s coverage of 'Those Wild, Wild Girls', the magazine arguing that the more one looked into the lives of young women 'the more apparent it became that social barriers were fast melting away' with 'factory girls . . . taking more and more interest in those recreations which have hitherto been considered the recreations of the middle class' (1 April 1957).

The prominence of the image of the 'teenage girl' as a signifier of social change during the late fifties and early sixties was epitomized by the succession of 'girls next door' plucked from obscurity by British television and promoted as the nation's quintessential teenager. For example, in 1959 Susan Stranks featured as a 'typical teenager' on the first panel of the BBC's *Juke Box Jury*, while in 1962 Janice Nicholls, a sixteen-year-old office clerk, shot to fame in a similar role on ITV's pop show *Thank Your Lucky Stars*. The ultimate 'Joanne Public' of British youth, however, was undoubtedly Cathy McGowan, a nineteen-year-old secretary from Streatham picked as a 'typical teenager' to present ITV's pop flagship *Ready, Steady, Go!* in 1963. Indeed, dubbed 'Queen of the Mods' by the popular press, McGowan attained the status of cultural icon, with the sale of Cathy McGowan shirts, jeans, stockings, record players and even movable Cathy McGowan dolls.

The late fifties and early sixties also saw a crop of young female singers promoted as 'ordinary teenagers'. Outstanding in this respect was Helen Shapiro. Born and brought up in London's East End, Shapiro signed to Columbia Records at the age of fourteen and between 1961 and 1962 released a series of successful pop singles. Filmed in school uniform as she waved good-bye to her friends at Clapton Girls' School and embarked on her show-business career, Shapiro's public persona was based on her qualities of 'conventional' adolescence – her photo-sessions and press releases stressing her essence as 'a typical teenager of the day'. The 'ordinary' teenage girl also raised her beehive in British films of the period. Shapiro, for instance, starred in light-hearted pop vehicles such as *Play It Cool* and *It's Trad Dad* (both 1962), though it was in 'kitchen sink' realism that the 'teenage girl' became most prominent as a social type. Representative was the career of Rita Tushingham who, after making her debut in *A Taste of Honey* (1961), went on to play a series of gritty, working-class girls in films such as *That Kind of Girl* (1963), *A Place To Go* (1963) and *The Leatherboys* (1963), as well as featuring in tales of 'swinging London' like *The Knack* (1965) and the satirical *Smashing Time* (1966). Testimony to the salience of such 'ordinary teenage girls' as an embodiment of the period's images and ideologies came in 1962, when the Variety Club of Great Britain's award for 'Most Promising Newcomer' was shared by both Shapiro and Tushingham.

'Teenage Rampage': Young Women and Pop Culture

One of the greatest weaknesses of earlier histories and sociologies of youth culture was the limited coverage accorded to female experiences. Studies of spectacular subcultures, in particular, reinforced 'stereotypical' images of women as passive and inactive.[3] Here, young women tended to be mentioned only insofar as they were dependent upon or deviant from masculine patterns of behaviour, girls' activities often treated as a mere footnote to the principal areas of interest – the dramatic acts of delinquency or stylistic innovation perpetrated by 'the lads'.

Certainly, the masculine preoccupations of some subcultures worked to marginalize female participation. The boots'n'braces culture of the skinheads during the late sixties and early seventies, for example, was preoccupied with the exploration of expressions of masculine identity and,

girls.
↓

as such, tended to circumscribe the active involvement of young women.[4] Nevertheless, girls were not, by any means, excluded from the pageant of post-war youth subcultures. In the fifties, for example, stiletto-heeled and multi-petticoated girls could be found jiving alongside Teddy boys in most local coffee bars and dance halls. Other subcultural milieux proved to be especially accessible to young women. The constructions of gender within mod subculture during the early sixties, for example, were sufficiently ambiguous to allow young girls an especially visible and active presence, while the acid house and rave scenes of the late eighties and early nineties represented dance-oriented cultures of comparable accessibility. Within these scenes women tended not to be located at the level of production – in terms of organizing events or being involved in music making – yet many women were prominent on the dance-floors of eighties' and nineties' club culture. The communal atmosphere of the rave seemed to erode the preda-tory sexual relations of traditional night-club life and for many women the rave scene opened up access to the kind of thrills and pleasures that had previously been the preserve of masculine subcultures.[5]

Overall, however, traditional gender divisions have tended to be repro-duced within the sphere of youth culture – young women facing a range of economic and social constraints to which their male counterparts have not been subject. For example, although girls undoubtedly made gains from post-war shifts in the labour market, their disposable income has been consistently less than that of young men, imposing greater limits on access to leisure and the 'raw materials' of cultural activity. Moreover, the sexual division of labour (especially within working-class families) has also meant that from an early age women have taken on child-care and domestic responsibilities not usually expected of young men. As a consequence, young women's leisure has been qualitatively as well as quantitatively different from that of men. Female leisure has been more predominantly structured around the family and the private sphere of the home so that the times, locations and nature of leisure have merged with those of domestic work.[6] This home-centredness of young women's cultural life, furthermore, has been accentuated by the tendency for parents to police their daughters' leisure more strictly than that of their sons, while a regu-latory male presence within domains such as the street, the pub or the football ground has further militated against female participation in the 'public' side of subcultural activity and expression.

The recognition that young women occupy social and cultural locations different from those of their male peers led, in the 1980s, to a growing body of feminist research into the ways that girls interact among themselves and form distinctive cultures of their own.[7] Rather than seeing girls simply as appendages to male subcultural activity it was argued that young women inhabited *their own* cultural structures. Instead of the male-dominated world of public subcultures, girls' cultural spaces were presented as being chiefly concentrated within the private realm of the home. The bedroom in particular was cited by theorists as a key site of girls' cultural life, the bedroom being 'the place where girls meet, listen to music and teach each other make up skills, practice their dancing, compare sexual notes, criticize each other's clothes and gossip' (Frith, 1978, p. 64). The growth of such a 'bedroom culture' was greatly facilitated by post-war rises in living standards and shifts in demography and housing which saw trends towards both smaller family units and more privatized patterns of family life. Nevertheless, though young women have certainly enjoyed a degree of independence and freedom within the 'bedroom culture', it would be misleading to present their cultural activity as taking place more or less exclusively within the realm of the private. While it is true that patriarchal regulation has pronounced the terms under which girls have appeared in public spaces, they have rarely been excluded altogether. Instead of simply sitting in their bedrooms since 1945, then, teenage girls have actively participated in numerous public arenas.

Rather than being absent from street cultures, young women's presence may simply have attracted less attention from agencies of social control and sociological research. Girls' involvement in deviant youth gangs, for example, has gone largely uncharted, only attracting interest at times of heightened public concern such as that which followed the street robbery of actress Elizabeth Hurley by a group of four teenage girls in November 1994. Indeed, there now exists a growing body of contemporary research to suggest that many young women do participate in 'deviant' activities usually associated with men – though the extent of girls' involvement in crime, drinking, fighting and drug-taking tends to be obscured by legal and welfare responses which interpret this behaviour as 'pathological' rather than 'delinquent'.[8]

More generally, the street has always been an important focal point of young women's cultures, a role enhanced by the development of town centres and shopping complexes from the sixties onwards. Such public arenas have afforded young women an important cultural space where they have been able to wander around the shops or simply 'hang around', chatting to their friends. Throughout the fifties and sixties coffee bars were also pivotal within the public cultures of young women. Places where girls could see and be seen, coffee bars offered relative sanctuary from the confines of the home, the workplace and the official institutions of youth provision. During the late sixties the role of the coffee bar in girls' lives was displaced by the disco and increasingly the town centre pub, but their function has been much the same – a public space in which young women can socialize and express a cultural identity.

Popular music has represented another important cornerstone in young women's post-war cultural formations. The thousands of young amateur musicians spawned by the skiffle boom in the fifties and the beat explosion of the sixties were, however, almost exclusively male. Where girls have been most crucial in the sphere of popular music is in their capacity as consumers. In 1949 an eighteen-year-old clerical worker explained to interviewers the important place of pop music in her life:

> I go to the jazz club, dancing, tennis, swimming and listening to gramophone records. On Saturday I went to the Bebop Club in the evening . . . I packed up my boyfriend because he didn't like me going to Bop clubs . . . I don't disagree with my parents except about 'Bop'. That's the only thing: Mother can't stand that, but I like it . . . What do I want out of life? Just a nice husband, a baby, a house and 'bop' records.[9]

This enthusiasm often assumed proportions that took social commentators aback. For example, writing in *Picture Post* in 1954 Robert Muller was astounded by reactions to 'crooner' stars like Dickie Valentine, Frankie Vaughan and David Whitfield that came from the gallery audience:

> They are mostly young girls up there, splashing in a crazy pool of adoration. Usually, they are 'unescorted', sitting hunched forward . . . half-open mouths emitting a strange, continuous symphony of sound . . . And when the song is ended, the arms go into action, flapping and tearing the air. Hands are whipped together. And above the shrieks, and the moans, and the sighs, you hear the frenzied appeals: 'Oh Frankie!'; 'Oh Dickie!'; 'Oh – !' (*Picture Post*, 7 August 1954)

Of course, female fanaticism over male performers was not unique to the post-war era. Film stars such as Rudolph Valentino attracted similar displays of excitement and devotion during the twenties and thirties. During the fifties, however, this kind of behaviour became more specifically associated with the relationship between teenage girls and pop musicians, the period witnessing the birth of a new cultural phenomenon – the 'teenybopper'. Since Johnny Ray and Tommy Steele in the mid-fifties successive performers and pop groups have been the focus for zealous shows of admiration from large groups of young women. High-points were obviously reached in the early sixties with the scenes of near hysteria that attended any public appearance by the Beatles or the Rolling Stones, yet the heyday of the teenybopper probably came a decade later. During the early seventies a staggering array of pop idols competed for the attention of teenage fans. American stars like David Cassidy and the Osmonds (especially brothers Donny and 'Little' Jimmy) were regularly greeted by thousands of chanting fans upon their arrival in Britain, though home-grown talent like Scottish band the Bay City Rollers were also famous for their devout legion of tartan-clad female followers. Meanwhile, the rise of glam rock (with its fusion of rock guitars, implausible silver costumes and androgynous pantomime theatrics) was also important in generating a whole catalogue of teen heartthrobs – with stars like David Bowie, Marc Bolan, the Sweet, Slade and Gary Glitter.

The teenybopper has traditionally been the subject of popular ridicule – the very term having derisive and pejorative connotations. A particularly misogynistic broadside came in 1964 when Paul Johnson, writing in *New Statesman*, launched a vitriolic attack on fans of the Beatles. For Johnson the Fab Four's following revealed 'a bottomless chasm of vacuity':

> Huge faces, bloated with cheap confectionery and smeared with chain-store make-up, the open, sagging mouths and glazed eyes, the hands mindlessly drumming in time to the music, the broken stiletto heels, the shoddy, stereo-typed, 'with it' clothes: here apparently, is a collective portrait of a generation enslaved by a commercial machine. (*New Statesman*, 28 February 1964)

Johnson's comments were obviously permeated by male chauvinism, yet many feminist authors have also been critical of the teenybopper. While applauding the imperviousness of teenybopper culture to male intervention, several feminist theorists have been critical of practices which they see as socializing young women into the subordinate gender role of 'adoring female in awe of the male on a pedestal' (McRobbie and Garber, 1976, p. 221). However, like many aspects of women's post-war culture, perhaps the teenybopper has been unjustly trivialized and dismissed. After all, the experience of being a teenybopper has offered young women opportunities for friendship and communal solidarity, as well as an avenue through which to participate in symbolic displays of collective power. While 'teenybop' culture has had its private, 'bedroom' dimension, it has also afforded young women the chance to enter public spaces *en masse*, overstepping the bounds of conformity in a transgression of everyday norms. So, in this respect, the faces on the posters are themselves not especially important. Indeed, the ephemeral fame of pop stars like Bros and Kajagoogoo bear testimony to the notoriously short shelf-life of many teen idols. Instead, girls' real obsession has been with the public display of collective power and the sense of group solidarity that are offered by teenybopper culture. For example, Sheryl Garratt's autobiographical account of her experiences as a Bay City Rollers fan during the 1970s describes how her screams came not from meaningless hysteria but from 'defiance, celebration, and excitement . . . It was us against the world and, for a while at least, we were winning' (Garratt, 1984, pp. 142–5). In this argument we should not, perhaps, go quite as far as a group of American feminists who have interpreted Beatlemania as 'the first and most dramatic uprising of *women's* sexual revolution' (Ehrenreich et al., 1987, p. 11). Fans of the Beatles and the Bay City Rollers were not a revolutionary vanguard. Any 'opposition' articulated within 'teenybop' offers only an oblique challenge to patriarchal domination and falls far short of direct confrontation with the origins of inequality and oppression. Nevertheless, for all its shortcomings, 'teenybop''s potential for the cultural empowerment of young women should not be underestimated.

During the late eighties and early nineties a new wave of young, energetic 'boy bands' came to the fore. Groups such as New Kids on the Block, Take That, Boyzone and East 17 excited crowd responses redolent of sixties' Beatlemania, yet they were not straightforward reproductions of the 'teenybop' idols of the sixties and seventies. Compared with their predecessors, the 'boy bands' of the eighties and nineties were much more explicit in terms of their sexual appeal – often appearing stripped to the waist, their well-oiled physiques shown off in sensual and provocative dance sequences. This 'sexualization' of 'boy bands' was constituent in wider shifts taking place in the representation of the male body in popular culture. During the 1980s and 1990s masculinity came to be increasingly displayed as an object of pleasure and desire – an objectification of male sexuality which, some feminist theorists argued, offered greater measures of cultural empowerment to female audiences.[10]

During the eighties and nineties further important shifts seemed to register in the realm of teenage girls' culture. According to Angela McRobbie, the emergence of a new range of girls' magazines such as *Just Seventeen* in the 1980s was representative of a general 'unhinging' of traditional stereotypes of passive femininity.[11] Whereas earlier magazines such as *Jackie* were suffused with stifling ideologies of romantic love as a prerequisite for happiness and success, in the pages of *Just Seventeen* femininity emerged as an altogether less rigid category – a form of female identity marked by a greater measure of self-esteem and autonomy.

In the field of pop performance young women also began to engineer more assertive and even rebellious forms of feminine identity. In the late 1970s the rise of punk rock (see chapter 8) provided a fertile space for the politicization of sexuality and female identity, brash female artists like the Slits and Siouxsie Sioux enacting transgressive forms of femininity in their unconventional hair and clothing styles and their assertive stage performances. During the eighties the erotic videos and stage-shows of artists like Madonna further challenged traditional, passive notions of female identity, while in the early nineties the American underground rock scene saw the emergence of the 'Riot Grrrl' movement – a loose alliance of all-women bands and individual women artists who made loud, confrontational music that self-consciously developed a feminist critique of the patriarchal power structures of the rock establishment.[12] Although the 'Riot Grrrl' movement certainly exerted an influence on the British music scene, it was essentially a phenomenon of the American music underground. Yet mainstream British pop also saw moves by young women into highly visible, confident and often defiant musical styles. The late nineties, for example, saw an all-girl fivesome, the Spice Girls, spring to the forefront of pop stardom. In many respects the Spice Girls were a perfectly conventional vehicle of mainstream pop. Recruited, modelled and marketed by a team of producers and record company moguls, their album, 'Spice', sold over three million copies in 1996 while their single, 'Wannabe', reached number one in the singles' charts of twenty-seven countries. The Spice Girls' image, however, recast many of the qualities conventionally associated with female pop artists. Although their dictum of 'Girl Power' amounted to little more than an advertising slogan, the Spice Girls' strident, feisty stage personas embodied many of the changes that had taken place in the possibilities for women's public self-expression over the preceding twenty years. The Spice Girls' blend of brazen cheek, fun-seeking energy and confident sexuality elaborated a version of feminine identity which, in some respects at least, transgressed traditional norms and conventions, laying claim to a cultural visibility and assertiveness which had previously been the province of male-dominated youth subcultures.

Notes

1   See Pam Taylor, 1979, 'Daughters and mothers – maids and mistresses: domestic service between the wars', in John Clarke, Chas Critcher and Richard Johnson (eds), *Working Class Culture: Studies in History and Theory*, London: Hutchinson, pp. 121–40.

2   Further discussion of the impact of the imagery of 'youth' on the field of women's fashions during the early sixties can be found in Elizabeth Wilson and Lou Taylor, 1989, *Through the Looking Glass*, London: BBC, pp. 157–63; Jennifer Harris, Sarah Hyde and Greg Smith, 1986, *1966 And All That: Design and the Consumer in Britain 1960–1969*, London: Trefoil, pp. 109–32.

3   For a critique of these accounts see Angela McRobbie, 1980, 'Settling accounts with subcultures: a feminist critique', *Screen Education*, no. 34, pp. 37–49.

4   According to Mike Brake, one of the central features of post-war subcultural style has been the exploration of various forms of masculine identity. See Mike Brake, 1985, *Comparative Youth Culture*, London: Routledge and Kegan Paul, pp. 178–83.

5   These freedoms and pleasures encountered by young women in the dance scenes of the late eighties and early nineties are explored in Maria Pini, 1997, 'Women and the early British rave scene', in Angela McRobbie (ed.), *Back to Reality? Social Experience and Cultural Studies*, Manchester: Manchester University Press, pp. 152–69.

6   For discussion and analysis of the various factors which work to circumscribe young women's participation in the spectacle of youth subcultures see Rachel Powell and John Clarke, 1976, 'A note on marginality', in Stuart Hall and Tony Jefferson (eds), *Resistance Through Rituals: Youth Subcultures in Post-War Britain*, London: Hutchinson, pp. 223–30; Sarah Marshall and Carol Borrill, 1984, 'Understanding the invisibility of young women', *Youth and Policy*, no. 9, pp. 36–9; Sheila Scraton, 1987, ' "Boys muscle in where angels fear to tread" – girls' subcultures and physical activities', in John Horne, David Jary and Alan Tomlinson (eds), *Sport, Leisure and Social Relations*, London: Routledge and Kegan Paul, pp. 160–86.

7   Examples of this approach can be found in Angela McRobbie, 1978, 'Working

class girls and the culture of femininity', in Women's Studies Group (ed.), *Women Take Issue: Aspects of Women's Subordination*, London: Hutchinson, pp. 96–108; Angela McRobbie and Trisha McCabe (eds), 1981, *Feminism for Girls: An Adventure Story*, London: Routledge and Kegan Paul; Christine Griffin, 1985, *Typical Girls: Young Women from School to the Job Market*, London: Routledge; Angela McRobbie and Mica Nava (eds), 1984, *Gender and Generation*, London: Macmillan; Sue Lees, 1986, 'A new approach to the study of girls', *Youth and Policy*, no. 16, pp. 20–7.

8   For studies which highlight the extent of female involvement in 'deviant' social behaviour see Lesley Shacklady Smith, 1978, 'Sexist assumptions and female delinquency', in Carol Smart and Barry Smart (eds), *Women, Sexuality and Social Control*, London: Routledge and Kegan Paul, pp. 74–83; Rob Mawby, 1980, 'Sex and crime: the results of a self-report study', *British Journal of Sociology*, vol. 31, no. 4, pp. 525–43; Anne Campbell, 1981, *Girl Delinquents*, Oxford: Basil Blackwell; David Riley, 1986, 'Sex differences in teenage crime; the role of lifestyle', *Home Office Research Bulletin*, no. 20; Anne Campbell, 1986, 'Self-report of fighting by females', *British Journal of Criminology*, vol. 26, no. 1, pp. 28–46.

9   Mass Observation, 1949, *A Report on Teenage Girls*, File Report 3150.

10 Further discussion and analysis of the potential for female autonomy and control in the realm of popular culture is elaborated in Lorraine Gamman and Margaret Marshment (eds), 1988, *The Female Gaze: Women as Viewers of Popular Culture*, London: Women's Press.

11 These arguments can be found in Angela McRobbie, 1991, '*Jackie* and *Just Seventeen*: girls' comics and magazines in the 1980s', in Angela McRobbie, *Feminism and Youth Culture: From 'Jackie' to 'Just Seventeen'*, London: Macmillan, pp. 135–88; Angela McRobbie, '*More!* New sexualities in girls' and women's magazines', in McRobbie (ed.), *Back to Reality?*, pp. 190–209.

12 A detailed account and analysis of the 'Riot Grrrl' movement can be found in Joanne Gotlieb and Gayle Wald, 1994, 'Smells like teen spirit: riots grrrls, revolution and women in independent rock', in Andrew Ross and Tricia Rose (eds), *Microphone Fiends: Youth Music and Youth Culture*, London: Routledge, pp. 250–74.

6 'The Boys Are Back in Town': Youth Subcultures and the 'Return' of Class Conflict

'Skinhead Moonstomp': Subcultures, Conflict and Class in the Early Seventies

By the mid-sixties the confident post-war rhetoric of growth and prosperity had begun to falter. Attempts were made to shore up social and political consensus, most obviously with the 'corporatism' of Harold Wilson's 1964 Labour government and its calls for short-term 'belt-tightening' and the subordination of sectional demands to the 'national good', but by the end of the decade successive wage freezes and cuts in public expenditure had become symptomatic of growing economic strife and industrial unrest. In this context the ideologies of affluence and classlessness, which had been such a feature of fifties' social comment, became increasingly untenable. The working class had certainly obtained higher standards of living during the fifties and early sixties, but it became clear that decreases in relative inequality had been limited and the basic contours of class relations in Britain remained essentially intact.[1] The sixties, moreover, saw the 'rediscovery' of poverty, a series of studies revealing that 'affluence' had been far less broadly based than many had supposed.[2] Similarly, notions of young people's 'classless affluence' and the rise of a homogeneous 'culture of youth' were steadily revealed as a myth, research increasingly pointing to the continued relevance of economic class as a key influence on youngsters' social experiences and cultural preferences.

As an issue for enquiry, 'class' was never entirely evacuated from studies of post-war youth. For example, official research such as the Crowther Report of 1959 and the Robbins Report of 1963, as well as studies such as J. W. B. Douglas's *The Home and the School* (1964), all registered concern at the continual 'failure' of working-class children to realize their educational potential. By the late sixties, meanwhile, studies by Barry Sugarman (1967) and David Hargreaves (1967) had demonstrated that class background was crucial in determining secondary school pupils' cultural preferences and orientations. David Downes's (1966) work on youths from London's East End, meanwhile, also attested to the persistence of social class as a determinant of young people's cultural patterns – especially in the sphere of leisure which, according to Downes, represented the pre-eminent focal point in the lives of working-class youngsters for whom school was a meaningless drudge and work represented nothing more than a source of income. By the end of the decade, then, structural inequality had begun to re-establish itself at the centre of youth studies, a development which was at least partly indebted to shifts within British youth culture itself, the period seeing the appearance of much starker divisions in the field of youth style and music.

The mod subculture of the early sixties had developed from within the south-eastern working class, mod argot and ritual reflecting many core values and concerns of the parental working class. Nevertheless, the mods' flamboyant style of conspicuous consumption meant they could be easily incorporated within a discourse of classless affluence. In the late sixties, however, no such co-option was possible with the skinheads, whose self-conscious invocation of a 'traditional' working-class heritage was irreconcilable with notions of disappearing social divisions in the culture of British youth.

The skinhead style first began to make its presence felt within British youth culture in the mid-sixties.[3] A measure of disagreement exists as to the specific location of the skinhead's roots, some commentators citing Glasgow or the north-east of England as the origin of the distinctive 'uniform' of steel toe-capped work boots, rolled-up jeans, braces and convict-style cropped hair,[4] while others point to the East End of London as the skinhead's birthplace.[5] Irrespective of its exact geographical origin it seems certain that the skinhead 'look' first developed as a 'harder-edged' branch of the sixties' mod scene. The actual term 'skinhead' first came into general circulation in 1969 through its usage by the popular press, but in reality it is impossible to pinpoint changes in youth culture with any kind of temporal precision, one subcultural style merging seamlessly into another. In fact, youngsters wearing boots and sporting closely cropped hairstyles could be found within mod circles as early as 1964, though by the later sixties the 'skinheads' had begun to evolve into a more identifiably distinct subcultural group.

Even so, important elements of continuity always linked the skinheads to the mods, particularly with regard to musical preference. Like the mods before them, skinheads favoured American soul and Jamaican ska. Jamaican artists such as Desmond Dekker and Prince Buster were particular skinhead favourites and record companies like Island, Trojan and Pama sprang up in Britain to meet the growing demand for ska and reggae that came not just from the West Indian community, but also from an increasing number of white youngsters. Like the mods, skinheads also drew on elements of black culture as a source of fashion and style. A crucial cultural reference point were Jamaican rude boys, the hustlers and small-time gangsters of the slums of West Kingston, whose 'street cool' apparel of two-tone 'tonic' suits, 'pork pie' hats and wrap-around dark glasses found echoes in both mod and skinhead style (see chapter 9). In other respects, though, skinhead subculture differed markedly from that of mod, especially in the skinheads' projection of a rawer, more abrasive form of masculine identity and the way in which football became a focal point of the skinheads' cultural universe.

Aggressively partisan behaviour is not a feature unique to post-war football. Since the modern game's inception in the late nineteenth century there has been a long and connected history of fights between players, violence between supporters and attacks on game officials.[6] Only after 1945, however, did disturbances at football matches begin to become more specifically associated with younger sections of the crowd. The national press first made regular reference to 'hooligan gangs' operating in relation to football during the 1966/7 season, a period in which segregation by age was becoming more pronounced in league football grounds. Groups of young men increasingly began to stake out the football terraces as their own territory, acting in ways which either deliberately or inadvertently discouraged the presence of older spectators, phenomena closely associated with the rise of the skinhead. Strident support of a local football side was congruent with the skinheads' assertion of a stylized proletarian aesthetic and their celebration of traditional loyalties and aggressive masculinity.

Attending football games *en masse*, groups of skinheads laid claim to grounds in a manner unknown to previous generations, taking the names of the terraces as their own – for example the Chelsea 'Shed', Arsenal's 'North Bank' or 'the Loft' at Queens Park Rangers – and there developed an extensive network of violent rivalries between the various football 'ends', with shared memories of past victories and defeats and complex cycles of retribution.[7]

By the mid-seventies the skinhead style had become an anachronism, yet violence by younger sections of the football crowd remained a problem. The late seventies and eighties, in fact, seemed to witness a heightened development and 'refinement' of football 'fighting crews' – with the emergence of an 'elite' group of hooligan gangs such as Leeds' 'Service Crew', West Ham's 'Inter-City Firm', Millwall's 'Bushwhackers', Chelsea's 'Head-Hunters', Portsmouth's '6:57 Crew' and so on. Assessing the true level of organization within such groups, however, is problematic. The nature of their group structure and hierarchy has tended to be distorted by sensationalized press reports of 'disciplined hooligan armies ravaging the land', while the rise of 'casual' subcultural style on football terraces during the mid-eighties saw hooligan groups themselves anxious to exude an image of business-like efficiency (see chapter 11). Even so, it seems likely that the improvements that took place in police strategies of surveillance and control in and around football grounds from the late seventies demanded a greater degree of planning and foresight on the part of football hooligan gangs – though possibly not of the order suggested in the most melodramatic press reports. However, if this period did see a trend towards more firmly bounded, formally organized 'gang' structures this would mark a major departure from the historical traditions of British youth culture.

In America there exists a long history of sociological research highlighting the urban presence of formally organized, delinquent youth gangs.[8] In contrast, hierarchical and tightly knit gang structures have been rare among British working-class youngsters. More typical of British youths' collective alliances have been less formally structured and more loosely organized 'cliques' or casual 'fraternities of the street'.[9] These looser, more informal bonds have typified the group allegiances of British youth, from the nineteenth century 'scuttlers' through to post-war groups such as the Teddy boys and the skinheads. Rather than any notion of rigid gang structure, the central unifying force within these groups has been a strong sense of local identification and neighbourhood solidarity. In the mid-1990s these patterns, in some areas at least, seemed to be shifting. In 1995 the murder of headmaster Philip Lawrence by a knife-wielding teenager highlighted the existence of a more formally structured gang culture in north and west London. With their membership primarily made up of Chinese youngsters, gangs such as the Wo Sing Wo (WSW) and the 14K took their names from established groups of Triad gangsters, the youngsters emulating their criminal heroes in the way they drew up a system of secret oaths, subscriptions and hierarchies. These patterns of organization, however, were the exception rather than the norm and informal networks, based on local friendships and affiliations, remained more typical of British 'gang' culture. Nevertheless, bonds of loyalty have always been powerfully felt and have generated an intense sense of 'proprietorship' over neighbourhood 'turf' and local solidarity in the face of incursions by 'outsider' groups. More often than not these 'outsiders' are youngsters from surrounding neighbourhoods or nearby communities, themselves members of a different 'street fraternity', who may have strayed into the wrong part of town. At times, however, this 'us verses them' sense of local unity has also embraced a marked dimension of racial hostility, particularly in the context of the post-1945 collapse of many local economies. All too often blame for local socio-economic decline has been displaced from the deep-rooted political and economic causes onto more readily identifiable targets such as immigrant communities and minority ethnic groups (see chapter 9).

Working-class youths' symbolic appropriation of their locale's physical spaces has also led to confrontation with the forces of social control. Again, this confrontation has a history stretching back to the late nineteenth century when many sections of the working-class community regarded the police as 'a plague of blue locusts' (Storch, 1975) who posed a threat to the traditions of working-class street culture. Young people in particular were brought into conflict with the majesty of the law through the criminalization of street pastimes (such as football, gambling or simply loitering on street corners) which were perceived as a threat to public order.[10] The post-1945 period has seen strikingly similar conflicts between the forces of law and the street culture of young people. In 1989, for example, Home Office researchers voiced concern that at night many town centres seemed to operate 'like a vast semi open-air party for large groups of young people' with a 'noisy and violent street-culture [that] took over the streets . . . at weekends' (Tuck, 1989, p. 72). Conflict between working-class youth and agencies of social control over the 'legitimate' use of public space, then, has been a recurring feature of modern Britain's urban landscape. However, post-1945 changes in police occupational structure may have helped to increase tension between the two sides. As some commentators have observed, trends towards the 'juvenilization' of local police forces may have tended to reduce the scenario of law enforcement to 'a battle between two rival gangs, both composed of young, single, working-class males, each seeking territorial control over the class habitat – but with the difference that one mob have the full weight of the state behind them, the other only themselves and their mates to fall back on' (Cohen, 1981, p. 131).

Angels with Dirty Faces? Subcultural Theory and 'The Meaning of Style'

By the seventies, then, notions of British youth as a homogeneous and economically prosperous cultural group were proving increasingly difficult to sustain. In their place social researchers began to pay greater attention to the influence of social class and dimensions of conflict within the lives of young people. A seminal study in this respect was Phil Cohen's (1972) attempt to relate shifts in the form of post-war youth culture to more general transformations taking place within the ecologies of many traditional working-class neighbourhoods.

According to Cohen, major changes had taken place in the fabric of working-class life after 1945. Rather than 'disappearing', however, he argued that working-class forms of cultural reproduction and representation had been *disrupted*. In particular, he contended, institutions that had traditionally formed the material basis of working-class life – extended kinship networks, the local economy and focal points within the working-class neighbourhood (such as the local pub and the corner shop) – had been destabilized and restructured. Cohen argued that post-war patterns of rehousing and redevelopment had been central to these processes – the development of new towns and large estates on the outskirts of London in the fifties, followed by the building of new estates on the site of old inner-city slums in the sixties, tending to undermine and decompose traditional neighbourhood ecologies and communal structures. Moreover, these transformations had been accompanied by the collapse of traditional labour markets and the contraction of many local economies, leading to the steady polarization of labour. On the one hand there emerged highly skilled, relatively well-paid jobs associated with new industrial sectors and technologies, but on the other there remained the routine, low-paid and unskilled jobs associated with the residue of the declining staple industries.

Cohen contended that the impact of these changes was felt by the working class as a whole, but was mediated by generational position. The disintegration of community structures, he argued, intensified pressures on the 'nucleated' working-class family with the result that tensions within working-class culture tended to manifest themselves in the form of generational conflict. In these terms Teddy boys, mods, skinheads and all the other post-war subcultural permutations could be understood as various attempts to resolve symbolically the wider contradiction between traditional working-class puritanism and the newly emergent ideologies of hedonistic consumption. The mods, for example, represented an exploration of the upwardly mobile, consumption-oriented working-class lifestyle that began to emerge during the post-war decades, while the skinheads represented a symbolic reassertion of more traditional proletarian values and culture.

Cohen's work represented a bold attempt to apply a sophisticated historical perspective to the inter-generational relationships of the post-war working class. Nevertheless, his thesis was open to a number of criticisms. Firstly, because Cohen's analysis was heavily dependent on the example of the post-war fortunes of London's East End, it tended to lose sight of the way that working-class communities more generally were in a state of transition *before* 1945. In many parts of the country, for example, the patterns of redevelopment that Cohen located in the fifties had already begun between the wars, with nearly a fifth of British workers rehoused during the twenties and thirties. Similarly, the processes of 'decomposition' of the structures of the working-class neighbourhood that Cohen saw as taking place during the fifties and sixties were in evidence three decades earlier, with many of the new inter-war estates being accused of a shortage of cultural facilities and a lack of 'communal spirit'. Furthermore, Cohen's whole notion of the post-war 'fragmentation' of working-class life may have been unduly pessimistic, underestimating both the ability of 'old' class structures to survive and the ability of communities to generate new sources of unity over time.

Where Cohen's work was crucially influential, however, was in its

approach to subcultural style. Instead of treating Teddy b
heads as simple fads or fashions, Cohen presented their stylis
as important purveyors of social meaning, intrinsically lir
patterns of cultural change. Indeed, during the seventies and eighties such
a perspective became a touchstone within studies of British youth culture,
represented above all in the various contributions made by members of the
Centre for Contemporary Cultural Studies (CCCS) at Birmingham
University and the development of what came to be known as 'subcultural
theory'.[11] Drawing on a rich blend of cultural theory and semiotics, the
CCCS group extended and built upon Cohen's original terms of analysis,
arguing that subcultural style could be understood as a 'magical' or 'ritu-
alistic' expression of social experience. Originally influenced by Marxist
and neo-Marxist theoretical perspectives, the Birmingham authors saw
young people as locked into class-based struggles and conflicts fundamental to modern capitalism. Working-class youth, in these terms, shared
the same general set of subordinations as their parent culture, yet their
experience of these inequalities was given particular inflection through
their position in relation to education, work and leisure. In response to
their subordination, therefore, working-class youngsters were seen as
drawing not only on elements of their parent culture (for example working-
class argot, neighbourhood ties and particular kinds of masculine and
feminine identity) but also on elements derived from other cultural sources
(in particular the products of the various fashion and music industries). In
this manner, working-class youngsters were presented as constructing a
cultural, or *sub*cultural, response pertinent to their material life experiences. This approach did not simply evacuate age in favour of class as a
focus for analysis, rather it sought to examine 'the relations between class
and age, and more particularly the way in which age acts as a mediation of
class' (Murdock and McCron, 1976, p. 24).

The CCCS theorists gave a generally positive, at times even enthusiastic, account of youth subcultures. Central to the CCCS thesis was the
notion that subcultural styles were strategies of symbolic resistance to
ruling class power structures. Youth subcultures were interpreted as forms
of cultural insubordination, expressions of defiance and rebelliousness as
working-class youths appropriated articles, artefacts and icons and
symbolically reworked them to take on new, threatening and subversive
meanings. The effect of this approach was to turn subcultural styles
into texts – various semiotic techniques being employed to 'read' the

subversive meanings implicit within the skinhead's boots and braces or the punk's finely coiffured mohican. In attempts to explain how subcultural formations appropriated cultural artefacts and subverted their 'original' meanings two analytical concepts emerged as especially important – the ideas of bricolage and homology. Originally developed in the field of anthropology, the notion of bricolage was used to denote the way in which objects were taken up by subcultural groups and recontextualized to communicate fresh meanings. The mods, for example, were seen as appropriating a commodity such as the motor scooter – formerly a plain and respectable means of transport – and transforming it into 'a weapon and a symbol of solidarity' (Hebdige, 1976, p. 93). Homology, also a concept borrowed from anthropology, was used to denote the way that disparate stylistic elements – for example, music, clothes and activities – coalesced to form a coherent symbolic expression of a subcultural group's way of making sense of itself and its place in the world. In these terms the elements of a subcultural style 'fitted' together 'homologically', the different parts combining together in a structured ensemble that produced 'an organized group-identity in the form and shape of a coherent and distinctive way of "being-in-the-world"' (Clarke et al., 1976, p. 54). To illustrate this notion of 'homological fit' Paul Willis (1978) offered the examples of the rockers – whose love of motor-bikes and commitment to fast rock'n'roll was 'homologous' with their stress on activism and immediate gratifications – and the sixties' hippies, whose use of hallucinogenic drugs and preference for progressive rock was 'homologous' with their introspection and pseudo-mysticism. In this way, then, subcultural theory used techniques of semiological analysis to understand 'the selection of certain symbols (clothes, hairstyles, locations and so on) which are relevant to the focal concerns of the group in question, their investment with the meanings of the group, and their use to form a distinctive whole to symbolically express that group's self conception and focal concerns' (Clarke and Jefferson, 1976, p. 152).

Dick Hebdige, in particular, emerged as a luminary of these approaches. For Hebdige, subcultural style represented an 'oblique gesture of refusal' where 'the objections are lodged, the contradictions displayed . . . at the profoundly superficial level of appearance: that is, at the level of signs' (1979, p. 17). Borrowing from the work of cultural theorist Umberto Eco, Hebdige presented subcultural style as a kind of 'semiotic guerrilla warfare' (1979, p. 105), stressing the resistance he saw as inherent in the way established patterns of meaning, signs and codes were subverted and thrown into disorder by the radical dissonance of subcultural style. As the CCCS authors admitted, however, there were always limits to this form of 'resistance'. No haircut, no matter how startling, could bring the capitalist order to its knees. Confined to limited realms of social life – most obviously leisure – subcultural 'resistance' was inevitably partial and tangential and, as Hebdige himself put it, 'no amount of stylistic incantation can alter the oppressive mode in which the commodities used in subculture have been produced' (1979, p. 130).

The CCCS authors' contribution to the study of British youth culture was invaluable, representing one of the most impressive and far-reaching contributions to the post-war sociology of British youth. Their restoration of class as a crucial factor in the mediation of young people's life experiences was vital in displacing the more conservative perspectives that had held sway during the fifties and early sixties. Nevertheless, the CCCS approach was itself vulnerable to criticism.[12] 'Subcultural theory' was, in many respects, the product of a particular historical moment – a response to a context in which class divisions between British youth styles were thrown into particularly stark relief. For example, in their survey of musical tastes among London youths in the early 1970s, Graham Murdock and Robin McCron (1973) found a conspicuous divide separating middle-class youngsters, who mainly subscribed to the culture of the school and educational success (with a small minority developing a taste for progressive rock and the underground press), and working-class youths who threw themselves into the immediacy and group solidarity of skinhead subculture. In the late seventies, meanwhile, punk rock's dramatic stances of alienation and revolt made it easy for theorists to decode youth style in terms of resistance and subversion. Youth cultures of the eighties and nineties, however, seemed to be less dramatically bisected along lines of social class, while themes of 'resistance' were much less clearly pronounced within cultural forms such as acid house and rave (see chapter 12).

In some respects, perhaps, the Birmingham theorists were also over-eager to present youth subcultures as meaningful strategies of 'opposition'. Accounts such as Paul Willis's (1977) study of working-class secondary school pupils tended to generate an overly romantic view of their subjects, many of whom were aggressively sexist and racist in their attitudes and behaviour. The CCCS authors were, themselves, also aware that their fixation with the deviant and the spectacular laid them open to criticism (Clarke et al., 1976, p. 16). Indeed, the sensational subcultural groups on which so much analysis of post-war youth has been based – the Teddy boys, skinheads, punks and so on – have hardly been representative of the bulk of British youngsters. The vast majority of young people have always been much more 'mundane' in their apparel and activities. In fact, surveying the sheer volume of literature dealing with dramatic youth subcultures since 1945, it is tempting to conjecture that never, in the field of social history, has so much been written by so many about so few. In contrast, most young people have been comparatively 'normal' and 'ordinary' in their cultural orientations and stylistic preferences. Even where youngsters have become involved in a spectacular subcultural movement, relatively few have entered the 'pure' or 'undiluted' subcultural groups that are described in the literature. Instead, most have adopted only a limited range of subcultural trappings – perhaps wearing a tee-shirt or buying a record – rather than making a wholehearted commitment to a subcultural lifestyle. In reality, then, the line dividing 'mainstream' and 'non-conforming' youth is blurred, impossible to draw with any kind of clear-cut precision.

The CCCS authors' tendency to present youth subcultures as well defined and 'tightly bounded' is also open to question. Indeed, it is probably more appropriate to see subcultural movements as fluid and amorphous formations. Young people's attachments to such groups have invariably been fleeting and transient, individuals wandering across a range of identities and affiliations according to different social contexts, making few permanent cultural attachments. Indeed, so far as stylistic subcultures have developed any degree of cohesion or definition, it is intervention by the media and consumer industries that has been of foremost importance. Certainly, young people themselves have been involved in stylistic inception and the generation of subcultural movements. However, the Birmingham theorists tended to inflate these dimensions of self-creation, arguing that commercial exploitation only occurred in the wake of a spontaneous moment of subcultural innovation. In reality, though, these instants of 'authentic' stylistic 'creation' are elusive and it is difficult to pin down historical moments in which a 'pure' subculture existed entirely independent of the machinery of the commercial market.

Where the subcultural theorists did consider the role of the market it was primarily in negative terms. In the work of the CCCS authors intervention by commercial industries was equated with the 'neutralization' of youth style, returning once meaningful and 'oppositional' subcultures to the fold of bland and unthreatening consumerism. Within subcultural theory the notion of 'incorporation' arose to denote a cycle in which cultural responses generated at a 'street level' by subordinate youth were subsequently exploited and recuperated by a commercial apparatus – spontaneous and 'authentic' subcultural styles being repackaged and resold in a form void of the original dimensions of meaning and resistance. This model, however, set up a fairly elitist and unconvincing polarity between creative, 'meaningful' subcultures on the one hand and, on the other, a diluted, 'synthetic' 'mainstream' youth culture. Instead of emphasizing youth's agency in the construction of cultural frameworks (as subcultural theory originally intended) this approach simply confirmed the passivity of the vast majority of young people.[13] 'Meaning' and 'resistance' were confined to a small coterie of 'style rebels', while those youngsters who relied on high-street fashion stores and town centre discos for their cultural 'raw materials' were implicitly presented as gullibly buying into a 'defused' 'consumption style'. More recent versions of subcultural analysis, however, have been less disdainful of the commercial market, emphasizing instead a creative dimension to practices of consumption in which individuals actively select and appropriate the raw texts and artefacts made available by the commercial market to engineer their own cultural identities.[14]

Generally, then, it is more accurate to present post-war subcultures as locked into ongoing relationships with the media, commercial entrepreneurs and market institutions. As Stanley Cohen (1972, p. 34) observed of youth subcultures during the early 1960s, the stylistic opposition between mods and rockers was initially indistinct and ill-defined, only being formalized, lent substance and popularized through media coverage. Even a group as apparently 'authentic' as the skinheads were, at least partly, the product of media stylization and commercial exploitation. The skinhead 'movement' simply would not have coalesced into a recognizable form without intervention from entrepreneurs and retailers and would have quickly disappeared had it not been galvanized and given momentum by exposure in newspapers, on television and in pulp fiction such as Richard Allen's series of 'skinhead' novels.

Many accounts of post-war youth subcultures have also overlooked the dynamic quality to their styles. All too frequently subcultural forms are discussed as though they were immutably fixed phenomena, frozen statically at a particular point in history. In reality nothing could be further from the truth. Constant change and flux have been endemic to the universe of youth subcultures. Styles have continually developed over time, making sense in different ways for different groups of youngsters at different historical moments. The skinhead style, for example, has invariably been reduced to a simple caricature of shaven heads, braces and Dr Marten boots when the style actually shifted quite dramatically over a period of time. By the end of the sixties the emergence of the suedehead marked a sublime variation on the skinhead theme, a less severe, crew-cut hairstyle being coupled with a more fastidious fashion sense – including a preference for city gents' Crombie overcoats, accessorized with a black umbrella. Bowler hats even made an appearance after they had been sported by the futuristic hooligans featured in the film *A Clockwork Orange* (dir. Stanley Kubrick, 1971). The suedehead style itself quickly metamorphosed, giving way to the 'smooth' styles that dominated youth fashion during the early seventies. The seventies 'smoothies' marked a shift towards a more narcissistic form of masculine identity, taking their cues from the 'harder' end of glam rock and from a new generation of young, flamboyant football stars like George Best, Charlie George and Stan Bowles, whose lifestyles were more akin to jet-setting playboys than professional sportsmen. Here, the distinction between 'subcultural' and 'mainstream' youth styles became especially blurred. Rather than a discrete subcultural 'uniform', the 'smooth' image of long hair, flared trousers and sleeveless 'tank top' pullovers was a hallmark of more general youth trends in the early seventies. Indeed, any attempt to differentiate sharply between subcultural 'style' and mainstream 'fashion' within postwar youth culture is fraught with difficulty. Such a typology is artificial and contrived, imposing a set of clear sectarian divisions on a scenario which has more often been characterized by fluidity and a lack of precise boundaries.

'Boogie Nights': Dance Culture in the Seventies

By the early to mid-seventies the field of British popular music had become deeply fragmented. One key feature of the period was the rise of a collection of weary progressive rock performers such as Yes and Emerson, Lake and Palmer – bands whose album-oriented output and artistic pretensions catered for a growing 'hip' middle-class audience. Associated with the rise of this 'seriously minded' progressive rock was the growth of a more reflective, 'intellectual' style of popular music journalism. This was pioneered by the launch of the music paper *Sounds* in 1970, its approach imitated by rivals *Melody Maker* and *New Musical Express* and paralleled on television by the launch of BBC2's *Old Grey Whistle Test* in 1972. Alongside the progressive scene there also developed a coarser and 'heavier' set of rock conventions – epitomized by bands such as Deep Purple and Led Zeppelin and their fusion of a rhythm'n'blues derived guitar style with a bludgeoning beat and throaty vocals. A darker cousin to heavy rock also arose in the form of bands such as Black Sabbath whose combination of demonic iconography and beer-swilling braggadocio laid the basis for a heavy metal tradition that remained a feature of youth culture and popular music throughout the eighties and nineties.

Overall, however, the musical genre that wielded the greatest influence on British youth culture in the early seventies was black American soul, together with the disco boom that it spawned. American soul artists on the Motown and Atlantic labels had been popular in Britain during the mod era of the early sixties, but in the early seventies a new wave of activity based around Sigma Studios in Philadelphia began to make an impression on the British charts. 'Philly soul', which entwined vocal harmonies with rich orchestration, became increasingly popular and was played extensively both in clubs and on the growing number of commercial radio stations. Although American records provided the basis of the soul boom, black British artists also began to establish an indigenous soul tradition. Pre-eminently, the band Hot Chocolate had a string of over twenty hits in the seventies and even enjoyed some success in the American soul charts. White British artists also began to explore the soul idiom, the careers of Rod Stewart, Bryan Ferry and David Bowie all registering the influence of American soul.

American soul music also held sway over the grassroots cultures of many British youngsters during the 1970s. In the London club scene the profile of soul had receded during the late sixties as the mod subculture declined. In contrast, soul maintained its grip on youth culture in parts of the Midlands and (especially) in many northern cities and towns. Northern soul, as it became known in the early seventies, grew up around a network of clubs that included the Twisted Wheel in Manchester, the Mecca

Ballroom in Blackpool and, most famously, the Casino in Wigan.[15] Northern soul 'weekender' and 'all-niter' dance sessions played host to a fanatical enthusiasm for the most obscure and esoteric American soul sounds. Devotees devised complex and often acrobatic dance routines to accompany their favourite records, intense personal dedication becoming a trademark of the northern soul subculture. Although music and dance were the cornerstones of northern soul, the scene also generated its own style of dress. Comfortably loose clothes were essential for ease of movement and so 'baggies' were heavily favoured – high-waisted trousers, flared widely at the ankle to show off the wearer's fancy moves as he strutted his stuff on northern dance floors. Although hugely influential in cities like Leeds, Liverpool and Manchester, northern soul had relatively little impact further south. Consequently the style never captured the imagination and patronage of the London-based media industries and tended to maintain a comparatively localized, almost subterranean existence. The wider disco scene, in contrast, exploded to become the defining phenomenon of mid-seventies' youth culture.

As a musical form the disco sound was distilled from a range of sources. These encompassed the sensual finesse of 'Philly soul', the emphatic basslines of American funk and the quick-paced, soulful guitar rhythms of popular black film soundtracks such as Isaac Hayes' score for *Shaft* (1971). In American black and gay clubs in the early seventies DJs began layering and overlapping records, phasing them in and out to create a continuous cycle of music as a background to energetic and erotic dancing marathons. The disco scene rapidly boomed in the United States, quickly being taken up-market by fashionable night-clubs such as Manhattan's Studio 54. The British singles' charts also registered the rise of disco. Gloria Gaynor's 'Never Can Say Goodbye' reached number two in 1974 and was followed by an array of disco hits. Disco's popularity was given a further lease of life in 1978 by the release of the film *Saturday Night Fever* (dir. John Badham), a tale of young Brooklyn rough-necks whose lives centred on the weekend thrills of the night-club and the dance floor. Breaking box office records on both sides of the Atlantic, the film powerfully re-energized the disco scene. In its wake threadbare dance halls were refitted and refurbished as glitzy discotheques and mobile disco systems increasingly displaced live music as an attraction at pubs and clubs.[16]

The British disco boom owed a less direct debt to black and gay culture than its American equivalent. As the American disco beat was transplanted to British high streets and dance floors many of its original ethnic and sexual overtones were lost. Nevertheless, though the British disco scene was primarily a white, heterosexual province in which traditional gender identities and patterns of behaviour remained the norm, the disco experience of the seventies continued to be an arena in which divergent identities and cultures could be articulated. Moreover, the growth of British disco was concomitant with a burgeoning gay club scene based around venues such as Heaven (in London's Charing Cross Road) which came to set the pace for heterosexual night-club panache during the eighties.

During the seventies, therefore, the cultures and fashions of British youth underwent considerable transformation. By the middle of the decade skinhead style had all but disappeared. In its place there arose the more 'casual' sensibilities of the white 'soul boys' who packed the dance floors of the seventies' disco scene. These formations, however, were largely the province of working-class youngsters. Middle-class youth, in contrast, were more frequently drawn to the various counter-cultural movements that had risen to prominence during the sixties. The rise of a youth-based counter-culture in post-war Britain had a spectacular public profile and continues to infuse popular conceptions of the period, yet has been subject to surprisingly little serious historical scrutiny. Sociologically oriented accounts of the period have also tended to deal more exclusively with the subcultural formations of working-class youth, giving only limited coverage to the primarily middle-class counter-cultures. This, then, is an oversight which the next chapter will begin to address.

Notes

1 Surveying post-war socio-economic trends in the mid-seventies John Westergaard and Henrietta Resler found little evidence of a dawning 'post-capitalist' era, detecting instead an overall pattern of 'continuing inequality'. See John Westergaard and Henrietta Resler, 1976, *Class in a Capitalist Society: A Study of Contemporary Britain*, Harmondsworth: Pelican, p. 43.

2 Several studies stand out as especially important here. See R. M. Titmuss, 1962, *Income Distribution and Social Change*, London: Allen and Unwin; Brian Abel-Smith and Peter Townsend, 1965, *The Poor and the Poorest*, London: G. Bell.

3 For informed and well-documented histories of the development of skinhead style see Nick Knight, 1982, *Skinhead*, London: Omnibus; George Marshall, 1991, *Spirit of '69: A Skinhead Bible*, Dunoon: ST Publishing.

4 This account is offered in David Robins, 1984, *We Hate Humans*, Harmondsworth: Penguin, p. 46.

5   This alternative is preferred by a wider range of commentators and cultural historians. See, for example, Jeremy Bugler, 1969, 'Puritans in boots', *New Society*, vol. 14, no. 372, pp. 761–2; Susie Daniel and Pete McGuire (eds), 1972, *The Paint House: Words From an East End Gang*, Harmondsworth: Penguin, p. 11; John Clarke, 1973, 'Football hooliganism and the skinheads', Occasional Paper no. 42, CCCS, University of Birmingham, p. 12.

6   The most comprehensive account of the history of hooliganism and violence in relation to British association football is provided in Eric Dunning, Patrick Murphy and John Williams, 1988, *The Roots of Football Hooliganism: An Historical and Sociological Study*, London: Routledge and Kegan Paul.

7   An insightful account of the rise of the culture of the football 'ends' in the early 1970s can be found in David Robins and Philip Cohen, 1978, *Knuckle Sandwich: Growing Up in the Working-Class City*, Harmondsworth: Pelican, pp. 133–41.

8   For an anthology of work that highlights the key themes and issues raised in the sociological analysis of American gang culture see C. Ronald Huff (ed.), 1990, *Gangs in America*, London: Sage.

9   Discussion of the informal and loosely structured nature of British neighbourhood 'gangs' is provided in Peter Scott, 1956/7, 'Gangs and delinquent groups in London', *British Journal of Delinquency*, vol. 7, pp. 4–25; David Downes, 1966, 'The gang myth', *The Listener*, vol. 75, no. 1933, pp. 534–37; David Downes, 1966, *The Delinquent Solution*, London: Routledge and Kegan Paul, pp. 116–23; Peter Willmott, 1966, *Adolescent Boys of East London*, Harmondsworth: Pelican, pp. 29–43; Anne Campbell, Steven Munce and John Galea, 1982, 'American gangs and British subcultures: a comparison', *International Journal of Offender Therapy and Comparative Criminology*, vol. 26, pp. 76–89.

10   A detailed account of confrontations between working-class youngsters and the agencies of social control during the early twentieth century can be found in Stephen Humphries, 1981, *Hooligans or Rebels? An Oral History of Working Class Childhood and Youth, 1889–1939*, Oxford: Blackwell.

11   Three texts, in particular, stand out as central to the development of 'subcultural theory' in Britain during the late 1970s: Stuart Hall and Tony Jefferson (eds), 1976, *Resistance Through Rituals: Youth Subcultures in Post-War Britain*, London: Hutchinson; Paul Willis, 1978, *Profane Culture*, London: Routledge and Kegan Paul; Dick Hebdige, 1979, *Subculture: The Meaning of Style*, London: Methuen.

12   One of the best critiques of subcultural theory has been provided by Stanley Cohen in 'Symbols of trouble', his introduction to the revised (1980) edition of *Folk Devils and Moral Panics*, Oxford: Blackwell.

13   A cogent critique of this aspect of subcultural analysis is elaborated in Gary

Clarke, 1990, 'Defending ski-jumpers: a critique of theories of youth sub-cultures', in Simon Frith and Andrew Goodwin (eds), *On Record: Rock, Pop and the Written Word*, London: Routledge, pp. 81–96.

14   The key text in this respect is Paul Willis, 1990, *Common Culture*, Milton Keynes: Open University Press.

15   As yet there exists relatively little writing on the history and development of northern soul during the early seventies. Nevertheless, an animated and engaging autobiographical account of life on the northern soul circuit is provided in Pete McKenna, 1996, *Nightshift*, Dunoon: ST Publishing. A meticulously documented history of the Wigan Casino can be found in Russ Winstanley and David Nowell, 1996, *Soul Survivors: the Wigan Casino Story*, London: Robson. For additional discussion of the music and style of the northern soul subculture see Iain Chambers, 1985, *Urban Rhythms: Pop Music and Popular Culture*, London: Macmillan, pp. 137–8; Ted Polhemus, 1994, *Streetstyle*, London: Thames and Hudson, pp. 84–5.

16   For a more detailed account of these developments see Sarah Thornton, 1995, *Club Cultures: Music, Media and Subcultural Capital*, Cambridge: Polity Press, pp. 43–8.

7 'All You Need Is Love': Counter-Cultural Youth and Social Change

'What Do You Want If You Don't Want Money?' The 'Beat Generation' and the Ideals of the Counter-Culture

Throughout the two decades following the end of the Second World War middle-class youngsters were relatively marginal to the universe of British youth culture. With less disposable income than their working peers, and often alienated from the subcultural world of groups such as the Teddy boys, middle-class youth did not make its cultural presence felt in Britain's youth 'spectacle' until the rise of the counter-culture during the mid-sixties. The term 'counter-culture' is, however, problematic. Rather than a homogeneous, coherent social formation, the post-war counter-culture is better seen as a diverse range of loosely related anti-establishment, non-conformist and bohemian factions. Tracing the genealogy of such movements, moreover, is a complex task. During the twenties and thirties there had been upper-middle-class youth cultures in the form of 'bright young things', 'flappers' and student cliques, but these are hardly commensurate with the radical and unorthodox groupings that arose thirty years later. Bearing a closer resemblance were the left-wing political circles which began to appear in British universities between the wars.[1] Even these, however, were distinguished primarily by their politically militant stand rather than the cultural and stylistic innovations characteristic of movements during the fifties and sixties. The counter-cultural lineage is better traced to movements such as Dada and surrealism – artistic and literary avant-garde groups that arose in Europe between the wars and employed deliberately startling creative strategies to scrutinize and question western culture's aesthetic and social values. Such movements, however, revolved around a relatively small nucleus of artists and writers and it was not until the 1950s that such attitudes and concerns began to find a more broadly-based resonance – the generic term 'beatnik' coming to denote a disparate range of unconventional and radical groups of young people.

The immediate origins of what has come to be known as the 'Beat Generation' lay in post-war Paris and the avant-garde intelligentsia that frequented the street cafés of the Left Bank and the Boulevard St Michel. From this intellectual core there began to evolve a much wider social movement espousing a creed of existentialism and individual expression, providing a reference point and a set of images subsequently drawn upon by groups of disaffected middle-class youngsters around the world. This was especially the case in North America where the writings of Allen Ginsberg, Neal Cassidy, William Burroughs and Jack Kerouac pioneered and eulogized the beats' 'on the road' ethos and lifestyle, the term 'beat' probably first being coined by Kerouac as way of connoting a state of mind that was at once melancholy and beatific. More precisely, the beat milieu was distinguished by the focal concerns of creativity and introspection, beat culture encompassing jazz, poetry, literature, eastern mysticism and drugs – a quixotic mixture that prefigured the counter-cultural scene which was to blossom in the late sixties.

The British beat experience has been the subject of scant academic attention. This omission is perhaps surprising since, although they were comparatively few in number, the British beats had a significant impact on the public consciousness, especially in the geographic areas on which they converged. These tended to be places where the cultural ambience was more relaxed or risqué, hence Soho became a principal beat locus, as did a number of British seaside resorts. For example, in 1960 television reporter Alan Whicker was dispatched by the BBC's *Tonight* programme to report on Newquay's sizeable beat community, and it was perhaps predictable that Brighton (with its artistic and cosmopolitan traditions, beach and occasional sunshine) emerged as Britain's answer to Greenwich Village – the American beats' spiritual home in New York. In Brighton in 1962 midsummer saw as many as a hundred beatniks (or 'beachniks' as they were dubbed by the local press) congregate on Brighton's lower promenade, the youngsters easily identifiable through their scruffy appearance, long hair and old clothes. The beats' style made explicit their philosophy of existentialism and disengagement from what they saw as the shallow, suffocating routines of wider society. Beats saw themselves as imaginative dissidents and cultivated the image of the pauperized intellectual, thread-bare jackets and fishermen's jerseys being set off by goatee beards and horn-rimmed spectacles in a montage of studied dishevelment.

Although there were comparatively few women among British beatniks, beat culture was far from being an exclusively male preserve. In an auto-biographical essay historian Sheila Rowbotham, for example, has recalled her time as a seventeen-year-old 'incipient existentialist', with a taste for black eye-liner and white make-up, black stockings and skirts and the largest black sweaters she could find (Rowbotham, 1985, p. 189). Indeed, whereas working-class subcultural groups like the Teds and skinheads largely embraced fairly traditional notions of gender, the masculine iden-tities generated by the beats were more complex. Certainly, the literature of figures such as Kerouac could be boorish and misogynistic, though the behaviour of individual beats often eschewed traditional gender roles and identities. On a superficial level, at least, many male beats repudiated the aggressive, dominant virtues attached to established masculine norms, experimenting instead with a more passive and benign form of male iden-tity. As a Brighton youth worker observed in 1966, 'Much has been discussed of the violent potential of youth today, but I suggest that the beatniks are showing a different reaction – that of quiet withdrawal and non-interference.'[2]

In his study of beat enclaves in New York, Ned Polsky (1971) drew attention to the beats' reverence for those that the 'straight' society had labelled deviant – especially the street-wise hustlers of the black ghetto. The seafronts of British holiday resorts, however, were not known as a twilight world of black 'hipsters' and 'hep cats' and, though British beats revelled in an iconography of 'otherness' (exemplified in their penchant for the 'authentic' sounds of trad jazz), the image of the black hustler was much less pronounced within their cultural reference points. The British beat scene also differed from its American cousin in the nature of its political orientations. New York beats, Polsky observed, were '*anti*political', vigor-ously opposed to any form of organized political movement (Polsky, 1971, pp. 159–60). British beats certainly shared this animosity to conventional politics yet, in contrast to the American experience, there did exist an orga-nized 'political' movement that made marked inroads into the British beat scene – the Campaign for Nuclear Disarmament (CND). Formed in

January 1958 from the Direct Action Committee Against Nuclear War (which had existed since 1954), CND drew much of its strength from the simplicity and single-mindedness of its aims. The movement's lack of a formal ideology enabled a range of anti-establishment sentiments to become enlisted behind a single cause defined as a straightforward choice between 'good' and 'evil'.[3] In this way CND became a focal point for youth groups adopting postures of disillusionment with traditional values and conventional party politics and ranks of duffle-coated youngsters strumming acoustic guitars turned CND's Aldermaston marches into events of carnivalesque festivity. Much of CND's significance, then, lay in its role as a movement of cultural politics that held special appeal for sections of the nation's youth. As such CND can be seen as a precursor to the radical political movements that became a marked feature of the counter-culture during the late sixties. Indeed, the degree of continuity linking the beats of the late fifties and early sixties with these later movements is often underestimated. Rather than representing a sudden explosion of counter-cultural activity, the events of 1967–70 are more properly seen as a climax to trends that had been underway for nearly a decade.

Though the beats, and the hippies after them, conceptualized themselves as existing beyond the nomenclature of socio-economic analysis, many researchers have drawn attention to their class-specific origins and focal concerns. The Birmingham CCCS theorists, for example, argued that it was possible to make a fairly precise differentiation between the *sub*cultural groupings of working-class youth and the *counter*-cultures of their middle-class peers (Clarke et al., 1976, pp. 60–1). Subcultures (Teddy boys, mods and so on) generally reproduced traditional working-class values and patterns of behaviour, for example drawing on identifications with local neighbourhoods and representing a leisure-oriented and fairly temporary episode in the lives of their members. The counter-cultures, in contrast, were more diffuse in their structure and concerns. They were more 'individualized' (local identifications and group solidarities playing little role in their cultural make-up) while the stark polarity between work and leisure characteristic of working-class subcultures was much less pronounced in the counter-cultural environment. Additionally, compared to leisure-based subcultures such as mod, counter-cultures tended to exercise a deeper and more long-lasting influence on their members' lives and cultural orientations. More fundamentally, the counter-cultures differed from subcultural formations in so far as they did not represent a revolt from 'below' so much as an attack from 'within'. That is to say, the counter-cultures were derived from within the dominant formation itself, representing, in essence, 'a revolt of the unoppressed' (Musgrove, 1974, p. 19). Indeed, this 'revolt' was only made possible through the opportunities afforded by the material resources and relative freedoms found within the dominant culture. As Mike Brake has wryly observed, the very notion of 'dropping out' pre-supposes a location in the class structure from which to drop – and ultimately return (Brake, 1980, p. 86).

Theoretical models, however, can lose sight of the complexities of social reality. Young people's cultural preferences could never be 'read off' from their class position with the ease suggested in much sociological literature. For example, while many beatniks did come from relatively well-to-do, middle-class backgrounds, the beat culture comprised youngsters from diverse social origins, including numbers of young drifters whose impoverishment signified genuine hardship rather than middle-class affectation. A degree of socio-economic heterogeneity, then, has to be acknowledged within many post-war youth movements. Indeed, though less immediately evident, a degree of social diversity has also existed within ostensibly 'working-class' subcultural formations – these groups embracing a minority of (usually male) middle-class affiliates who use their working-class peers as a reference group and a source of stylistic inspiration.

'Tune In, Turn On and Drop Out': The Hippy Trip of the Late Sixties

Though a degree of social diversity must be acknowledged within the post-war counter-cultures, it remains the case that these movements were, for the most part, middle class in both composition and ideological orientation – owing their existence to profound shifts in the nature of middle-class life and culture after 1945. For instance, one of the principal foundations of the growth of counter-cultural movements in the post-war period was the sustained expansion of higher education after 1945. In 1938 only 2.7 per cent of British school-leavers continued to full-time higher education, but by 1954 the figure had risen to 5.8 per cent and stood at around 8.5 per cent by 1962. However, even increases of this order were deemed insufficient. In 1963 the influential Robbins Report on higher education urged that, in view of the greater numbers of youngsters set to reach school-leaving age in the late sixties and early seventies, further expansion was imperative. Robbins set targets for 1973 of 219,000 university places, 122,000 teacher-training places in colleges of education and 51,000 places on advanced courses at technical colleges. By the beginning of the seventies these projections had been chiefly met, the total population of students in full-time education doubling between 1963 and 1971 to reach a figure of 457,000. From the early 1960s, then, higher education underwent considerable growth and reorganization – processes which embraced not only existing colleges, polytechnics and universities but also the establishment of the new 'red-brick' universities. In Scotland four such universities were founded – Strathclyde, Stirling, Heriot-Watt and Dundee – while in England charters were granted to Sussex, East Anglia, York, Essex, Kent, Warwick and Lancaster.

The Robbins Report had anticipated that this growth would lay the basis for a more meritocratic system of higher education, ameliorating what was seen as a regrettable 'wastage' of working-class talent. Despite these intentions, however, it was the middle classes who most successfully exploited the new educational opportunities. Among the multiplying numbers of students the fastest rates of growth took place among working-class youngsters but in absolute terms the middle class accounted for the greatest area of expansion, the character of the modern education system remaining 'a minimal education for the majority, with further opportunity for the minority' (Halsey, 1988, p. 291). Compared to working youngsters, students possessed a relatively low level of disposable income, yet higher education had its compensations – offering middle-class youngsters significant amounts of leisure time, coupled with the independence of living away from the parental home. Indeed, the post-war period saw an appreciable decline in numbers of home-based students, the proportion slumping from nearly 42 per cent of full-time students in 1938/9 to just over 16 per cent by 1971/2.

In the early sixties even living in halls of residence or lodgings did not guarantee absolute freedom. Many universities and colleges sought (with varying degrees of success) to monitor and control the leisure of their students through regulations and curfew systems. Nevertheless, living away from parental supervision, among a large number of youngsters in similar circumstances, still provided a new dimension of autonomy. This was especially true for young women, whose numbers increased from just over 30 per cent of Britain's student body in 1962 to more than 40 per cent by 1980. Nor should we overlook the influence of the liberal ambience to be found at many of the new universities. The sixties saw the rise of a new generation of radical academics who were willing to introduce more informal styles of teaching and more flexible approaches to learning in the academic environment. The relative freedoms of higher education, then, were a crucial influence on the cultural frameworks elaborated by sections of middle-class youth after 1945. Whereas working-class youth sub-cultures owed their heightened social profile largely to shifts in traditional labour markets during the fifties and early sixties, the most important foundation of the counter-cultures of the post-war period was the growing experience of 'studenthood' among the middle classes.

The expansion of higher education in the sixties further invigorated the counter-cultural movements that had begun to emerge during the previous decade. Again, focal concerns of the counter-culture were disaffection with (and symbolic disaffiliation from) 'mainstream' society and its institutions, a disenchantment with organized politics, an emphasis on creativity and expressivity and a desire for self-exploration through drugs, mysticism and 'journeys' through dimensions of both geography and consciousness. What was particularly striking about the sixties' counter-culture was its global character. By the end of the decade counter-cultural groups of various kinds had become a visible and vociferous feature of not only most western capitalist societies but also a growing number of countries within the Eastern Bloc. Nevertheless, it was from the United States that these movements took their cues and throughout the late sixties the counter-culture's spiritual home was always the West Coast of America – especially San Francisco.

During the 1950s San Francisco's North Beach area had already attracted a sizeable beat fraternity of writers, poets and artists, but during the sixties these groups steadily migrated to the formerly respectable neighbourhood of Haight Ashbury. By the end of the sixties 'the Haight' had become the counter-cultural capital of the world, its once prosperous townhouses populated by long-haired bohemians and its Fillmore and Avalon ballrooms playing regular host to a growing legion of progressive rock bands, including Jefferson Airplane, the Grateful Dead, Big Brother and the Holding Company and Quicksilver Messenger Service.[4] The Haight community also maintained the beats' use of drugs to push back the boundaries of the imagination. Lysergic acid diethylamide (generally known as LSD or 'acid') was especially favoured, many believing that the drug's hallucinogenic effects offered a unique doorway to a plane of consciousness that was free of all preconceptions. Belief in the ability of LSD to heighten the individual's degree of consciousness and maximize aesthetic potential led figures like Timothy Leary and Ken Kesey to experiment with and enthuse over the power of the drug, Kesey and his group of 'Merry Pranksters' touring the cities of the West Coast in their 'magic bus', introducing people to the 'Acid Test' – a phantasmagorical combination of electronic equipment, music and LSD.

In its attempts to generate an aesthetic lifestyle which broke through the constraints of respectable society, the British counter-culture bore many similarities to its American cousin.[5] In both Britain and America counter-cultural strategies encompassed a wide-ranging engagement with media forms, far surpassing the beats' earlier endeavours. This was especially evident in the prodigious output of the underground press. In Britain the lead was taken by *International Times* (or simply *It*, launched in 1966) and *Oz* (launched in 1967). Respectively, these periodicals had achieved print runs of around 50,000 and 20,000 by 1968 and were complemented by a stream of comparable national and local ventures. More than simple information sheets, the very form of the underground press explored the imagery of dissent and opposition through the use of fantastic visuals and striking symbolism. The same strategies could also be found in a range of cultural initiatives, from 'alternative' posters and films to the various experimental projects of the Arts Lab movement. Music, of course, also figured prominently in the British counter-culture. In 1966 venues such as the Roundhouse and UFO became hubs of the burgeoning London underground scene, while the rise of 'art rock' – in the form of later albums by the Rolling Stones and the Beatles and the output of new bands such as Cream, Soft Machine, and Pink Floyd (who made their first major appearance at the party to launch *It* and who were regulars at UFO) – sought to redefine popular musical practice through an espoused commitment to individual and 'anti-commercial' creativity.

Loosely organized 'happenings' of various kinds were also important focal points within the counter-culture. Festivals, concerts and other gatherings all helped to generate a sense of group identity and played a key role in maintaining commitment to 'alternative' lifestyles. In January 1967 100,000 people attended the first 'Gathering of the Tribes' or 'Human Be-In' in San Francisco's Golden Gate Park, followed in June by a three-day pop festival in Monterey, featuring an all-star line-up that included many of the progressive rock performers that had emerged from the San Francisco scene. On 15 August 1969, meanwhile, a gathering of 500,000 assembled on farmland at Bethel, New York, for a gathering that became a cultural landmark. The Woodstock Music Festival represented a high point in the history of the counter-culture, bringing together such musical luminaries as Jimi Hendrix, Jefferson Airplane, Canned Heat, the Who and Credence Clearwater Revival. Britain, meanwhile, saw similar convocations. In January 1967 Pink Floyd topped the bill at the 'Giant Freakout' at the Roundhouse followed, in April, by 'The 14 Hour Technicolour Dream' held at Alexandra Palace and, in August, by the three-day 'Festival of the Flower Children' at Woburn Abbey. The late sixties also saw a series of enormous free concerts in Hyde Park – Pink Floyd in 1968, Blind Faith in June 1969 and, the following July, the Rolling Stones (attracting a crowd estimated at between 250,000 and 500,000). This was also the heyday of the Isle of Wight Festivals, with performances by Bob Dylan and the Band in 1969 and the last appearance of Jimi Hendrix attracting a crowd of at least 200,000 in 1970.

The counter-culture's preoccupation with self-expression and 'authenticity' also registered at the level of style. During the sixties the beatniks' avant-garde pretensions were increasingly fused with the exotic and psychedelic fashions peddled in the growing legion of London boutiques. Cheesecloth shirts, beads and flared denims were complemented by 'ethnic' kaftans and Afghan coats in a pot-pourri of patchwork and tie-dye. The term 'hippy' was increasingly coined by the media to describe any group of outlandishly attired, long-haired and non-conformist young people – though it was a term rarely accepted by the youngsters themselves. Indeed, the moniker 'hippy' tended to obscure more than it revealed, glossing over the complex divisions and differences within the counter-cultural scene. From the perspective of the counter-culture's members themselves, moreover, their movement encompassed something more meaningful and more socially pertinent than could be adequately accounted for by glib media labels.

'Children of the Revolution'? The Politics of the Counter-Culture

The counter-cultural movements of the late sixties captivated many commentators on the political Left. To some, the dimensions of bohemian cultural dissent, coupled with an increasing militancy among students, seemed to represent a foundation upon which a movement of wider social and political revolution might be built. In America, for example, Theodore Roszak (1970) interpreted the counter-culture as a revolutionary vanguard with the potential to rehumanize society, returning to people the individual freedoms lost through the rise of technocracy and the institutions of industrial capitalism. In a similar vein Charles Reich (1972) described how the counter-culture was spawning a 'new consciousness' that would eventually reshape western civilization through its values of community and harmonious self-expression. Marxist theorist Herbert Marcuse was equally enthralled. Marcuse was deeply critical of modern capitalism, especially its obsession with consumption which he saw as an exercise in authoritarian manipulation and materialistic conformity. In the sixties counter-culture, however, he found solace. For Marcuse (1972), these non-conformist youth movements represented society's most progressive and creative elements, their 'new sensibility' holding out the possibility of radical social transformation. Equally, many on the British Left also enthused over what they interpreted as the emergence of a mass movement of radical politics. Gareth Stedman Jones and his associates, for example, waxed lyrical over the rise of radical politics on British campuses and what they saw as 'the complete and militant solidarity of students' (*New Left Review*, May–June, 1967).

On closer inspection, however, notions of the sixties counter-cultural movements as agencies of opposition with the power to fundamentally restructure society seem rather exaggerated. Throughout the sixties these movements never attracted more than a small minority of the young, contemporary research testifying time and again to the 'conventionality' of most youngsters. From their empirical investigation of the political attitudes of British youth during the mid-sixties, for instance, Philip Abrams and Alan Little (1965) concluded that young people were largely following paths established by their parents in terms of political orientation and commitment. Furthermore, celebrations of 'complete and militant solidarity' among British students were especially misleading. In his study of students in Manchester and Oxford during the early sixties, Ferdynand Zweig found most of his subjects to be characterized by conformity and passivity and to be, on the whole, 'honest, sincere young men [sic] taking their studies very seriously' (Zweig, 1963, p. xiii). Even in the militant heartland of the London School of Economics, Tessa Blackstone and her colleagues found that the sit-in of 1967 involved only 36 per cent of registered students, while no more than 18 per cent stayed on the premises over one or more nights (Blackstone et al., 1970). From research conducted at Durham University in 1970, meanwhile, Stanley Cohen and Alan Waton uncovered 'a picture somewhat inconsistent with the dominant image of the typical student', with 'an extremely low involvement in any form of political activity' and radicalism steadily decreasing 'as action, commitment and confrontation are demanded of the student' (Cohen and Waton, 1971).

Throughout the late sixties, moreover, the political and cultural responses of British youth continued to be bisected along lines of social class. Certainly there was a working-class presence within the counter-culture and there were many working-class student radicals strident in their opposition to the status quo. On the other hand, however, there were more conspicuous groups of working-class youngsters who were actively hostile to the counter-culture and radical politics in general. In London in October 1968, for example, one of the largest demonstrations against the Vietnam war faced barracking from an angry gang of two hundred skinheads, the demonstrators' cries of revolutionary solidarity with 'Ho, Ho – Ho Chi Minh!', eliciting from the skinheads the taunts of 'Enoch! Enoch!'[6] and 'Students, Students! Ha! Ha! Ha!'

Many counter-cultural activists were convinced that the skinheads' reputation for rowdy rebelliousness made them a likely ally in the struggle against the establishment. The underground journal *It* even gave skinheads 'their own' (rather unconvincing) page. Entitled 'Yell', the page ran for several issues and included coverage of football and reggae, together with calls for skinheads and 'hairies' to 'get to know each other better'.[7] These efforts, however, failed to apprehend adequately the class-based nature of the skinhead/'hairy' opposition. The skinheads' marked antipathy for (and frequent physical attacks upon) hippies and students derived chiefly from deeply felt class antagonisms. For many working-class youngsters the counter-culture was simply a luxury of the affluent middle class, the self-indulgence of the hippies and the 'effeminacy' of aspects of their style standing as anathema to young men who made a fetish of traditional working-class puritanism and machismo.[8] As members of an East End skinhead gang told social researchers in 1972:

> Them dirty 'ippies, poncing off us all the fucking time. We 'ave to work and pay taxes and things, all these 'ippies are on the dole and don't do nothing and thieve and that . . . You notice that a lot of rich people turns 'ippie. They 'ave been spoilt. It's just to be the opposite of their parents, that's all it is. Their mum's got money and all this and they say 'give your money away' and all that. (Daniel and McGuire, 1972, pp. 70–2)

The strategies of 'opposition' adopted by the counter-culture are also open to a degree of criticism. As Mike Brake has observed, the 'politics' of the counter-culture often amounted to little more than an absorption in 'art' and 'individualism' and thus tended to evade rather than confront the structural sources of inequality (Brake, 1980, p. 100). All too often expressive values and idealism were the extent of the counter-culture's 'subversion'. Retreatism and disengagement took the place of activism and confrontation in ineffectual (and often pretentious) gestures that were exemplified, in May 1969, by John Lennon and Yoko Ono recording 'Give Peace a Chance' from their hotel bed at the end of their ten-day 'Bed-In' protest against the Vietnam war. Faced with Lennon's extended repose it is unlikely that the establishment was thrown into a state of fearful panic.

In other respects, too, the counter-culture's 'radicalism' often proved to be a thin veneer. Despite its egalitarian sloganeering, sexual inequality remained pronounced within many areas of the counter-culture. The hippy scene tended to reproduce traditional sexual divisions of labour, while the 'sexual revolution' was defined largely in male terms, 'sexual liberation' often amounting to little more than an intensification of the sexual exploitation of women.[9] Furthermore, notwithstanding its scorn for materialism and capitalist 'bread-heads', the sixties' counter-culture was often a resounding market success. From its inception the counter-culture was 'a nice little earner' for a network of 'hip capitalists' who marketed everything from psychedelic posters to illicit drugs. Indeed, in some instances these enterprises proved phenomenally lucrative, Richard Branson's 'alternative' record business serving as the launching pad for his Virgin business empire.

In these terms, rather than being a movement *against* dominant ideologies, the counter-culture can be seen as a movement *within* middle-class culture. Though superficially incompatible with the dominant order, the counter-culture's libertarian ethos of 'doing your own thing' can be seen as actually celebrating many of the core values of classical liberalism and petit bourgeois individualism. In many respects the sixties counter-culture represented not so much an 'alternative' lifestyle as an adaptation of the traditional middle-class ideologies of self-improvement, freedom of expression and entrepreneurship.[10] Indeed, although the counter-culture was subject to its share of negative stereotyping by the media, dominant responses were often ambiguous. The hippies' hedonistic lifestyle and even their drug-taking were never universally condemned, but were often accorded respect and even a degree of admiration. In 1968, for instance, in its series 'The Restless Generation', *The Times* praised hippy communes such as the Tribe of the Sacred Mushroom for generating 'a fresh approach to living' that provided its members with 'livelihood and fulfilment' (*The Times*, 18 December 1968).

The ambiguity of dominant attitudes to the counter-culture became especially apparent in relation to the Rolling Stones' drug trial of 1967. Following a tip-off from the *News of the World*, Sussex police had raided Keith Richards' farmhouse in West Wittering and arrested Richards, Mick Jagger and their friend Robert Frazer for drug offences. In June 1967, amid a blaze of publicity, they appeared before magistrates at Lewes and were found guilty of possession of illegal drugs, Jagger being sentenced to three months' imprisonment and Richards twelve, though both were granted bail pending an appeal against their sentences. Dominant responses, however, were mixed. Rather than denouncing the Stones, large sections of the establishment actually rallied to their defence. On 1 July William Rees-Mogg published an editorial in *The Times*, asking 'Who Breaks a Butterfly on a Wheel?', defending Jagger and Richards and attacking their sentences as draconian and inappropriate. At the end of the month, mean-while, two Members of Parliament, along with doctors, poets, artists and the authors Graham Greene and John Piper were among signatories of a full-page advertisement in *The Times* calling for the legalization of mari-juana. On 31 July Jagger and Richards' appeals met with success and the two rock stars walked free from the court. Rather than facing media vilifi-cation, however, Jagger was whisked by helicopter to appear on Granada Television's current affairs programme *World in Action*. Here, he joined with Rees-Mogg, Lord Stow Hill (a former Labour Home Secretary), Dr

John Robinson (the Bishop of Woolwich) and Jesuit leader Father Corbishley in a group discussion on the nature of personal liberty – Rees-Mogg later recalling how he had been impressed by Jagger and was fascinated by the way 'all his arguments turned on those classic propositions that people ought to be absolutely free and that there ought to be as little government as possible . . . Straight John Stuart Mill!' (Taylor, 1987, p. 128).

The rise of the counter-culture, then, can in many respects be seen as symptomatic of changes taking place within the dominant cultural order. Just as subcultural groups like the mods and the skinheads sprang from working-class lifestyles in a state of transition, the counter-culture issued from a bourgeois culture struggling to adapt itself to the new social and economic contours of the post-war environment. The traditional middle-class world that had emerged during the eighteenth and nineteenth centuries – with its emphasis on the work ethic, moderation and decorum – was increasingly out of step with a form of capitalism that now prioritized consumption, hedonism and immediate gratification. The counter-culture, therefore, fulfilled a pioneering role, initiating and experimenting with new cultural forms and lifestyles more appropriate to the post-war social and economic climate, ultimately giving the dominant order much greater dimensions of adaptability and flexibility.[11]

Here, a link can be established with what theorist Pierre Bourdieu (1984) has identified as the rise of a new petit bourgeois way of life or 'habitus' in modern capitalism. Contemporary western society, Bourdieu contends, has seen the rise of 'cultural intermediaries', a new bourgeoisie formed from those whose occupations deal with the production and dissemination of symbolic goods and services. The members of this emergent group stand apart from traditional bourgeois structures in their preoccupation with the attributes of style, distinction and refinement – their narcissistic obsession with 'lifestyle' and self-expression making them an ideal consumer group. Though Bourdieu sees this faction as a characteristic feature of the eighties and nineties, their roots can be traced to the counter-culture of the sixties. The nineties' ideologies of self-expression and personal 'liberation' can be seen as developing out of the counter-culture's concern for self-exploration and individual freedom, while many of those who emerged as 'cultural intermediaries' during the eighties and nineties were exactly those 'beautiful people' who had been busy 'hitting a major groove' twenty years earlier.

Nevertheless, the Utopian politics of the counter-culture should not be dismissed out of hand. Always a mass of contradictions, the counter-culture's 'adaptive' functions should not be allowed to obscure totally its dimensions of genuine opposition and dissent. As Dick Hebdige (1989, pp. 87–8) argues, the politicization of issues of culture and identity that took place within the sixties' counter-culture paved the way for an upsurge of movements that, during the following decades, placed questions of gender and sexuality firmly on the political agenda. Moreover, during the late sixties themselves aspects of the counter-culture represented an oppositional force to be reckoned with, its gestures of disaffiliation and militancy feeding into the atmosphere of crisis and confrontation that hung over Britain throughout the period.

Street-Fighting Men: Youth Culture Amid the Breakdown of Consensus

During the late sixties and early seventies changes in the fabric of British youth culture took place against a background of growing social and political conflict. The politics of consensus, already proving difficult to sustain during the mid-sixties, began a more rapid disintegration towards the end of the decade. Harold Wilson's Labour government of 1964 had sought to address the deep-seated weaknesses of the British economy through the modernization of industry and the application of the 'white-hot heat of technology', but results had been disappointing. Between 1964 and 1970 annual average rates of growth remained low while rising imports led to a balance of payments deficit and a crisis of confidence in sterling. In the face of these problems the government sought to reduce spending through restraint, holding wages down and raising import duties. Yet a dockers' strike in May 1966 brought trade to a virtual standstill. Facing a massive trade deficit the government devalued the pound in November 1967 and the following year cut public spending by £750 million. Although the balance of payments gradually improved, Britain's economic problems remained pronounced and industrial relations steadily deteriorated. Unofficial 'wildcat' strikes became a particular problem and the media increasingly conjured with images of militant shop-stewards conspiring to undermine British industry. Problems in economic management and industrial relations were paralleled by difficulties in foreign affairs, the hollowness of Britain's claims to being a world power becoming increasingly evident. During the sixties fractures began to appear in the multiracial ideals of the Commonwealth while Britain's application for membership of the European Economic Community faced steadfast opposition from de Gaulle's French government in 1967. In Northern Ireland, meanwhile, the rise of a Catholic civil rights movement was met by a violent backlash from Protestant factions, compelling the British government to send troops into Belfast and Londonderry in 1969 in a bid to maintain order and protect the cities' Catholic populations.

By the end of the sixties, then, an atmosphere of discord and friction had come to characterize British society. The ideologies of affluence, prosperity and consent which had articulated social relations during the fifties and early sixties were now untenable, giving way to political programmes more visibly confrontational and coercive. Symptomatic was the 1970 general election victory of the Conservatives under Edward Heath. With a pledge 'to change the course of history of this nation, nothing less', Heath weaved together an ethos of free market individualism and a commitment to tougher measures of law and order which set a tone for the political agendas that followed during the subsequent two decades. Within these agendas, moreover, 'youth' featured as a recurring motif. During the fifties and early sixties a negative stereotyping of youth had already figured as a vehicle for more general debates around the perceived detrimental consequences of cultural change. From the late sixties this negative stereotyping became more marked, groups of young people being portrayed as part of a more pervasive and subversive 'enemy within'.

Historical precision is not easy in the field of youth culture. The styles and music that shape its existence evolve and mutate in ways that defy easy generalization. Analysing the development of the counter-culture is especially problematic since, as we have already seen, it was always a loose alliance of disparate factions rather than a coherent and unified social formation. Nevertheless, during the late sixties it is possible to detect a broad shift in the British counter-culture, the rhetoric of 'peace' and 'flower power' being displaced by that of street-fighting and political protest as the 1967 'Summer of Love' gave way to 1968, the year of revolts. In contrast to the vague, bohemian philosophies of 'love' and spiritual communion characteristic of 1966/7, the end of the decade saw the evolution of stances more explicitly and self-consciously political. In the United States the rise of a more overtly political dimension to the counter-culture was manifested in an upsurge of student militancy and agitation against the increasingly unpopular war in Vietnam. The greatest impact of political radicalism, however, was felt in France where, in May 1968, a student occupation of university buildings in the Sorbonne was followed by a general strike and factory occupations involving over nine million workers. These events shook the French state to its foundation and came to an end only when President de Gaulle dissolved the National Assembly and played on fears of a Communist takeover to win a landslide election victory the following June.

Though not on the scale of events in France, virtually every country in western Europe saw episodes of student militancy and radical political opposition during the late sixties. In Britain CND was superseded by opposition to the Vietnam war as a cause for protest, the Vietnam Solidarity Campaign organizing several massive demonstrations outside the US Embassy in Grosvenor Square in 1967 and 1968. Student politics also developed a more radical hue. During the 1950s the National Union of Students (NUS) had been largely dominated by right-wing Labour representatives and as late as 1965 NUS leaders had happily dined with Harold Wilson at 10 Downing Street. In the late sixties, however, dis-illusion with the Labour Party, the escalation of fighting in Vietnam and frustration with the conservatism of its own executive combined to spur a grassroots move to the Left within the NUS – marked by the growing influence of groups such as the Radical Students Alliance (formed in 1966). The period also saw a series of fierce confrontations between student groups and the administrations of a number of universities and colleges. Most notably, the London School of Economics saw numerous sit-ins and demonstrations between 1966 and 1969 – events initially sparked by the appointment of Walter Adams (from the University of Salisbury in Rhodesia) as the LSE's new director, but which quickly came to embrace wider academic and political issues.[12] In the wake of events at LSE similar disturbances followed at institutions throughout the country, including universities in Birmingham, Manchester, Edinburgh, Bristol, Hull, Essex, Warwick and Hornsey College of Art.[13]

During the fifties and sixties there had already been a succession of moral panics in which the cultural forms and practices of working-class youth were presented as indicative of a general breakdown in the tra-ditional order and its values. During the late sixties the counter-cultural responses of middle-class youth began to figure more centrally within this imagery of decline. However, whereas working-class subcultures had been understood as socially delinquent *symptoms* of deterioration, the counter-culture (especially its more overtly political elements) was cast as an active *cause* of cultural degeneration and social instability.[14] Though responses were never exclusively negative, the late sixties and early seventies saw political comment and media coverage become appreciably more hostile towards counter-cultural movements, a critique that was paralleled by an increasingly repressive official treatment of social elements deemed either 'permissive' or 'subversive'.

Even in the early sixties there existed the seeds of a reactionary response to what was perceived as a rising tide of 'moral laxity' in British culture. In 1963, for example, Mary Whitehouse embarked on her crusade to 'clean up' the media, launching her National Viewers and Listeners Association. By the early seventies such movements had gained momentum through their high-profile public campaigning. In September 1971, for example, pop star Cliff Richard joined forces with eminent figures such as Lord Longford, the Dowager Lady Birdwood and Malcolm Muggeridge in support of the Festival of Light – a fundamentalist Christian crusade against 'moral depravity'. By the end of the sixties the proselytizing of these informal 'moral entrepreneurs' was paralleled by the introduction of formal measures of constraint and control by state agencies.

This shift towards greater official intervention and repression was marked, above all, by the implementation of more concerted measures against the counter-culture. The late sixties saw drug laws enforced with much greater determination, followed by police raids on the offices of underground publications such as *It* and the closure of clubs like Middle Earth and UFO after police raids had prompted landlords to withdraw leases. In 1970 the authoritarian offensive against the underground press continued, with *Oz* editors Richard Neville, Jim Anderson and Felix Dennis prosecuted, and subsequently imprisoned, for obscenity.[15] A more coercive set of official responses also made itself felt in the sphere of public order. In 1968 demonstrations against the Vietnam war were subject to aggressive and often brutal policing, with the intimidatory use of mounted officers and police 'snatch squads', while in February 1970 punitive prison sentences were passed on six defendants after police had battled with protesters objecting to the presence of representatives of the Greek military junta at the Garden House Hotel in Cambridge. In 1974 further violence erupted in Holborn's Red Lion Square as police clashed with demonstrators protesting against a meeting being held by an extreme Right-wing group, the National Front. In the midst of the skirmish a young protester, Kevin Gately, was killed, his death prompting an inquiry presided over by Lord Justice Scarman in 1975.

During the late sixties, therefore, negative social reactions to youth began to converge on groups of middle-class youngsters, with a backlash against the counter-cultures and the revolutionary ferment of 1968. The seventies, however, saw the thrust of reaction gradually return to more 'traditional' targets. A moral panic around mugging in the early 1970s, followed by the spectre of the 'inner-city rioter' at the end of the decade, saw the addition of a powerful 'racial' dimension to the negative stereotyping of youth.[16] More generally, the seventies saw working-class youngsters once again highlighted as the nation's most menacing folk devils – and as a consequence sections of working-class youth became subject to much harsher measures of control and discipline.

Throughout the early seventies disturbances at football grounds continued to attract spectacular media coverage. Particularly infamous reputations were carved out by the supporters of such clubs as Millwall, Leeds United and Manchester United (whose rowdier followers were dubbed the 'Red Army' by the press). As a consequence of perceived increases in the scale of football hooliganism a new battery of crowd control measures were introduced in British football grounds. During the late sixties police forces had experimented with 'mob squads', groups of officers who moved into the heart of terrace crowds to seize hooligan ringleaders, while magistrates had been encouraged to exercise the full measure of their powers in imposing fines on those arrested for offences at football grounds. During the seventies the football terraces themselves were divided up into more manageable, self-contained 'pens', while spiked perimeter fences began to be erected around pitches, the first at Manchester United's Old Trafford ground in 1974. Policy conferences, held at both national and regional levels during the early seventies, constantly reiterated the theme that football hooliganism was 'about to be beaten' – but this optimism proved ill-founded. More effective measures of crowd control on the terraces simply served to displace the problem to the immediate vicinity of football grounds and, later, city centres and points of transit such as railway stations and motorway service stations.

The mid-seventies also saw a new dimension to football violence as Britain increasingly began to export its hooligan problem. With a growing number of international fixtures and a reduction in the relative cost of overseas travel, it became common for large numbers of supporters to follow League sides and the national team to matches abroad. Well-publicized clashes between English fans and European supporters and police forces became a common occurrence during the seventies and early eighties. Matters climaxed at the European Cup Final held at the Heysel Stadium in Brussels in 1985. In full view of eighty million television viewers across the world thirty-eight people died and a further four hundred were injured in the panic that ensued as a phalanx of Liverpool fans charged at their Juventus rivals. In the wake of the disaster English teams were banned from competing in Europe, while the British authorities took an increasingly tough line in the control of football crowds and in the punishment of those convicted of football-related violence.

Notes

1   An outline of the nature and history of these radical groups is provided in Arthur Marwick, 1970, 'Youth in Britain, 1920–1960: detachment and commitment', *Journal of Contemporary History*, vol. 5, no. 1, pp. 37–52.

2   These observations can be found in Brighton Weekenders' Holiday Scheme, 1966, *Application For a Grant from the Youth Service Development Council*, Appendix 3, p. 5.

3   The nature of CND's political appeal is explored in Frank Parkin, 1968, *Middle Class Radicalism: The Social Bases of the British Campaign for Nuclear Disarmament*, Manchester: Manchester University Press.

4   A detailed history of life in 'the Haight' is provided in Charles Perry, 1985, *The Haight Ashbury*, New York: Vintage. One of the most authoritative accounts of the rise of progressive bands in this area can be found in Joel Selvin, 1995, *Summer of Love*, London: Plume.

5   Of the few histories of the British counter-cultural experience, one of the best is Elizabeth Nelson, 1989, *The British Counter-Culture, 1966–73: A Study of the Underground Press*, London: Macmillan.

6   This was a reference to Enoch Powell, whose political stand against immigration had made him a figure of notoriety during the late sixties.

7   A copy of 'Yell' is reproduced in Peter Stansill and David Zane Mairowitz, 1972, *Bamn! Outlaw Manifestos and Ephemera, 1965–70*, Harmondsworth: Penguin, pp. 70–2.

8   For further discussion of the skinheads' animosity towards the counter-culture see Eric Dunning, Patrick Murphy and John Williams, 1988, *The Roots of Football Hooliganism: An Historical and Sociological Study*, London: Routledge and Kegan Paul, pp. 169–73.

9   A powerful feminist critique of the sixties' 'sexual revolution' is provided in
     Sheila Jeffreys, 1990, *Anticlimax: A Feminist Perspective on the Sexual
     Revolution*, London: Women's Press.

10   For a more detailed elaboration of this argument see Stuart Hall, 1968, *The
     Hippies: An American 'Moment'*, Occasional Paper no. 16, CCCS, University
     of Birmingham, pp. 10–11.

11   This interpretation of the counter-culture as performing an 'adaptive' func-
     tion for bourgeois culture was originally forwarded by John Clarke, Stuart
     Hall, Tony Jefferson and Brian Roberts in their seminal essay 'Subcultures,
     cultures and class: a theoretical overview', in Stuart Hall and Tony Jefferson
     (eds), 1976, *Resistance Through Rituals: Youth Subcultures in Post-War Britain*,
     London: Hutchinson, pp. 65–6.

12   For contrasting accounts of student activism and unrest at the London School
     of Economics see Ben Brewster and Alexander Cockburn, 1967, 'Revolt at the
     LSE', *New Left Review*, no. 43, May–June, pp. 11–26; Paul Hoch and Vic
     Schoenbach, 1969, *LSE: The Natives are Restless: A Report on Student Power
     in Action*, London: Sheed and Ward; Harry Kidd, 1969, *The Trouble at LSE,
     1966–7*, London: Oxford University Press; Tessa Blackstone, Kathleen
     Gales, Roger Hadley and Wyn Lewis, 1970, *Students in Conflict: LSE in 1967*,
     London: Weidenfeld and Nicolson.

13   Accounts of the confrontations that took place at Essex, Hornsey and Hull can
     be found in Tom Fawthrop, Tom Nairn and David Triesman, 1969, 'Three
     student risings', in Carl Ogelsby (ed.), *The New Left Reader*, New York:
     Grove. For contemporaneous commentaries on student activism written by
     student radicals themselves see Alexander Cockburn and Robin Blackburn
     (eds), 1969, *Student Power: Problems, Diagnosis, Action*, Harmondsworth:
     Penguin. An excellent autobiographical account of the growth of militant
     opposition during the late sixties is provided in Tariq Ali, 1988, *Street
     Fighting Years: An Autobiography of the Sixties*, London: Fontana.

14   These arguments were originally developed by John Clarke, Stuart Hall,
     Tony Jefferson and Brian Roberts in 'Subcultures, cultures and class: a theo-
     retical overview', in Hall and Jefferson (eds), *Resistance Through Rituals*, p. 72.

15   The prison sentences passed on Neville, Anderson and Dennis were only
     dropped after a lengthy appeal. For a detailed account of the case see Tony
     Palmer, 1971, *The Trials of Oz*, London: Blond and Briggs. In a similar fashion
     the publishers of Søren Hansen and Jesper Jenson's *The Little Red Schoolbook*
     were convicted of obscenity in July 1971 in a case originally brought by Mary
     Whitehouse.

16   According to authors associated with the Birmingham Centre for Con-
     temporary Cultural Studies, the moral panic around mugging in the early
     1970s helped orchestrate consent for a political order which was increasingly

willing to rule through force and compulsion rather than consensus and consent. See Stuart Hall, Chas Critcher, Tony Jefferson, John Clarke and Brian Roberts, 1978, *Policing the Crisis: Mugging, the State and Law and Order*, London: Macmillan.

8 'Blank Generation': Cultures of Confrontation

The Mid-Seventies: A Context of Crisis

Thirty years after the end of the Second World War visions of social and political consensus had become a distant memory in Britain. In the early seventies inflation and unemployment rose, industrial relations deteriorated and, in 1973, increases in the cost of oil imports ruined any possibility of a favourable balance of payments. Edward Heath's Conservative government responded with spending controls and a policy of wage restraint which, in turn, was met by a series of overtime bans by miners, electricity workers and railwaymen. Fuel shortages worsened and industrial confrontation intensified, prompting the government to introduce a series of dramatic emergency measures to conserve power. Facing an all-out strike by mine-workers in February 1974, Heath finally called a general election in a bid to win a public mandate, though after a bitterly fought contest it was the Labour Party who managed to clinch a slim overall majority. However, despite Harold Wilson's pledge to 'get the economy right', the country's economic predicament did not improve. Inflation and unemployment continued their seemingly inexorable rise, recovery proving impossible as the world economy slipped into recession. The Labour Party had made political capital from claims that it could work successfully with the trade unions, but such attempts disintegrated as the scale of Britain's economic problems forced the government towards spending cuts and wage restraints in policies reminiscent of its Conservative predecessor. By the mid-seventies, then, an air of crisis and social polarization hung over Britain, a sense of discord which manifested itself at a symbolic level in the youth styles and subcultures of the period.

'Young, Loud and Snotty': The Polarization of British Youth Style

In the late sixties upper-class tastes and manners had been decidedly unfashionable. Counter-cultural pretensions had dictated that tweed give way to denim and that Oxbridge accents be buried under cockney affectation. The second half of the seventies, in contrast, saw upper-class panache return with a vengeance. In the pages of *Harpers and Queen* cultural commentator Peter York faultlessly catalogued a taxonomy of the period's style, coining the term 'Sloane Ranger' (after Sloane Square in Chelsea) to denote a new young, upper-middle class that, quite literally, wore its social status on its sleeve.[1] Sloane Ranger style was that of up-market conservatism, taking many of its cues from younger members of the aristocracy and the royal family. For women this meant a classically tailored look. Navy blue tights and skirts were teamed with Jaeger jackets or velvet blazers and accessorized with Gucci shoes and shoulder bags, strings of pearls and Hermés headscarves. Hair was elegantly bobbed or, occasionally, worn in a pony-tail. This 'classic' appearance was maintained in evening wear, the Sloane favouring a low-cut French or Italian frock for cocktail parties around the fashionable night-spots of Kensington and Knightsbridge or, for more formal get-togethers, a taffeta ballgown set off by a velvet choker. Initially a label reserved for upper-middle-class young women, the Sloane Ranger found her counterpart in similarly 'class-conscious' young beaux. The male of the species sported expensive, yet tastefully understated, suits accompanied by Barbour raincoats and flat caps in an image evocative of rural manor houses and the country gentry, the Sloane style embodying 'the thousand-year infatuation of the English upper middle-classes for what it imagines is the style of its betters' (York, 1980, p. 62).

York's Sloane Ranger was, of course, a caricature. Yet his observations were made with consummate accuracy, vividly catching the nuances of a new bourgeois style that was proud to proclaim its 'insider' status. The Sloanes' ostentatious flaunting of their upper-middle-class prestige, then, was symptomatic of the wider social and political polarization of British society during the mid-seventies. The period's general sense of turbulence, social antagonism and conflict, moreover, was further dramatized by the emergence of a subculture and musical style that laid vociferous claim to an alienated 'outsider' status.

Punk rock first burst into the British public consciousness in December 1976. Facing a last-minute gap in its running order, an early evening chat show on Thames Television booked the Sex Pistols, then a recently formed and little-known band, to fill a short interview spot at the end of the programme. The Sex Pistols had just released their first single, 'Anarchy in the UK', and the intention was to provide a brief and innocuous commentary on the band and what appeared to be a new, rebellious subculture emerging on the fringes of British pop. However, baited and egged-on by the programme's host, Bill Grundy, the band and members of their entourage sneered, swore and generally made themselves as disruptive as possible on live television. The profanities themselves were comically irreverent ('. . . shit. Oh, sorry, a rude word', 'What a fucking rotter' and so on), but the humour of the incident disappeared in the subsequent media uproar. The following day a feeding frenzy broke out among Britain's tabloid newspapers, with headlines such as 'The Filth and the Fury' and 'Foul Mouthed Yobs' casting the Sex Pistols and their associates as immoral degenerates, a baleful influence on British youngsters and stark testimony to the nation's cultural debasement. There followed one of the most intense moral panics since the early sixties as promoters cancelled the Sex Pistols' concerts, the BBC refused to play their music and a succession of record companies washed their hands of the group.[2] Predictably, such media exposure simply drew more attention to the band and their fellow travellers, the Sex Pistols' records soaring to the top of the charts and punk style becoming one of the most influential aesthetics of the late twentieth century.

As with the Teddy boys, mods and skinheads before them, the media distorted and embellished the punks' behaviour. However, punks' incendiary appearance and demeanour certainly seemed to signal confrontation and antagonism. Punk plundered the vaults of British youth subcultural style. Drape jackets, drainpipe trousers, work-boots and leather jackets all found a place in a ripped and torn collage held together by safety pins, buckles and zip fasteners. Hair was short, spiky and sometimes dyed. Slogans were stencilled onto shirts and trousers and the iconography of sexual fetishism (studded leather, PVC, bondage straps, stiletto heels) combined in a style that embodied a sense of transgression and alienation.[3] Dissonance was also evident within punk music. Fast, distorted guitar refrains and electronic feedback complemented aggressive and nihilistic lyrics in songs which made a virtue of raw brevity.[4] Even the names of punk singers and musicians (Johnny Rotten, Sid Vicious, Poly Styrene, Rat Scabies) and punk bands (the Sex Pistols, the Clash, the Damned, Generation X) expressed a challenge to the established tastes and conventions of the pop music establishment. As the year of the Queen's Silver Jubilee began, therefore, shifts in subcultural style dramatized at a symbolic level the wider collapse of social and political consensus, young punks appropriating 'the rhetoric of crisis which had filled the airwaves and the editorials throughout the period' (Hebdige, 1979, p. 87).

Initially, it was easy to take punk's guttersnipe stance at face value. Commentators presented punk as 'dole-queue rock' (Marsh, 1977), the expression of a generation that had been dispossessed and disowned – the flotsam and jetsam of desolate high-rise wastelands and decaying inner-city estates. Closer scrutiny, however, revealed that punk's origins were rather less lumpen. There were, certainly, individual punk musicians with working-class (even petty criminal) backgrounds, but the bulk of those who frequented early punk clubs like the Roxy and the Vortex tended to be art students and middle-class youngsters from London's commuter-belt. A retinue of the Sex Pistols' earliest followers, for example, were known as the 'Bromley contingent', their members hailing from this south London suburb and its surrounding area. Indeed, the 'outsider' posture of Britain's initial punk 'moment' is best seen as a piece of radical theatre, a calculated attempt to inflame and outrage establishment sensibilities.

Although punk's iconoclastic rhetoric poured scorn and contempt on the sixties' hippies, many of those involved with the management and promotion of the first punk bands had, themselves, been either embroiled in or influenced by the ideas and programmes of the bohemian counter-culture. The idea that European avant-garde movements such as Dada, Lettrisme and Situationism were an influence on British punk rock in the late seventies has been dismissed as 'bollocks' by John Lydon who, as Johnny Rotten, was the Sex Pistols' lead singer (Lydon, 1994, p. 4). According to Lydon, the rise of the Sex Pistols was chaotic and unplanned – a product of fortuitous circumstances and the individual talents of the band members rather than the outcome of any overarching strategy of artistic sedition. Indeed, authors such as Greil Marcus have tended to romanticize and inflate the role of avant-garde artistic philosophy in seventies' punk,[5] obscuring the way in which the movement was always an unstable conglomeration of diverse concepts and influences. Nonetheless, although their role should not be overstated, the aesthetics of radical art were clearly an inspiration in the ideas and work of figures such as Bernard Rhodes, manager of punk band the Clash; Jamie Reid, the Sex Pistols' graphic designer; and (especially) Malcolm McLaren, the Sex Pistols' Faginesque mentor.

Throughout the sixties McLaren had drifted through an array of art colleges, revelling in their radical milieux and developing a particular fascination for the ideas of the French Situationists. Established in 1957, the Situationist International had been a group of avant-garde radicals who drew on a range of philosophical and artistic cross-currents to elaborate a critique of contemporary culture.[6] For the Situationists the whole experience of life in modern capitalism was intrinsically alienating, with people reduced to mere spectators of a world in which genuine participation had been precluded. In this 'society of the spectacle', it was argued, authentic experience could only be glimpsed through moments of artistic expression and political struggle – the Situationists developing strategies of *détournement* in which existing symbols, images and texts were usurped and reworked in an attempt to subvert the banalities of everyday life. Situationism, then, sought to manipulate the media's symbolic and visual language, endeavouring to turn the passively experienced 'spectacle' of everyday life into a 'situation' in which structures of repressive control were thrown into sharp relief and possibilities for action and change became discernible.

The Situationist ethos was a tangible force in French student politics throughout the sixties, its influence readily visible in the pamphlets, practices and sloganeering of May '68, while in America Situationist ideas inspired radical groups such as the Yippies, the Motherfuckers and Black Mask. In British radicalism Situationist ideas had a lower profile, though were taken up by small 'groupuscules'[7] such as the Kim Philby Dining Club and King Mob. Various accounts exist as to the extent of Malcolm McLaren's involvement with these groups, though it is certain that he participated in at least one of King Mob's 'situations' – members of the group, one dressed as Father Christmas, invading Selfridges' toy department in December 1968 and handing out toys to bewildered children.

The manifestos and pranks of groups like King Mob were a crucial influence on McLaren, persuading him of the possibilities of radical subversion through the manipulation of the media and popular culture. In particular

McLaren became captivated by the subversive potential of youth sub-cultures and, in partnership with Vivienne Westwood (whom he had met at Harrow School of Art in 1965) he opened a clothes shop – 'Let It Rock' – in London's King's Road in 1971, selling fifties' Teddy boy clothes and memorabilia. Then, during a visit to New York, McLaren became impressed by the high energy and outrageous sleaze of an art/rock scene that was developing around a band called the New York Dolls and on his return to London he set about revamping the King's Road premises. Trading under a new name, 'SEX', the shop specialized in rubber and leather clothes inspired by the subterranean world of sado-masochism and sexual fetishism, reflecting McLaren and Westwood's enthusiasm for style and fashion as strategies of provocation and outrage. A further visit to America saw McLaren manage the New York Dolls for the final six months of their career and on his return he began to prepare a similar project, encouraging the musical aspirations of four youngsters who had gravitated to his shop, intrigued by its audacious clothes designs. Taking inspiration from the name of McLaren's emporium, the foursome (John Lydon, Glen Matlock, Steve Jones and Paul Cook) soon became known as the Sex Pistols, McLaren recruiting several of his former Situationist co-conspirators to produce the publicity and promotional material which helped galvanize the band's meteoric rise to notoriety during 1976 and 1977.[8]

Punk's bohemian lineage, therefore, cannot be disputed. At the same time, however, like all sub- and counter-cultural movements, punk's origins were nebulous. From Britain punk also drew inspiration from the camp histrionics of glam rockers such as David Bowie and Marc Bolan, as well as the coarse rhythm'n'blues of bands like Eddie and the Hot Rods and the 101ers, who had emerged in London's 'pub rock' scene of the mid-seventies. Additionally, punk drew on an extensive roster of influences from the United States. Especially inspirational was the high-octane guitar distortion of early sixties' 'garage' rock, the jagged fury of Detroit bands like the MC5 and the Stooges and the artistic experiments of the Velvet Underground. A more immediate set of influences came from the rock'n'roll 'trash' of the New York Dolls and (most obviously) the rise, during the mid-seventies, of a New York club scene dominated by performers such as Patti Smith, Television, Blondie and the Ramones.[9] Indeed, it is arguable that the latter's raucous minimalism represented the most enduring influence on the musical style adopted by British punk bands. Avant-garde libertarianism, then, may have been a feature of the initial punk 'project', but it stood as just one influence among many. Moreover, after the Sex Pistols' acrimonious implosion amid a disastrous tour of America in 1978, there came to the fore a second wave of punk fans and performers (for example, the UK Subs, the Angelic Upstarts, the Anti-Nowhere League and the Exploited) on whom the finer points of Situationist theory were somewhat lost. This later manifestation of punk was unconcerned with avant-garde strategies of subversion through the manipulation of the media. Instead, there developed a milieu that owed a much greater debt to the buzz-saw guitars of American punk bands, the boisterous camaraderie of the English football terraces and the bawdy sing-alongs of the English music-hall.

Compared with earlier subcultural formations, the Teddy boys or skinheads for example, music and music-making were much more central features of punk. Punk's ethos of do-it-yourself improvisation spawned an army of fresh-faced 'one chord wonders' in a swell of amateur musicianship evocative of the skiffle and beat booms of the fifties and sixties. In addition, the national and local punk scenes were chronicled by an array of crudely photocopied and stapled together 'fanzines' such as *Sniffin' Glue* and *Ripped and Torn*, the verve of individual enthusiasts providing the energy for a literary culture that was, in many ways, evocative of the sixties' underground press. Echoes of the sixties' counter-culture were also found in the legion of small-scale, independent record shops and record labels begot by seventies' punk. Independent record companies like Stiff, Chiswick and Small Wonder found stimulus in the punk explosion and were followed by a horde of smaller confederates, all independently promoting and distributing their artists.[10] However, like their counter-cultural predecessors, the punk 'independents' were often closer to 'hip capitalists' than avant-garde revolutionaries. Indeed, rather than dethroning the corporate record moguls, punk (like progressive rock of the sixties) actually represented a massive spur to the popular music industry, generating new tastes and markets and operating as an important marketing and research organ for the major labels.

'Church of the Poison Mind': New Romanticism, 'New Pop' and the Early Eighties

Like the subcultural formations that came before it, punk was never a static, unified entity but a continually developing fusion of different factions and influences. Any sense of a coherent punk 'movement' or punk 'identity' was largely the outcome of media simplification and commercial marketing strategy. By the early eighties punk's inherent instability had become unmistakable, the scene breaking down into a diverse series of camps and contingents. In September 1979, for example, 'The First Futurama Science Fiction Festival' in Leeds showcased performances by Public Image Limited, Cabaret Voltaire, Joy Division and several other artists who made up the core of punk's bleakest and most avant-garde strand. Many of the leading lights of this offshoot of punk cohered around northern independent labels such as Factory Records, launched by media personality Tony Wilson and his associates in 1979 to cater for the north-west's flourishing music scene (see chapter 12).

Many of punk's more dandyesque elements resurfaced in London clubs such as Hell, Billy's and, especially, Blitz. Held on Tuesday nights in a Covent Garden wine bar, Blitz became the epicentre of a London club culture which cultivated an air of exclusivity and excess. The scene was dominated by a subcultural clique who turned their backs on seventies' despondency, instead revelling in peacock displays of outrageous hedonism. Many of the new romantics, as they became known, came from the same art school and design backgrounds as the original punks but, instead of a downwardly mobile proletarian image, they established a vogue for foppish indulgence in a West End recreation of Weimar Berlin. The new romantics loathed the mundane. Their style was one of fantasy and preening arrogance, frilly-fronted fencing shirts, kilts, braided tunics and pantomime dame chic being set off by layers of white face powder, mascara and sculptures of heavily lacquered or back-combed hair. Musically, the new romantics returned to the lavish theatrics of David Bowie and Roxy Music, though new romantic bands such as Spandau Ballet and Visage also drew on the experimental forays of European electronic musicians like Kraftwerk, these groups' synthesizer-based anthems dominating the sound of early eighties' pop.

According to Peter York, the style of the new romantics caught the flavour of wider changes taking place in British life and culture during the early eighties.[11] Just as punk symbolically played out the sense of crisis and conflict that prevailed during the late seventies, new romanticism seemed to dovetail with a new phase in the nation's political climate. For York, new romanticism's brash excesses and desire to throw off the stylistic baggage of the past found a political counterpart in the new brand of free market Conservatism emerging from right-wing think-tanks like the Institute of Economic Affairs and the Centre for Policy Studies. Here, York's reading of style possibly begins to over-reach itself, yet there are certainly parallels to be drawn between new romanticism and the new political order that dawned during the 1980s. Like the new romantics, the new free market Conservatives saw themselves as swash-buckling mavericks and (again, like the new romantics) they had an unshakeable set of convictions which were poised to bury the traditions of the past, launching a new era of self-assured individualism. In the case of the new romantics this brashness and self-interest registered in a commitment to a narcissistic and flamboyant subcultural style. In the case of the new Conservatives it registered in a commitment to free market competition and processes of deregulation that would thoroughly transform British social and economic life.

Unlike its political counterpart, new romanticism had run its course by the mid-eighties. In its place the most introspective elements of punk sought refuge in a morose 'gothic' subculture. The 'gothic' image was indebted to fifties' ham horror, combining a deathly pallor with a taste for dusty, black Victoriana and a predilection for gloom-laden guitar rock (exemplified in the ponderous releases of gothic bands such as the Sisters of Mercy, the Mission and Fields of the Nephilim). In contrast, punk's early interest in radical art reappeared in a new, up-beat pop aesthetic. In 1983 music journalist Paul Morley joined forces with Trevor Horn, formerly a musical accomplice of Sex Pistols manager Malcolm McLaren, to form record label Zang Tumb Tuum (or ZTT, the name taken from a First World War futurist poem). In their various pop projects Morley and Horn drew on many of the avant-garde ideas that had originally informed punk, using new technological processes of sound and image production to undermine notions of authorship and authenticity. Frankie Goes to Hollywood, ZTT's most successful artists, scored a trilogy of number one hits in 1984, though the record company's sharp marketing skills were of even greater significance. In its approach to merchandising ZTT mockingly blurred the distinction between authenticity and artifice, its promotion campaigns (which began an eighties' trend for slogan tee-shirts) playfully satirizing the processes of commercial calculation and 'hard sell' that underlay the entertainment and media industries. However, as Simon Frith (1990) argues, it remains an open question as to whether Morley and Horn's Situationist-inspired scam actually added up to a radical critique of contemporary culture, or was simply co-opted into the mainstream sales strategies of corporate business.

As well as continuing many of the avant-garde preoccupations of early punk, 'new pop' also probed questions of gender and identity originally explored by glam rock artists such as David Bowie. These issues had also been present within punk and new romanticism, both scenes embracing marked elements of androgyny and a close association with gay subcultural style, but 'new pop' pushed the themes much further. Singers such as Boy George and Marilyn (both former 'faces' of the new romantic scene) took cross-dressing into the high street, while openly gay bands like Bronski Beat won acceptance in the pop mainstream.[12] ZTT's Frankie Goes to Hollywood, meanwhile, caroused with an imagery that made explicit use of a host of gay and sado-masochist signifiers. In its own way, then, the 'new pop' of the early eighties was radical and subversive – mischievously deconstructing the commercial processes of the pop industry and gleefully undermining traditional representations of gender and sexuality.

Radical politics of a different kind was articulated in another offshoot of punk. In the late seventies, disillusioned with what they saw as a commercial 'watering-down' of punk's original ethos, a number of activists sought to give material substance to punk's political rhetoric. Based around Crass, a group of anarchists who dabbled in music and performance art, there developed a version of punk more aggressively committed to libertarian politics. Rather than making impishly subversive incursions into the commercial pop industry, Crass and their followers saw themselves as staying true to the 'authentic' spirit of punk. From a commune in Epping Forest Crass handled all their own affairs, promoting their own concerts, financing like-minded artists and releasing a series of insurrectionary records throughout the early eighties. By 1984 the members of Crass had moved on to new projects, but their fusion of hippy idealism and punk sensibility pioneered a style which was given more fully formed expression by the 'New Age travellers' of the late eighties and early nineties (see chapter 12).

Amid the cultural fall-out from punk there also emerged a series of 'retro' styles and revivals, beginning with ska, mod and psychedelic revivals in the late seventies and early eighties. The vogue for 'retro' styling was especially prominent in advertising geared to the youth market, advertisers increasingly reviving and reworking the mythologies and representations of the recent past, epitomized in 1986 by a marketing campaign for Levi's 501 jeans which gently parodied fifties' youth lifestyles.[13] A penchant for quotation and pastiche also became a pronounced feature within British subcultural style, the fascination for 'retro' imagery reaching a high point in the late eighties and nineties. During the early and mid-nineties, for example, youth style was dominated by a fascination for sixties' aesthetics, a revival of mod élan coinciding with a renaissance in British guitar music in which 'Britpop' bands such as Blur and Oasis consciously toyed with the genres and iconography of the mod era. Rather than simple exercises in fond nostalgia, however, these reworkings were innovative and creative in the way they fused together elements of the past and the present. Nineties' mod, for example, was not a straight copy of its sixties' forebear, the 'original' Fred Perry shirts and Harrington jackets finding a place alongside modern trainers and sportswear. This 'hybridization' of youth style could be cited as an example of a new 'postmodern' blurring of cultural boundaries (see chapter 13), yet it should be remembered that processes of resurrection and reconfiguration have not been unique to the eighties and nineties. In the seventies, much of the impact of punk style derived from the way it ransacked the subcultural past in a riotous mix of historical references – from the biker's leather jacket to the Ted's brothel-creeper shoes. Indeed, rather than being novel features of the late twentieth century, practices of 'quotation' and appropriation should more accurately be seen as intrinsic characteristics of the entire history of British subcultural youth style.

Notes

1   Peter York's articles 'The Sloane rangers' and 'Sloane ranger man' can be found in an anthology of his writings from the period. See Peter York, 1980, *Style Wars*, London: Sidgwick and Jackson.
2   There now exists an enormous range of texts outlining the Sex Pistols' brief but explosively influential musical career. One of the earliest, yet still one of the most informative, is Fred and Judy Vermorel, 1978, *The Sex Pistols: The Inside Story*, London: Star Universal. Additionally, a thoroughly researched and meticulously detailed account of the Sex Pistols and their entourage can

be found in Jon Savage, 1991, *England's Dreaming: Sex Pistols and Punk Rock*, London: Faber and Faber.

3 A contemporaneous survey of the late seventies' punk scene can be found in Caroline Coon, 1977, *1988: The New Wave Punk Rock Explosion*, London: Omnibus Press. The definitive semiological reading of punk style is provided in Dick Hebdige, 1979, *Subculture: The Meaning of Style*, London: Methuen.

4 The best 'musicological' survey of punk style is provided in Dave Laing, 1985, *One Chord Wonders: Power and Meaning in Punk Rock*, Milton Keynes: Open University Press.

5 Greil Marcus's most grandiose claims for the influence of avant-garde art on punk rock can be found in Greil Marcus, 1989, *Lipstick Traces: A Secret History of the Twentieth Century*, Cambridge, Mass.: Harvard University Press. Marcus is prone to the quixotic in many of his observations, yet his writings still contain many elements of insight and perception. A collection of his best writings on the punk phenomenon can be found in Greil Marcus, 1993, *In the Fascist Bathroom: Writings on Punk, 1977–92*, Harmondsworth: Penguin. Alternatively, an uncompromising and acerbic critique of Marcus's perspective is provided in Stewart Home, 1995, *Cranked Up Really High*, London: Codex.

6 For an accessible introduction to the history and nature of Situationist thought see Sadie Plant, 1996, 'The Situationist International: a case of spectacular neglect', in Stuart Home (ed.), *What Is Situationism: A Reader*, Edinburgh: AK Press.

7 'Groupuscules' was a term coined in France during May 1968 to denote the array of radical sects that sprung up amid the student disturbances in Paris.

8 A more extensive account of the relationship between punk and Situationism can be found in Simon Frith and Howard Horne, 1989, *Art into Pop*, London: Routledge, pp. 123–61.

9 The most detailed and accurate accounts of the American punk scenes of the mid- and late seventies can be found in Roman Kozak, 1988, *This Ain't No Disco: The Story of CBGB*, London: Faber and Faber; Clinton Heylin, 1993, *From the Velvets to the Voidoids: A Pre-Punk History for a Post-Punk World*, Harmondsworth: Penguin; Legs McNeill and Gillian McCain, 1996, *Please Kill Me: The Uncensored Oral History of Punk*, London: Little, Brown.

10 A survey of the growth of independent record labels in Britain during and after the late seventies can be found in Johnny Rogan's introduction to *The Guinness Who's Who of Indie and New Wave Music*, 1992, Enfield: Guinness, pp. 5–9.

11 Peter York elaborated these themes in a television series produced for the BBC in 1995. His comparison of the new romantic subculture with the eighties' ethos of free market individualism can also be found in the volume

produced to accompany the series. See Peter York, 1995, *Peter York's Eighties*, London: BBC, pp. 8–39.

12   A well-observed account of the rise of 'new pop' figureheads Culture Club is provided in Dave Rimmer, 1985, *Like Punk Never Happened: Culture Club and the New Pop*, London: Faber and Faber.

13   An analysis of the meaning and significance of the revival of fifties' styling during the 1980s is offered in Janice Winship, 1986, 'Back to the future: a style for the eighties', *New Socialist*, July/August, pp. 48–9.

9 'Dread, Beat an' Blood': Race, Racism and Post-War Youth Culture

'Exodus': The Context and Impact of Post-War Immigration

Immigration is not, of course, a feature unique to British post-war development. For centuries Britain has been a destination for both immigrants and refugees fleeing religious or political persecution, and the existence of minority ethnic communities has long been an aspect of life in many British cities and towns. Since the beginning of the twentieth century, for example, black enclaves had developed in ports such as Liverpool and Cardiff, and in cities such as Manchester and London's East End. Economic depression during the twenties and thirties provided little incentive for immigration to Britain, but the outbreak of war saw increasing numbers of West Indians, Africans and Asians recruited into both the Allied armed forces and British industry, a process which laid the basis for subsequent patterns of immigration.

As post-war reconstruction got underway, and as the British economy steadily expanded during the fifties and sixties, labour shortages quickly became pronounced. Above all, it was in the less profitable, and often labour-intensive, sectors of the economy where these shortages were most severe. As the workforce was attracted to the most prosperous employers – for example, the motor industry, telecommunications and finance – less profitable industries such as public transport, the health service and textiles struggled to compete for the labour of British workers. These employers, therefore, gladly absorbed those workers from the New Commonwealth who were gradually coming to Britain in search of employment. Indeed, some industries went further and actively recruited abroad. In 1956 London Transport began recruiting staff in Barbados (and in Trinidad and Jamaica ten years later), while the health service welcomed nurses from the West Indies. The British Hotels and Restaurants Association also recruited workers from Barbados, while official encouragement was given to the employment of workers from the Indian subcontinent.[1] With their British citizenship guaranteed by the 1948 Nationality Act, numbers of immigrants from the West Indies, Africa and Asia steadily increased from about 2,000 in 1953 to around 130,000 in 1961 (see table 9.1), many of these people settling in areas of Britain where labour shortages were greatest – for example Greater London, the West Midlands and Manchester.

The post-war expansion of minority ethnic communities has had a major impact on national culture and politics in general, but has had particular ramifications in the field of youth culture. Many of the immigrant settlers of the fifties and sixties were themselves aged in their early twenties or younger and, as a result, Britain's non-white population has been relatively youthful compared to the national total. Additionally, the dimensions of institutionalized racism and discrimination to which immigrant communities have, as whole, been subject have often manifested themselves most tangibly in relation to these communities' youngest members. Encountering prejudice in education and employment, and subject to strategies of policing that have frequently been oppressive and intimida-

Table 9.1   Estimated net immigration from the New Commonwealth, 1953–1962

	West Indies	India	Pakistan	Others	Total
1953	2,000	—	—	—	2,000
1954	11,000	—	—	—	11,000
1955	27,000	5,800	1,850	7,500	42,650
1956	29,800	5,600	2,050	9,350	46,800
1957	23,000	6,600	5,200	7,600	42,400
1958	15,000	6,200	4,700	3,950	29,850
1959	16,400	2,950	850	1,400	21,600
1960	49,650	5,900	2,500	–350	57,700
1961	66,300	23,750	25,100	21,250	136,400
1962[a]	31,800	19,050	25,080	18,970	94,900

[a] First six months up to introduction of controls.
Source: House of Commons, 1976, *Commonwealth Immigration to the United Kingdom from the 1950s to 1975: A Survey of Statistical Sources*, Library Research Paper no. 56, London: HMSO.

tory, black youngsters have responded by generating subcultural formations which have given a sense of collective solidarity to groups of young people facing a racist and hostile society. Moreover, black youth subcultures and their associated styles have, in turn, been a key influence on the cultural adaptations and styles generated by white youngsters. Though they have often seemed separate and autonomous, black and white youth cultures have always been deeply connected, engaged in processes of aesthetic dialogue and exchange which have played out, at a symbolic level, the wider patterns of relation between the two communities.[2] Indeed, according to Dick Hebdige, the prominence of 'race' as an organizing principle within British youth culture has meant that the entire array of subcultural styles can be read, in themselves, as 'a phantom history of race relations since the War' (Hebdige, 1979, p. 45).

City of Spades: Race, Racism and Youth in the Fifties

With growing immigration during the fifties and sixties African and West Indian cultural life burgeoned in many British cities. Indicative was the first Mardi Gras (later more firmly instituted as the Notting Hill Carnival) held at Paddington Town Hall in 1959. The vitality of calypso and jazz clubs, meanwhile, captivated white commentators such as Colin MacInnes, whose 'London Trilogy' of novels (*City of Spades* (1957), *Absolute Beginners* (1959) and *Mr Love and Justice* (1960)) romantically portrayed a vibrant night life among London clubs like the West End Rendezvous Club, the Sunset club in Soho and many others in Brixton, Whitechapel and Paddington. This milieu, however, was not populated exclusively by young immigrants. Many white youngsters, fascinated by what seemed to be an exotically alluring lifestyle, were also drawn to black jazz clubs. In 1954, for example, *Picture Post* reported on Cy Laurie's Jazz Club in Soho, a focal point of the capital's trad jazz scene where 'debutantes and barrow boys – students, artists, mechanics, incipient stockbrokers – white and black – in narrow trousers, loose shirts, and knotted neckerchiefs – sweat together in the groove' (10 July 1954).

Since the forties, jazz had attracted a significant white audience in Britain, though by the early fifties its following had begun to fragment into a series of mutually suspicious camps. The rawer-edged sounds of New Orleans jazz appealed especially to seriously minded aspiring musicians and devotees of the nascent beatnik scene, these youngsters attributing a sense of creative 'authenticity' and 'sincerity' to their music. For some this form of jazz also seemed to embrace qualities of dissent, a symbolic defiance of both the establishment's prim decorum and the commercial market's shallow cynicism. Hence the early fifties saw the Young Communists establish the Challenge Jazz Club in Holborn, with George Webb's Dixielanders as their house band.[3] During the late fifties trad jazz also provided the soundtrack to CND's Aldermaston marches, while Eric Hobsbawm, one of Britain's leading historians of the Left, wrote a weekly column as jazz critic of the *New Statesman*.[4] Less esoteric forms of jazz, on the other hand, became a feature of white working-class youngsters' leisure. A jazz boom in the early fifties was underpinned by the enthusiasm of youngsters who were less concerned with attributes of creative integrity or social protest than with the vivacious rhythms of a dance music that provided a lively background to the fun of Saturday nights. Indeed, before the arrival of rock'n'roll in the mid-fifties, Britain's Teddy boys could be seen hoofing it up in local dance halls to the throbbing sounds of hot jazz.

Despite their ardour for some types of jazz (and later for black rock'n'roll performers such as Chuck Berry and Little Richard), British Teddy boys had a reputation for vicious racism. Above all it was the riots in Nottingham and Notting Hill during August and September 1958 that forged this reputation. These 'riots' are, in fact, better seen as a series of violent and racist street attacks by white mobs. The incidents were usually brief but involved large numbers of people, the press reporting hostile crowds of up to 4,000 participating in the Nottingham disturbances, while groups of several hundred were involved in some of the Notting Hill attacks.[5] Between 30 August and 3 September hundreds of arrests were made in connection with the disorders and West Indian politicians flew to London to confer with government ministers and to tour the riot-hit areas.

The 'riots' in Nottingham and Notting Hill propelled the issues of race relations and immigration to the forefront of public debate. The press, politicians and community leaders were unanimous in their condemnation of the attacks and widespread approval greeted the punitive sentences passed on nine youths convicted of assault during the disturbances. However, although the perpetrators of violence were unequivocally denounced, dominant responses tended to interpret the disorders as defensive actions by local populations that felt increasingly threatened by levels of black immigration. Sensationalist media coverage fed a climate of alarm in which campaigners for tighter immigration controls won a growing measure of public support. Thus the groundwork was laid for the 1961 Commonwealth Immigrants Act, the first in a series of pieces of legislation which steadily increased restrictions on immigration from the Commonwealth. In this way, as Peter Fryer (1984, p. 382) argues, the unstated assumption developed that it was black people themselves who were the cause of 'racial problems' – a theme which dominated public debate around issues of 'race relations' throughout the sixties and seventies.

The role played by young people in the Nottingham and Notting Hill disturbances was not lost on the media. After the incidents in Notting Hill *The Times* (3 September 1958) noted that, of fifteen defendants appearing before Tower Bridge Court, 'all except one were in or just out of their teens' and the newspaper speculated that, at least partly, the troubles could be explained as 'the latest manifestation of that youthful ruffianism, long endemic in both areas, which has variously expressed itself in raids on post offices, the wrecking of cinemas and cafés, and gang clashes and stabbings.' *Punch* (10 September 1958) took a similar line, with a cartoon depicting two pugnacious, drape-suited Teddy boys admiring a display of Ku Klux Klan robes in the window of a gentlemen's outfitters (see figure 9.1). Media responses to the 1958 'race riots', then, drew together a powerful blend of fears and stereotypes. Implicit in newspaper and television coverage was the notion that the violent disorders were the inevitable consequence of an 'alien' presence in British cities and, as such, the only remedy lay with a tighter control of immigration. Complementing the tacit racism of this analysis was the rhetoric of concern around youth, crime and delinquency that had become a firm feature of the late fifties. By exploiting the familiar themes of violence and criminality that had already sedimented around the Teddy boy, the media effectively drew a veil over the institutional dimensions to racism and discrimination. Instead, a small group of working-class youngsters became 'a scapegoat for respectable British society to cover up its own failures and prejudices in dealing with its immigrant population' (Rock and Cohen, 1970, p. 314).

Media coverage of the 'riots' of 1958 was palpably distorted and partial, yet it remains the case that Teddy boys perpetrated numerous racist attacks during the late fifties. This may seem strange given that many aspects of the Ted's style – the drape jacket, for example, or rock'n'roll music – actually traced their origins to the cultural expressions of black American

Figure 9.1   'The latest style', *Punch*, 10 September 1958

youngsters. Paul Gilroy and Errol Lawrence (1988, pp. 128–9) explain this paradox by arguing that white British Teddy boys did not, in fact, interpret their style as an engagement with black subculture. In the United States the rise of rock'n'roll was generated through the proximity of white youth to black culture, but such proximity was still not a prominent feature of urban life in Britain during the 1950s. As a consequence, whereas American cultural forms such as rock'n'roll could express an ambiguous and vicarious identification with black experience, these meanings were not available to British Teddy boys. Instead, the Teds received cultural forms such as rock'n'roll as expressions of *white* American culture, and the reproduction of racist common sense within the Teddy boy subculture went uncontested.

By the early sixties, however, black and white youth cultures were intersecting more fully in British cities. Yet, while the influence of black culture on the styles of white youngsters became more readily discernible, relations between them remained contradictory. Sixties' subcultures such as the mods and skinheads certainly drew inspiration from the perceived 'coolness' of their black peers, but they retained a measure of racism that became more overt and brutal by the beginning of the seventies.

'Pressure Drop': Rude Boys, Rastas and Resistance

The early sixties saw a network of West Indian clubs and record labels become well established in London and other urban centres, catering especially for the popularity of ska music among black British youngsters. Ska, sometimes known as Bluebeat after one of its key British distributors, was a frenetic dance music that drew influence from both American rhythm'n'blues and Jamaican musical forms like Calypso. The records of Prince Buster and Laurel Aitkin found a ready audience in London clubs like Carnaby Street's Roaring Twenties, and as early as 1963 some 15,000 records were entering Britain from Jamaica each month (Marks, 1990, p. 106). As in the Caribbean, sound systems also began to appear in British cities. These mobile discotheques, known for their charismatic DJs and enormous speaker systems, became an essential feature of West Indian clubs and late-night gatherings. One of the first British sound systems was Duke Vin's in London's Ladbroke Grove, though by the late sixties a new wave of younger sound systems had taken the lead, for instance Sir

Coxsone's in Brixton and Count Shelly's in Dalston.[6] Between them the sense of competition was keenly felt and weekends would see rival sound systems, each with their own band of young supporters, battle for the reputation as the loudest, coolest looking and most dynamic entourage in the country.

Alongside these sound systems the Jamaican rude boy style also began to make itself felt within black British youth subcultures. Living on the street corners of Jamaica's shanty-towns, the archetypal rude boy or 'rudie' existed beyond dominant society's routines and disciplines, instead relying on his wits to hustle a living from gambling, drug dealing and pimping (Hebdige, 1987, pp. 71–4). Renowned for his guileful street-smartness and hair-trigger temper, the rude boy's sartorial panache matched his reputation – gangster-style suits and leather jackets set off by a pair of dark shades and a 'stingy brim' hat. The rude boy was canonized in many of the period's popular ska records, the figure of 'rudie' becoming a folk hero as his violence and criminality were glamorized and taken as marks of defiance and rebellion. Prince Buster, for example, was famed for a string of anthems which both championed and gently satirized the rude boy, Buster taking on the guise of Judge Dread, a dour magistrate determined to stamp out the rudies' hell-raising. The rude boys of West Kingston gained further notoriety from the release of the Jamaican film *The Harder They Come* (dir. Perry Henzell, 1972), ska musician Jimmy Cliff playing a street-hustling desperado locked into a struggle with urban corruption and exploitation. With its popular soundtrack, the film revived interest in the rude boy cult in both Britain and Jamaica, and rudie style continued to be influential throughout the seventies. By the end of the decade, however, it was increasingly complemented by influences drawn from elsewhere in Jamaican culture – specifically the beliefs and symbols of Rastafarianism.

The religious tenets of the Rastafarian movement draw upon key elements of Christianity, yet employ biblical metaphors to elaborate a critique of contemporary western society and culture. Central to Rastafarian beliefs are the writings and teachings of black activist Marcus Garvey, founder of the Universal Negro Improvement Association in 1914. Garvey's arguments for the descendants of black slaves to return to their African homeland won a large measure of support among black communities worldwide and his ideas retained influence after his death in 1940. Garvey's prophecies regarding a future African king were especially influential on the Rastafarian movement. Garvey had entreated black people to 'Look to Africa for the crowning of a black king for He shall be the Redeemer' and the coronation, in 1930, of Haile Selassie as Emperor of Ethiopia seemed to vindicate his prediction. Declared Ras Tafari, the Living God, Selassie was proclaimed a black messiah by many Jamaican preachers and a new religious movement began to cohere. Though not a systematic theology in the traditional sense, Rastafarianism developed a world-view based on religious convictions and rituals. Beards and long, 'dreadlocked' hair were worn as symbols of Christ and the Prophets, *ganja* (marijuana) was smoked as a holy sacrament, and the red, green and gold of the Ethiopian flag were taken as the Rastafarian's symbolic colours. Drawing from the Old and New Testaments, the term 'Babylon' was coined to denote the whole complex of western institutions. In this way Rastafarians established an identity between the Babylonian and Roman civilizations of biblical history and contemporary western society which, they argued, conspired to dominate, oppress and enslave black people.

Initially a small collection of sects on the margins of poor Jamaican society, Rastafarianism began to attract more followers during the 1960s, the looseness of its creed able to embrace a diversity of opinions and attitudes. The profile of Rastafarianism was also raised by the emergence of reggae as a musical form. The rhythmic drumming played at Rastafarian gatherings began to influence Jamaican record producers such as Lee 'Scratch' Perry who was trying to move away from vigorous ska riffs that were beginning to sound tired and clichéd. Instead, slower, heavier rhythms came to the fore, reggae beginning to displace ska as the most popular sound among Jamaican youth. Many of the younger reggae artists, meanwhile, began to adopt the beliefs of Rastafarianism, with the consequence that Rasta themes and imagery gradually became a characteristic feature of reggae numbers.

In the forging of this identity between Rastafarianism and reggae Bob Marley and his band the Wailers played a seminal role. Marley, who had already worked for several years in the Jamaican music industry, adopted the Rastafarian faith in the late sixties, wearing the Ethiopian colours, growing the long dreadlocks that became his trademark and performing songs which were increasingly militant in tone. Marley, in turn, owed much of his stardom to the work of Chris Blackwell, founder of Island Records, one of the most successful reggae labels of all time. Blackwell, the son of a white Jamaican plantation owner, realized that a potentially huge market for reggae existed among white rock audiences who would eagerly consume the genre's stridency. Backed by the full force of Island's publicity machine, Marley enjoyed phenomenal commercial success, emerging as reggae's first superstar.[7]

In Britain the combination of reggae's menacing bass lines and the political militancy of Rastafarianism appealed to black youngsters struggling to elaborate a cultural identity in a racist environment.[8] The particularly explicit and intrusive experience of racism, Michael Brake (1985, p. 143) argues, gave black British youth subcultures a more inflammably rebellious edge to their collective identities than that found among their white counterparts. A combination of bigoted discrimination and frustrated ambitions encouraged the growth of oppositional subcultures among many second-generation West Indian youths, these subcultures offering black youngsters an alternative set of values, aspirations and hierarchies – together with a rationale for resistance to, rather than assimilation within, dominant white society. In rude boy style this resistance took the form of a commitment to the subterranean values of the underworld and a refusal to be excluded from the dominant images of the good life – the rudie's defiance registering in the 'flashy' way he flaunted his illicit money and leisure. Rastafarianism, in contrast, was more militant and overtly political in its strategies of opposition. Facing growing levels of unemployment and more aggressive strategies of policing, black British youngsters took up Rastafarian symbols as an expression of black cultural consciousness and as an avenue of collective resistance (Hebdige, 1979, pp. 30–45). Whereas many West Indian immigrants of the fifties came with the faith that Britain would deliver jobs, homes and respectability, their children harboured little of this confidence. Instead, they were faced with the stark realities of racism and urban decay and adopted dreadlocks, Ethiopian colours and loose-fitting army fatigues as a symbolic form of opposition to a society in which they felt alienated and disaffected. Nor was their opposition solely symbolic. At the 1976 Notting Hill Carnival, black (together with many white) youths turned their frustrations against the police, fighting a series of running street battles in rehearsal for the many long, hot summers that would follow in the early eighties (see chapter 11).

The post-war self-definitions and cultural expressions of black British youth have, therefore, drawn on a plurality of black histories and politics. According to theorists such as Paul Gilroy (1987, pp. 154–6), patterns of post-colonial migration have created a dispersal or 'diaspora' of black peoples, an intricate web of cultural and political connections linking black communities around the world. Black British youngsters, then, have drawn inspiration from a diverse range of African-American and Caribbean cultures, adapting and reconfiguring these cultural expressions to distinctively British experiences and meanings. During the seventies it was Rastafarian and rude boy influences from the Caribbean that were foregrounded within black British subcultures, though the eighties and nineties saw African-American styles become much more visible. Here, the influence of rap and hip-hop culture was crucial.

The antecedents of rap lie within improvised vernacular poetry that has long been a central feature of the oral traditions of African-American culture.[9] The more direct precursors of contemporary rap, however, were politicized, African-American poets such as Gil Scott Heron, Amiri Baraka and the Last Poets who, during the late sixties and early seventies, experimented with a fusion of music and poetic verse. During the mid-seventies rap was further developed in the South Bronx area of New York where DJ Kool Herc, a Jamaican émigré, introduced American dance floors to the Jamaican practice of 'toasting' – improvised speaking over dub versions of records in a humorous and syncopated way. Kool Herc was a major influence on a generation of black DJs and artists, for example Grandmaster Flash and Afrika Bambaataa, whose records fed into the rich and developing hip-hop culture of music, dance and graffiti street art. During the late eighties rap's focus increasingly shifted to Los Angeles where a new form of 'Gangsta rap' emerged – the violent gang culture of the city producing a form of rap that was preoccupied with the imagery of hustling, high-rolling drug-dealers. Throughout the eighties and nineties all these styles and variants of black American rap and hip-hop culture infused the cultural expressions of black British youngsters, the urban experience of black America influencing and informing black British responses to changing patterns of social and political life.

'Babylon's Burning': Youth, Race and Politics in the Seventies and Eighties

Throughout the post-war period subcultural style represented a meeting ground between black and white youth. For many white youngsters black culture provided an important set of stylistic raw materials and reference points, this interplay of ethnicities becoming especially visible during the

1970s – a period in which racial issues more generally came to figure prominently on the political agenda.

During the seventies, as Rastafarian influences became more discernible
within black British youth style, reggae also became the staple of British
sound systems. However, aside from stars such as Marley and rather
insipid imitations by white performers, reggae made only a limited impact
in the mainstream of British pop. The separatist aura of Rastafarianism,
combined with the growing use of specifically Jamaican argot and heavy
over-dubbing, meant that until the late seventies reggae largely appealed
only to black audiences and was mainly confined to an underground scene
of Saturday night 'blues' parties and small independent record labels. With
the rise of punk, however, reggae found a growing white market. Though
they might seem unlikely confederates, during the late seventies the frantic
pace of punk and the brooding rhythms of reggae seemed to complement
one another. The oppositional themes of Rastafarianism and reggae found
a deep resonance in punk, seeming to mirror punk's aesthetics of revolt.
Many punks felt affinity with the Rastas' outsider status and their
disavowal of Britishness, and in reggae punks recognized an 'authentic' and
politically charged music that had developed outside the traditions of the
white rock establishment. Punk subculture, then, drew on black cultural
signifiers to give tangible expression to its sense of alienation and icono-
clasm. Where the mods and skinheads had obliquely reproduced the 'cool'
look and feel of the West Indian rude boys (Hebdige, 1979, p. 64), punks
were more explicit and direct in their appropriation of black style. Punk
musicians the Clash, for example, frequently poached the rhetoric and
symbols of Rastafarianism and, like many punk bands, added cover
versions of reggae numbers to their set. It also became common practice
for punk and reggae bands to share the same bill, the new interest in reggae
allowing struggling British reggae acts such as Aswad and Steel Pulse to
sign to major record companies (Marks, 1990, p. 111).

In its strong identification with the themes of subversion that it recognized in black subculture, punk can be placed within counter-cultural
traditions that have venerated black subculture as the 'authentic' voice of
rebellion. Just as white beats of the early sixties eulogized the black hipster
as a free-wheeling outsider unfettered by the confines of white society,
seventies' punks acclaimed the Rasta as a romantic hero untainted by
commercialism and corruption. This, of course, represented a highly selective mythologizing of black culture. Indeed, as Les Back (1994) contends,

this uncritical celebration of black subculture is implicitly racist in the way it invokes stereotypes of the 'Noble Savage' unsullied by the immorality of western civilization.[10] In the context of the late seventies, however, such romanticization had progressive potential, mobilized in the rise of a popular anti-racist movement which sought to unite black and white youngsters at a time when it seemed the extreme Right were about to win the allegiance of a significant segment of white British youth.

During the seventies and early eighties growing unemployment and the collapse of many local economies (see chapter 11) brought a deterioration in relations between factions of black and white working-class youth. To many within the hardest-hit sections of the white working class it seemed as though immigration had precipitated local socio-economic decline and the erosion of traditional neighbourhood structures.[11] In this context the racism of white youngsters cannot be dismissed simply as a product of ignorance and prejudice, but must be understood as a response to economic circumstances, derived from 'a perception of disadvantage among "us" who are vulnerable to the effects of inflation, the rise of unemployment and continuing housing shortage' (Phizacklea and Miles, 1979, p. 98).[12] During the 1970s this sense of insecurity, combined with working-class youth's traditional sense of territorial 'ownership' and hostility to 'outsider' groups, contributed to a rise in racial tension and violence in many inner cities.

The early seventies saw skinhead gangs, in particular, carve out a noto-rious reputation for their racist attacks. The skinheads' attitude to West Indian youth, however, was always ambiguous. Certainly, relations between the two groups were uneasy and fractious. Yet, as innovators of prestigious subcultural styles, black youngsters were often accorded a measure of respect by their white peers. Indeed, having drawn much of their image from West Indian colleagues at school and work, skinheads often gave conditional acceptance to local black youngsters. This 'insider' status, however, did not extend to Asian youth. As Phil Cohen (1972, pp. 29–30) observed, Asian youngsters were differentiated more sharply from white working-class culture and were perceived as lacking the qualities of masculine assertiveness revered by the skinheads. As a consequence, the Asian community became a focus for the skinheads' fears and anxieties and were singled out for brutal attention.

Throughout the post-war period the racist sentiments of sections of white, working-class youth prompted a range of extreme right-wing and neo-fascist movements to regard this group as a potentially fertile recruiting ground. In 1958, for example, the National Labour Party and the White Defence League sought political capital in the wake of the Notting Hill 'riots' and, since then, the extreme Right has found some of its strongest support among working-class youngsters. Although faction-alism and fragmentation dogged the extreme Right throughout the sixties, a revival in their fortunes came with the foundation of the National Front in 1967. With a political programme based on the compulsory repatriation of black and Asian immigrants, the National Front achieved a measure of electoral success during the seventies. Although the party never came close to winning a parliamentary seat, the Front could win approaching 10 per cent of the vote in some of its strongest areas of support – London's East End, the East and West Midlands, and parts of West Yorkshire. Elements of this support came from middle-class voters disillusioned by the Conservative government's failure to control trade unionism, but the bulk of the National Front's rank and file support came from the working class.[13] Working-class youth, in particular, were drawn to the National Front. In 1978 a study of white youths from Hackney and Shoreditch found that a quarter of the sample were committed to, or were prepared to support, the National Front (Weir, 1978), while six years later a similar survey found that 30 per cent of working-class youngsters named the National Front as either their first or second choice of political party (Cochrane and Billig, 1984). Indeed, the National Front was only too aware of these sympathies and capitalized on them by lowering its minimum age for membership to fourteen, leafleting outside schools and football grounds and launching a youth paper entitled *Bulldog*.

During the late seventies and early eighties racial tensions further inten-sified in Britain, a heightening that coincided with a resurgence of skinhead styles on the streets of British cities and towns. As in the late sixties, the skinhead's second coming was generated at the intersection between black and white youth culture, the focal point being a collection of ska bands from the West Midlands. The rock and reggae communities of Coventry and Birmingham had never been profoundly segregated from one another and from the casual exchange between the two there emerged an array of multi-racial bands whose music paid tribute to the ska musicians of the previous decade. Influenced by the 'do-it-yourself' ethos of punk, the Specials, the Selecter, the Beat and (from London) Madness came together under the independent Two-Tone record label, founded in 1978 by Jerry

Dammers. In his Two-Tone project Dammers aimed to promote local musical talent, but also sought to pioneer a new subcultural identity – a stylistic hybrid that would efface the growing divisions developing between black and white youth (Hebdige, 1987, pp. 106–14).

Commercially, the Two-Tone label was a phenomenal success. Two-Tone's releases punctuated the Top Ten throughout the late seventies and many of the label's artists were quickly signed up by major recording companies. Dammers' hopes for a new subculture that would unite black and white youth, however, were never realized. The Two-Tone image was widely taken up, yet Dammers' intervention into the field of youth politics was never able to overcome elements of racist antagonism – the racial ambivalence and contradictions of skinhead culture resurfacing in the ska revival. A racist contingent was a visible presence from the earliest Two-Tone concerts onwards, skinhead mobs greeting ska performers with chants of 'Sieg Heil'.

From the subcultural detritus left in the wake of punk there also emerged a much rawer, more abrasive manifestation of skinhead style. Here, the look was belligerently lumpen and the influence of the Jamaican rude boy was residual. The original skinhead crop was shaved even more severely, combat boots were worn virtually to the knee and the military-style, nylon M1A1 flying jacket became obligatory. This coarser version of skinhead style first surfaced at the beginning of the eighties, focused on

Figure 9.2 *Strength Thru Oi*, a notorious compilation album from 1981

the London clothes shop The Last Resort and a new surge of English punk bands that included the Cockney Rejects, the 4-Skins, and the Business. Known as 'Oi' (after the choral refrain common to many of its songs), this sub-genre was fast, furious and unrefined, taking punk's crude minimalism and proletarian posturing to even greater extremes (see figure 9.2). The early eighties saw 'Oi' become synonymous with extreme nationalism and violent racism. In some instances this was an unfair reputation, though 'Oi' bands such as Skrewdriver and Combat 84 made no secret of their political sympathies. Moreover, during the early eighties many skinheads were voluble supporters of the National Front and the British Movement (a more openly fascist group), providing an intimidatory phalanx to provocative marches through black and Asian neighbourhoods. As in the late sixties, skinheads also colonized British football terraces, games being regularly blighted by racist chanting and abuse of black players while hooligan gangs openly flaunted National Front badges and neo-Nazi emblems.

Racist and fascist activity, however, did not go unopposed. Facing a growing tide of racist violence, young Asians in Bradford and London began to form themselves into vigilante groups to defend their communities and sporadic sorties were made against fascist targets. In 1981, for example, Asian youths in Southall (an area of West London with a substantial Asian population) attempted to defend their neighbourhoods against incursions by gangs of skinheads. The British Left also responded to the threat of fascism, enlisting a full arsenal of cultural resources to undercut the extreme Right's appeal to youth. During the early seventies an informal network of anti-racist/anti-fascist groups had already begun to emerge, but were essentially small-scale and locally based. This changed in 1976 when a group of activists based around the Socialist Workers Party (SWP) wrote to the music press to protest against rock stars such as Eric Clapton, who had expressed his sympathy for the views of Right-wing MP Enoch Powell, and David Bowie, who had flirted with the iconography of fascism. Heavily inflected by the SWP's turgid Leninist rhetoric, the letter nevertheless made an important contribution in its call for youth culture and pop music to be mobilized in the campaign against racism. Rock Against Racism (RAR), the movement that followed, sought to put this into practice.[14] Kicking off in late 1976, local RAR groups began to organize events where black and white bands and their audiences could join forces under an anti-racist banner, and within a year RAR had organized over two hundred concerts. In its use of music and visuals RAR strategies harked back to the counter-cultural programmes of the late sixties, but it was from the punk idioms then in vogue that RAR drew inspiration for its style. The movement worked hard to entwine itself with the momentum of the punk scene and its magazine, *Temporary Hoarding*, was especially notable for the way it imitated the cut-up montages of punk fanzines, striking a chord with many young punk fans and making anti-racism a hip political stance.

In November 1977 an attempt was made to broaden the base of the anti-racist movement by launching the Anti-Nazi League (ANL). ANL was pitched as a wide political initiative, drawing support from a broad political spectrum and securing the endorsement of writers, academics, entertainers and sports stars. Where RAR strategy had addressed racism through engagement with a range of political issues and concerns, the ANL campaign modelled itself on the single-issue politics of CND, seeking simply to block the electoral aspirations of the National Front and expose the Nazi associations of its leadership. From this singularity of purpose ANL undoubtedly gained strength, though Paul Gilroy (1987, pp. 133–4) argues that in focusing on these narrower aims the chance to build up a more lasting movement of radical politics was lost.

Central to ANL strategy was the attempt to carry the anti-fascist struggle into the workplace via a host of occupational groups that ranged from Rail-workers Against the Nazis to Teachers and Architects Against the Nazis. Like RAR, ANL also made special efforts to win the support of youth and groups as diverse as School Kids Against the Nazis, Bikers, Football Fans and even Skateboarders Against the Nazis were initiated. Like RAR, ANL also sought to address youngsters through their own culture, producing an avalanche of popular magazines, badges and stickers. ANL also co-operated with RAR in the organization of several large demonstrations and 'Carnivals'. The first, in April 1978, attracted a crowd of 80,000 to a concert in Victoria Park headlined by leading punk and reggae bands in one of the biggest political rallies London had ever seen.

By the beginning of the eighties the electoral fortunes of the National Front had declined sharply. Victim to internecine squabbles and undercut by the Conservative Party's lurch to the right after 1979, the National Front returned to the fringes of the political system. However, RAR and ANL can also claim a measure of credit for the National Front's collapse. Through its engagement with the forms and language of contemporary youth culture, the anti-racist movement was able mobilize young people at a street level, and its ubiquitous presence crushed the National Front's recruitment drive. Its object apparently fulfilled, ANL was wound up in 1980[15] though RAR continued its activities into the eighties, cultivating an association with the developing Two-Tone scene.

For many, the RAR and ANL movements clearly demonstrated the possibilities of using youth culture and popular music as instruments of influence and mobilization. During the eighties a legion of campaigns followed in their footsteps. In 1984 Bob Geldorf assembled a collection of fellow pop stars to launch Band Aid, the charity's record sales and concert events raising millions of pounds for victims of famine in Ethiopia. Two years later a broad alliance of musicians, writers and artists initiated Red Wedge, an attempt to garner support for the Labour Party through music and comedy tours. Similar organizational strategies were even imitated by the extreme Right, the National Front launching its own (rather lacklustre) Rock Against Communism movement and the (equally unpropitious) White Noise record label.

Popular music is certainly a powerful emotional catalyst, but how far any of these movements had a profound impact on the political consciousness of British youngsters is open to question. Attempts by both Left and Right to intervene in the field of youth culture have had an uphill struggle against a robust suspicion of political manipulation. RAR and ANL, for example, certainly played a part in confounding the National Front's electoral ambitions and, for a time, youth subcultures were galvanized behind a movement of popular anti-racism. However, these groups were much less successful in transforming the long-term values and attitudes of British youth, a 1986 survey finding that two in five teenagers readily admitted to feelings of racial prejudice.[16]

Notes

1   For overviews of post-war patterns of immigration see Peter Fryer, 1984, *Staying Power: The History of Black People in Britain*, London: Pluto Press, pp. 372–6; Zig Layton-Henry, 1992, *The Politics of Immigration*, Oxford: Blackwell, pp. 9–14.

2   Simon Jones gives a detailed history of these processes of stylistic exchange in his study of black and white youth cultures in Birmingham. See Simon Jones, 1988, *Black Culture: The Reggae Tradition from JA to UK*, Basingstoke: Macmillan.

3 Paul Oliver (ed.), 1990, *Black Music in Britain*, Milton Keynes: Open University Press, p. 81.

4 Writing under the pseudonym Francis Newton, Eric Hobsbawm also produced a survey of contemporary jazz music and musicians. See Francis Newton, 1959, *The Jazz Scene*, London: MacGibbon and Kee.

5 For a more detailed account of these events and subsequent social and political responses see Robert Miles and Annie Phizacklea, 1984, *White Man's Country: Racism in British Politics*, London: Pluto Press, pp. 33–8.

6 For an account of the rise of sound systems in Britain during the 1960s see Dick Hebdige, 1987, *Cut'n'Mix: Culture, Identity and Caribbean Music*, London: Methuen, pp. 71–4.

7 An analysis of Island Records' marketing of Bob Marley to largely white audiences in Britain can be found in Roy Shuker, 1994, *Understanding Popular Music*, London: Routledge, pp. 50–2.

8 See Ernest Cashmore, 1979, *Rastaman: The Rastafarian Movement in England*, London: Allen and Unwin; Ken Pryce, 1979, *Endless Pressure: A Study of West Indian Life-Styles in Bristol*, Harmondsworth: Penguin, pp. 143–62.

9 The most detailed and informed histories of the development of rap music in America can be found in David Toop, 1991, *Rap Attack 2: African Rap to Global Hip Hop*, rev. edn, London: Serpent's Tail; Brian Cross, 1993, *It's Not About a Salary . . . : Rap, Race and Resistance in Los Angeles*, London: Verso.

10 For a penetrating analysis of the way in which mythologies of black 'authenticity' have infused the traditions of white rock music see Robert Pattison, 1987, *The Triumph of Vulgarity: Rock Music in the Mirror of Romanticism*, New York: Oxford University Press.

11 White working-class perceptions of the impact of immigration on traditional neighbourhood structures during the post-war period are discussed in Phil Cohen, 1972, 'Subcultural conflict and working class community', *Working Papers in Cultural Studies*, no. 2, Spring, p. 15; p. 30.

12 In a similar fashion Susan Smith, in her study of the Handsworth area of Birmingham, has shown how ethnicity and race often provide the most visible symbolic cues for understanding local socio-economic transformation. See Susan Smith, 1984, 'Negotiating ethnicity in an uncertain environment', *Ethnic and Racial Studies*, vol. 7, no. 3, pp. 360–73.

13 An examination of the basis of the National Front's electoral support during the 1970s is provided in Max Hanna, 1974, 'The National Front and other right-wing organizations', *New Community*, vol. 3, Winter–Spring, pp. 49–55; David Butler and Dennis Kavanagh, 1975, *The British General Election of October 1974*, London: Macmillan, p. 351; Christopher Husbands, 1975, 'The National Front: a response to crisis?', *New Society*, vol. 32, no. 658, pp. 403–5.

14   For an account of the development of anti-racist movements during the late
      seventies see David Widgery, 1987, *Beating Time: Riot'n'Race'n'Rock'n'Roll*,
      London: Chatto and Windus; Paul Gilroy, 1987, *'There Ain't No Black in the
      Union Jack': The Cultural Politics of Race and Nation*, London: Hutchinson,
      pp. 117–35.

15   In 1992 the Anti-Nazi League was relaunched in response to the electoral
      efforts of the British National Party, a political group on the extreme Right
      which had begun to make headway in local government elections. The activ-
      ities of ANL during the nineties, however, were small-scale compared to the
      high-profile campaign of the seventies.

16   Michael Williams, 1986, 'The Thatcher generation', *New Society*, vol. 75, no.
      1208, pp. 312–15.

10 'I Fought the Law': Youth and Agencies of Social Control

The Rise of the Youth Service: A History of Intervention

Since the late nineteenth century various agencies of social control have sought to penetrate and reconstruct young people's cultures. During the 1870s and 1880s, for example, voluntary organizations such as the Boys' Club movement and the Boys' Brigade were established by men of position and privilege who sought to use recreation as an avenue through which to imbue an ethos of discipline and 'respectability' among the working-class young.[1] In 1916 an official seal of approval was given to these voluntary organizations when the Home Office called together their representatives to form a Central Juvenile Organizations Committee, with a brief to liaise with educational bodies and co-ordinate the provision of recreational facilities for young people. Official agencies, meanwhile, also showed a greater willingness to intervene in the street cultures of working-class youngsters. Victorian and Edwardian Britain experienced mounting concern about the activities of urban youth, their apparent lack of parental or institutional control and a perceived rise in levels of juvenile delinquency. In response the police and courts were increasingly prepared to arrest and prosecute youngsters for behaviour formerly either tolerated or dealt with informally.[2]

Broadly speaking, the twentieth century has seen the co-existence of two competing responses to the problem of juvenile crime in Britain. On the one hand, a 'reformist' spirit has interpreted delinquency as a product of the culture and material circumstances of the offender. In these terms the role of custodial sentences is seen as the 'rehabilitation' of the young criminal, while the various institutions of the youth service are promoted as a means whereby socially acceptable value systems and patterns of behaviour might be inculcated among young people more generally. On the other hand, more authoritarian strategies of 'constraint' and 'control' have interpreted delinquency as the outcome of individual immorality, to which coercion and punishment are the most appropriate responses. These two traditions possess very different political and ideological bases, yet they share a common cause in seeking to effect a more comprehensive socialization of young people through greater intervention in their lives and culture. At different historical junctures one or other tradition has come to the fore, yet throughout the twentieth century both have, to some extent, always been discernible.

During the twenties and thirties 'reformist' approaches were ascendant in the criminal justice system. Rather than explaining delinquency in terms of individual criminal responsibility, official responses increasingly interpreted juvenile crime as a general symptom of the deficiencies of working-class culture, an outcome of this class's 'inadequate' modes of socialization.[3] A powerful influence, these themes underpinned the thinking of the 1927 Home Office Departmental Committee on the Treatment of Young Offenders, their findings paving the way for the Children and Young Persons Act of 1933. The 1933 Act was a comprehensive piece of legislation, raising the age of criminal responsibility from seven to eight, strengthening the powers of the Juvenile Court and raising the age of 'juvenile' criminals to seventeen. The spirit of the Act also affirmed the notion that juvenile crime was the consequence of social and cultural deficiencies in working-class life. Under the terms of the Act magistrates were directed to use the full battery of resources at their disposal to 'treat as well as punish' youngsters who came before them – even where no 'crime' had actually taken place. Delinquency, therefore, was attributed to the lack of satisfactory discipline within the working-class environment, the court becoming a site for arbitrating on matters of family socialization and parental behaviour – removal from working-class cultural influences coming to be seen as a panacea for the range of youth problems (Clarke, 1973, p. 15).

The implementation of the 1933 Act was a barometer of a growing concern with the cultural 'well-being' of the nation's youth. In 1938 continuing unease prompted the King George's Jubilee Trust to engage A. E. Morgan to survey the social situation of British adolescents.

Published as *The Needs of Youth* in 1939, Morgan's research reiterated inter-war concerns regarding youth unemployment and 'blind alley' jobs (see chapter 2). More significantly, however, Morgan also laid stress on 'the increasing problem of leisure, which in modern conditions has become of vital importance' (Morgan, 1939, p. 4). Anticipating perspectives that would become recurring themes in the post-war youth debate, Morgan contended that the work of the education system and voluntary youth bodies was being 'over-weighted by the vast power of publicity wielded by the vested interests of commercial amusement' and he claimed that youth had 'never before . . . been so captivated by the lust for exciting but passive pleasures' (Morgan, 1939, p. 416). Heralding concerns that would come further to the fore after 1945, Morgan averred that the only solution to these problems lay in a substantial strengthening of both the voluntary and official sectors of the youth service.

With only one in six teenagers in England and Wales attached to any form of youth organization in 1937, Morgan's proselytizing was symptomatic of a growing concern that youngsters' leisure was neither properly regulated nor adequately provided for. During the late thirties, and throughout the war, there followed mounting efforts to bolster the agencies of youth provision, both voluntary and state-sponsored. After 1945, and especially during the fifties and sixties, the cause took on renewed vigour. As increased earning power and an expansion of the commercial youth market delivered greater cultural autonomy to working youngsters, the provision of a comprehensive youth service that could furnish school-leavers with a more 'acceptable' range of leisure resources became a pressing social issue.

Off the Streets and onto the Table-Tennis Tables: The Growth of the Youth Service

The growth of young people's spending power in the fifties and early sixties was a cause for concern in many quarters. The greater economic enfranchisement of working-class youth, and the concomitant expansion of the commercial youth market, heightened long-held anxieties about the 'delinquent' propensities of working-class youth and the corrupting influences of 'mass' culture. As youngsters used the array of products offered by the new 'teenage' industries to engineer their own identities and cultures, dominant opinion became uneasy at the apparent 'abuse' of the fruits of the 'affluent society'. By 1960 voices in the press were suggesting that some form of control should be implemented on young people's earnings, with arguments that teenagers enjoyed 'tremendous spending power when they are obviously unfitted for it' (*Evening Argus*, 20 March 1960). Identical misgivings surfaced in a range of contexts and forums. Indicative was the British Medical Association's 1961 report on *The Adolescent*, with its arguments that 'not poverty but unaccustomed riches seems an equally dangerous inducement to wild behaviour, or even crime' (BMA, 1961, p. 6). Indeed, the BMA crystallized the post-war philosophies of the youth service in its speculation that:

> The exuberant adolescent may well need to have his [sic] leisure discreetly organised for him . . . An attractive alternative ought to be possible for the empty leisure hours which face too many young people when their day's work is finished – empty hours faced with empty heads, full pockets and high spirits. (BMA, 1961, p. 6)

The tasks ahead appeared onerous, yet the post-war decades saw the British youth service in a stronger position than at any time in its history. During the inter-war years the Central Juvenile Organisations Committee and its local equivalents had never operated with great efficiency and as a consequence, in 1939, the role of overseeing co-operation between Local Education Authorities (LEAs) and voluntary youth organizations passed to a more effective National Youth Committee. In plans for post-war reconstruction, meanwhile, the state-sponsored youth service's terms of reference were significantly extended. As we saw in chapter 3, the 1944 Education Act obliged LEAs to ensure the sufficient provision of recreational facilities for young people in their areas and a flurry of activity saw the establishment of local Youth Committees to discharge these responsibilities.

The post-war youth service was intended to function not simply as a palliative to delinquency, but as a fully integrated component within Britain's revamped education system. In March 1947, in a circular entitled *Further Education*, the Ministry of Education re-emphasized this aim, stressing that the youth service had now become an integral part in the national scheme of further education and as such should no longer be allowed to develop in isolation. Suggestions came from some quarters that membership of a youth club or similar organization should be made compulsory for all school-leavers, though these calls were never seriously considered by the state. Nevertheless, it was clearly the intention that the youth service should combine with the education system to provide an all-embracing apparatus that worked to socialize young people into the disciplines of the workplace, monitoring and orchestrating their leisure time and ultimately recruiting them into the processes of production. As a representative of the Ministry of Education explained to a meeting of the National Association of Juvenile Employment and Welfare Officers in 1946: 'We are moving away from the narrow conception of a youth service and are widening the field to include the whole of the educational needs of youth. The aim is to produce efficient workmen and good citizens' (*Brighton and Hove Herald*, 25 May 1946). With mounting demand for young people's labour from industry, the Youth Employment Service also became a key feature in this conception of a much broader, integrated youth service. In 1946 the Ince Committee recommended the Service be significantly extended and by the mid-fifties an enhanced and expanded Youth Employment Service was liaising with other elements of the youth service and the education system to channel as many as 40 per cent of school-leavers into their first jobs.[4]

The post-war expansion of voluntary and state-sponsored youth provision was undoubtedly well intentioned and certainly offered many young people concrete benefits and opportunities. At the same time, however, we should not overlook what Mica Nava terms 'the fundamentally regulatory and coercive features of state provision for young people' (Nava 1984, p. 8). Though cloaked in a language of 'care' and 'guidance', youth provision has always ultimately amounted to a mechanism of social control, geared towards the socialization and regulation of young people. It is in the history of provision for young women, moreover, that these regulatory functions most clearly reveal themselves. At the turn of the century girls were relatively marginal to the expansion of voluntary youth organizations. Certainly, the period saw the establishment of Working Girls' Clubs and the launch of organizations such as the Girls' Guildery in 1900, the Girls' Life Brigade in 1902 and the Girl Guides in 1910. Yet such bodies were much less prevalent than those seeking to recruit young men. Conceived as presenting much less threat to public order than their male peers, young women did not elicit comparable measures of surveillance and containment. Ironically, then, it is the very marginality of young women in relation to the institutions of state and voluntary youth provision that most glaringly reveals these bodies' regulatory dimension.

Compared with young men, young women have been subject to much tighter forms of surveillance and control within the home and the family. As a result girls have warranted comparatively little discussion or intervention from the formal and informal state apparatus (Nava, 1984, p. 11). On occasions where domestic surveillance has been judged inadequate, however, young women have elicited greater attention from the agencies of youth provision. For example, with the gathering pace of shifts in gender relations after 1945, official involvement in the socialization of girls became more pronounced. Restating the primacy of women's domestic role was one of the educational orthodoxies of the post-war era, encapsulated in John Newsom's *The Education of Girls* (1948) and its assertion that the future of women's education lay 'not in attempting to iron out their differences from men, to reduce them to neuters, but to teach girls how to grow into women and to relearn the graces which so many have forgotten in the last thirty years' (Newsom, 1948, p. 109). By the early sixties such views had begun to be undermined by growing concern at the 'wastage' of talent in British schools, the Crowther and Albermarle reports both calling for girls' education to be more related to the possibilities of a career. Nevertheless, during the fifties and much of the sixties, education for most young women remained oriented to a future of motherhood and domestic labour, assumptions that the youth service worked to reinforce. In 1953, for example, the National Association of Girls' Clubs and Mixed Clubs recommended to club leaders that they arrange 'Girls' Interest Groups' within their club programmes – the suggested topics for their meetings including 'Planning a wedding', 'Planning a children's party' and 'Washing and ironing'.[5]

Nevertheless, the central function of the youth service continued to be the socialization of young, working-class men. Youth clubs and voluntary youth organizations aimed to win working-class lads away from the 'corrupting' influences of street subculture and the commercial leisure market, drawing them into an environment where they could be more effectively supervised and controlled. As the fifties wore on, however, it became increasingly apparent that visions of a comprehensive, fully integrated youth service were not being realized. Doubts regarding the adequacy of the youth service began to surface in the work of researchers such as Pearl Jephcott, who pointed to the tendency for youth clubs to draw their memberships primarily from the more respectable sections of the working and lower middle class rather than the 'below average' child from the 'below average' home (Jephcott, 1954, pp. 110–11). Responding to concerns such as these, the Albermarle Committee was set up in 1958 to investigate the efficiency and effectiveness of Britain's youth service.[6]

Published as *The Youth Service in England and Wales* in 1960, the Albermarle Committee's report found the youth service to be in a critical condition. Insufficient funding had led to a scarcity of resources and a shortage of buildings and trained staff, the Committee estimating that only one in three British youngsters was affiliated to any kind of youth organization (Ministry of Education, 1960, p. 1). Following Albermarle's recommendations, therefore, there followed a thorough overhaul, expansion and professionalization of the youth service. Under a ten-year development plan millions of pounds were spent on new clubs and youth projects, while the pay and conditions of professional youth leaders were improved and a Youth Service Development Council was established to oversee future progress.

During the sixties the British youth service underwent considerable expansion, yet it was never a uniform nor smoothly functioning 'ideological machine'. The progress of the service was always impeded by internal rifts and by tensions between voluntary agencies and their official counterparts. During the 1950s acrimonious struggles took place over the level of grants made by the Ministry of Education to voluntary bodies and the youth service invariably bore the brunt of any cuts made in education expenditure. At a local level, voluntary organizations always guarded their independence jealously and vigorously resisted incursions by officialdom. Conflict between the state and voluntary organizations was especially pronounced in the antagonisms that developed between education authorities and religious bodies – the church fearing that its declining influence on the young would be further eroded by the expansion of the education system. The post-war youth service, then, was far from monolithic. Rather, it was plagued by a diversity of ideologies and concerns as different interest groups sought to pull the movement in conflicting directions.

Where the different agencies shared common cause, however, was in their determination to ensnare the section of working-class youth that had traditionally eluded their grasp. The issue of young people who were unaffiliated to any kind of provision had long preoccupied youth workers,[7] but in the wake of the Albermarle report the problem of the 'unattached' became a youth service fixation. One of the first acts of the Youth Development Council was to announce its readiness to consider grants for experimental projects aimed at reaching youngsters who stood beyond the orbit of existing youth work and a host of initiatives followed. A growth in the number of detached youth workers represented an effort to locate and make contact with 'the unattached' on their own ground, but the main feature of the period were attempts to move away from traditional youth club approaches towards more imaginative projects which, it was hoped, would be more attractive to 'unattached youth'.[8] Foremost among these efforts was the use of coffee bars staffed by youth workers as a setting for informal youth work. Taking inspiration from initiatives pioneered in the United States, these 'teen canteens' were seen as an ideal way to bring youngsters into the youth service fold and by 1966 at least twelve such projects were operating throughout the country.[9]

With the publication of its report, *Youth and Community Work in the Seventies*, in 1969, it was possible for the Youth Service Development Council to claim that many of Albermarle's recommendations had been met. Between 1960 and 1969 the number of full-time youth leaders had risen from 700 to 1,500, while the youth service had benefited from the initiation of a £28 million building programme, the increase of Department of Education grants from £299,000 to £1.9 million and those from local authorities from £2.58 million to £10 million, while the total number of youth groups that were assisted increased by 112 per cent (Youth Service Development Council, 1969, p. 12). Nevertheless, despite this period of major expansion, the grip on young people's leisure remained as incomplete as ever – the youth service still embracing no more than 29 per cent of 14–20-year-olds (Youth Service Development Council, 1969, p. 16).

Efforts by the youth service to penetrate the lives and culture of British youth, then, were much less than a total success. The principle of organization was alien to many working-class youngsters who resisted even the most guileful recruitment strategies. Tainted by the stigma of stuffy church halls and dreary middle-class convention, the agencies of official and semi-official youth provision simply could not compete against the excitement of dance halls and rock'n'roll and, as a consequence, youth organizations remained largely enclaves of respectable working- and lower-middle-class youth. Even where young people made use of the youth service this did not necessarily guarantee the taking up of its ideological baggage. Many youngsters had an instrumental orientation to the youth service, exploiting its amenities yet remaining resolutely ambivalent towards the 'education' and 'guidance' proffered by club leaders. Interviewing former members of Liverpool youth clubs in the early sixties, for example, researchers were disappointed to discover that their respondents had been attracted to clubs simply by the leisure facilities on offer. The youngsters had joined purely 'for somewhere to go at nights' and youth workers sadly reported that they 'could uncover nothing which . . . [the young people] might have gained of permanent value' (Guthrie, 1963).

Ultimately, then, the post-war youth service failed in the tasks it had set itself. Despite the increasing funds and resources at its disposal the youth service never made contact with more than a third of British youngsters, while many of those that the service was most anxious to organize steadfastly remained beyond its grasp. Moreover, while many youngsters were perfectly prepared to enjoy the amenities that youth clubs and similar organizations made available, these bodies found it much more difficult to wield any meaningful or lasting influence over their members' attitudes and behaviour.

'A Suitable Case for Treatment'? Post-War 'Reformism' in the Juvenile Justice System

During the fifties and sixties the ethos of 'reformism' that underpinned the post-war expansion of the youth service was also evident within trends taking place in the system of juvenile justice. Generally speaking, the juvenile justice system came to be perceived as a mechanism within a much wider framework of social welfare and treatment. Increasingly, errant youth came to be understood as deprived rather than depraved, in need of rescue and rehabilitation rather than simple punishment. Such a perspective was clearly discernible, for example, in the thinking of the Ingleby Committee. Established in 1956 to examine the operation of the Juvenile Court, the Ingleby Committee recommended that the age of criminal responsibility be raised to fourteen and that youngsters below this age should be subject only to welfare proceedings. Ingleby's liberalism reflected the widely held assumption that delinquency was a social anomaly located in pockets where 'classless' prosperity had yet to reach – a problem, therefore, which could be eradicated through the infusion of welfare resources to iron out the 'residues' of deprivation.[10] This, then, was the philosophy that lay behind the Children and Young Persons Act of 1963, with its raising of the age of criminal responsibility to ten and its empowerment of local authorities to allocate resources for the prevention of delinquency.

'Reformist' approaches to the treatment of young offenders were certainly in the ascendant during the post-war decades, yet punitive traditions were never entirely evacuated. Attendance Centres and Detention Centres, for example, were introduced by the Criminal Justice Act of 1948. At Attendance Centres young offenders were required to spend a proportion of their leisure time participating in compulsory activities, while Detention Centres were residential institutions whose regimes were strict, though sentences were shorter than those served at Borstals.[11] Authoritarian responses to the problem of juvenile crime could also resurface in reaction to particular events and circumstances. In the wake of an apparent upsurge of delinquency during 1958, for example, the Conservative government pledged itself to the institution of a new programme of 'short, sharp shock' regimes at Detention Centres, giving young offenders a punitive jolt of hard discipline. These, however, were relatively brief excursions into a more disciplinarian code of penology. For the most part the wider post-war context of political consensus and economic growth provided an optimistic environment in which notions of the 'treatment' and 'rehabilitation' of young offenders became established orthodoxies.

In 1965 the Ingleby Committee's 'reformist' sentiments were reiterated in the White Paper *The Child, the Family and the Young Offender*. The Paper's proposals were bold and imaginative, suggesting that the juvenile court should be replaced by a family panel composed of social and psychological experts and social workers. These ideas, however, proved too ambitious and foundered in Parliament. Nevertheless, the Paper's more modest successor engendered a greater measure of support. The 1968 White Paper *Children in Trouble* suggested the retention of juvenile courts, yet maintained a strong commitment to welfare by arguing that youngsters aged between fourteen and seventeen should, as far as possible, be dealt with without recourse to the criminal justice system. The proposals were influential, allowing the post-war spirit of reformism to culminate in the 1969 Children and Young Persons Act – a high-water mark in attempts to 'decriminalize' the treatment of juvenile offenders.

Under the terms of the 1969 Act the juvenile justice system remained essentially intact, yet it was anticipated that the criminalization and incarceration of the young would be minimized in several key respects. Firstly, the age of criminal responsibility was to be raised from ten to fourteen, substantially reducing the numbers of youngsters coming before the juvenile court and bringing Britain into line with many other European countries. Secondly, while magistrates retained their power to impose care and supervision orders on young offenders, it was to be social workers who had the ultimate responsibility for determining the appropriate manner for these orders to be implemented. It seemed likely, therefore, that fewer young offenders would be sent directly to custodial institutions. Lastly, the Act attempted to curtail the juvenile court's powers of custodial sentencing through the phasing out of Attendance and Detention Centres and their replacement by new Intermediate Treatment (IT) programmes. The details of the exact form that IT should take remained hazy, yet there was clear agreement that it should be a rehabilitative, and preferable, alternative to custody. In many ways the 1969 Act represented an uneasy compromise between the reformers and their opponents, yet it still stands as the legislatory apotheosis of 'reformist' traditions in British juvenile justice.

'You've Lost That Lovin' Feelin' ': The Turn to Authoritarianism

By the end of the sixties the social and political consensus that had underpinned the post-war spirit of 'reformism' had crumbled. The election of Edward Heath's Conservative government in 1970 signalled a move towards a state that was more markedly authoritarian in both tone and practice. Integral to this shift was the implementation of a more disciplinarian system of juvenile justice.[12] Although the 1969 Children and Young Persons Act was not abolished, the Act's intention of decriminalizing young offenders was nullified by the non-implementation of some of its key aspects. The age of criminal responsibility was not raised to fourteen and, although the development of Intermediate Treatment programmes went ahead, Attendance and Detention Centres were not phased out and incarceration remained a disciplinary option open to magistrates. The 1969 Act, therefore, failed in its bid to transform the treatment of young offenders and was instead absorbed into a system of juvenile justice whose powers became more pervasive and more punitive than ever before. Indeed, it is ironic that the 1969 Act, developed with the intention of keeping juveniles out of the criminal justice system, was followed by a major increase in the number of youngsters being sent to secure accommodation, with a 225 per cent increase in sentences to Detention Centres between 1971 and 1977 and a 70 per cent increase in Attendance Centre Orders (Tutt, 1980, p. 12).

The Labour governments of the seventies largely maintained the previous administration's policies and initiatives with regard to the juvenile justice system, authoritarian responses to delinquency undergoing further expansion with the election of Margaret Thatcher's Conservative government in 1979. The Conservatives' electioneering strategy had traded on social anxiety, politicizing the issues of crime and punishment to enlist support behind an 'authoritarian populism'[13] in which law and order became a central motif. In their juvenile justice policies the Conservatives sought to demonstrate their tough stand against crime, buoying up a government whose popularity, by 1980, was already rapidly fading. Once again a reinvigorated 'short, sharp, shock' regime was introduced to Detention Centres, giving young offenders aged between fourteen and twenty-one a taste of something akin to the discipline of the army glasshouse. Home Secretary William Whitelaw, meanwhile, delegated the drafting of the *Young Offenders* White Paper (HMSO, 1980) to Leon Brittan, an ex-barrister who was then a Minister of State at the Home Office. The subsequent Bill, a flagship within the government's law and order initiatives, stridently sought to placate the sabre-rattling of right-wing back-benchers and the agitation of magistrates, long resentful of the terms of the 1969 Children and Young Persons Act and what they saw as the erosion of their powers to deal with young offenders.

The 1982 Criminal Justice Act that followed marked a return to notions of the punishment rather than the 'treatment' of young offenders. Under its terms the hand of juvenile magistrates was significantly strengthened, control of the apparatus of juvenile justice passing away from social workers and back into the hands of the bench. The Act granted juvenile court magistrates greater powers to impose custodial sentences on young offenders, with the consequence that the youth custody population rose by 12 per cent between the end of May and the end of July 1983 (Pitts, 1988, p. 50). Institutions of juvenile custody, meanwhile, became more closely integrated within the mainstream prison system and when overcrowding dictated it became possible for young people to be placed anywhere within the system. This marked a major departure from the principle, in place for over fifty years, that young offenders should be treated differently from, and in institutions separate from, the adult prison population. Magistrates also received greater powers in the sphere of Intermediate Treatment, the 1982 Act introducing the Supervised Activity Order – effectively a strengthened form of IT in which the programme's duration and content was specified by the bench. With the 1982 Act, then, the tide had turned decisively against the 'reformist' spirit that had characterized much of the thinking within the juvenile justice system during the fifties and sixties. Notions of care and rehabilitation gave way to a greater stress on punishment and retribution and the first half of the 1980s saw a larger number of British youngsters receiving custodial sentences for markedly longer periods of time.

The general shift, during the seventies and eighties, towards a more coercive form of political state also had a profound impact on practices of urban policing. Facing both rising levels of violent crime and threats to public order (occasioned by an increasing number of bitter industrial disputes) many police forces developed elite groups of officers with specialized training and equipment. Squads such as the Metropolitan Police's Special Patrol Group were composed of highly mobile teams trained in a variety of roles (from rescue work to riot control and high-profile 'saturation' policing) and these groups developed a reputation for their uncompromising toughness. A consequence of these developments, however, was a drift towards more confrontational methods of policing, together with an increasing physical and social distance between the police and local communities.[14] These trends made an especially strong impact on black inner-city communities in general and black youngsters in particular.[15]

Under Section 4 of the 1824 Vagrancy Act the police were empowered to arrest a person on suspicion of loitering to commit an arrestable offence. These 'SUS' laws, as they came to be known, were used extensively in the black inner-city neighbourhoods of London, Liverpool, Greater Manchester and the West Midlands, but very little elsewhere – this selective implementation leading many to believe that police officers were using 'SUS' as a pretext for the harassment of black youths.[16] Indeed, during the early eighties Home Office studies showed that black youngsters were far more likely than their white peers to be stopped and questioned by the police.[17] Resentment at what was perceived as the excessively intimidatory policing of black neighbourhoods fed into a climate of hostility and suspicion between black youths and the police, the simmering tensions eventually culminating in a violent series of riots and urban disorders.

Police tactics, in themselves, should not be judged the underlying cause of the eighties' riots. The disorders had their roots in deep-seated socio-economic inequalities and processes of structural decline that had become a feature of life in British inner cities. With the economic recession of the late seventies and early eighties, inner-city neighbourhoods fell into decay. These areas became focal points of deprivation as the manufacturing industries that had been their economic base collapsed. Social polarization intensified as the expansion of service industries offset industrial decline in some areas but passed by the inner cities and their residents. Levels of inner-city unemployment soared, and were especially severe among black youths whose unemployment rates were twice that of white youngsters. Increasingly isolated from society's social and political mechanisms, a sense of angry alienation developed among black youths who felt unjustly disadvantaged and victimized. Indeed, after the Brixton disorders of 1981 local community activists challenged attempts to criminalize the events by deliberately replacing the term 'riot' with the term 'revolt' or 'uprising' – thereby underlining the disturbances' political context and presenting them as a conscious expression of social and political discontent.

Unemployment, poverty and hopelessness were the fundamental causes of the smouldering anger in Britain's inner cities, though it was the deteriorating relationship between black youth and the police that ultimately gave a sense of collective identity to these grievances.[18] The police, for many black youngsters, were the repressive agents of a hostile state and routine police operations came to be perceived as symbolic, or even actual, attacks on the black community. The police, therefore, became a focus for black youth's general sense of oppression and the most destructive riots were all precipitated by police operations that youngsters interpreted as racist attacks on their community. In April 1980, for example, a violent confrontation between police officers and a crowd of hundreds of black youths was sparked by a police raid on a café in the St Paul's area of Bristol. The following year more serious disturbances took place in the Railton Road area of Brixton in London. In an attempt to deal with growing levels of street crime the Metropolitan Police had launched 'Swamp '81', an operation which brought large numbers of officers to the streets of Brixton and Lambeth in a strategy of 'saturation' policing. The police, however, were already deeply unpopular in these neighbourhoods and their greater profile simply served to intensify local animosities. The incendiary atmosphere finally detonated on 10 April, and the two days of rioting that ensued resulted in extensive damage to property and vehicles, 200 arrests and over 200 people injured. In July further rioting followed in the Toxteth area of Liverpool. Even greater in scale and intensity, the Toxteth riots saw both black and white youngsters involved in fierce fighting, looting and large-scale destruction, the disorders notable for being the first occasion on which CS gas had been used to quell disturbances in mainland Britain. In the two weeks that followed more or less serious rioting broke out in some thirty British cities and towns, as well as in several parts of the capital.

Political reaction to the disturbances was initially hawkish, with virulent condemnation of the rioters. As the dust settled, however, strident rhetoric gave way to more considered perspectives. In response to the scale of the disorders the Home Secretary announced an inquiry into the circumstances of the riots and the role played by the police in the course of events. Headed by Lord Scarman (who was able to draw on his experience of the earlier investigation into the Red Lion Square disturbances of 1974), the twenty-six-day inquiry's findings were, in many respects, surprisingly liberal in tone. Though it was accepted that nothing could excuse the behaviour of the rioters, Scarman gave careful attention to the events' wider socio-economic context and the experiences of discrimination, unemployment and deprivation that had generated such a sense of resentment and anger among many black youngsters.[19] The only real solution to these feelings of disillusionment and bitterness, Scarman argued, lay in the introduction of resolute and far-reaching measures to deal with the problem of racial disadvantage. Furthermore, while Scarman praised the police for the way they dealt with the riots, he argued that tensions between officers and minority ethnic groups could be ameliorated only through the improvement of police recruitment, training and practice.

Responses to Scarman's recommendations were on the whole positive, yet were ultimately limited in scope and substance. In the wake of the riots the police sought better equipment and wider powers to deal with rioters, though many forces also attempted to liaise more effectively with local communities and made affirmative efforts to curb racism among their officers. In government policy, meanwhile, the regeneration of Britain's inner cities was accorded greater urgency. Michael Heseltine was appointed Minister with special responsibility for Merseyside and for a year worked with a task force of civil servants and representatives of local business to engender economic and social revival within Liverpool's most deprived neighbourhoods. More generally, the government significantly increased economic assistance to areas of deprivation. Spending under the Urban Aid Programme rose from £202 million in 1981/2 to £338 million in 1984/5, while funding to voluntary schemes to combat racial disadvantage doubled during the first half of the eighties. Many of these initiatives were imaginative and thoughtfully targeted, yet the scale of decline in British inner cities was such that they had marginal impact on levels of social and economic hardship. Without a more fundamental and comprehensive strategy to alleviate inner-city deprivation and unemployment further riots became inevitable.

Notes

1   Many other comparable bodies were also set up during the period, including the Church Lads' Brigade in 1891, the Jewish Lads' Brigade in 1895, the Catholic Boys' Brigade in 1896 and the Boy Scouts movement, set up after the publication of Baden-Powell's *Scouting for Boys*, in 1908. From the 1880s, meanwhile, the various cadet forces of the armed services also increasingly sought recruits from the urban working class. See John Springhall, 1977, *Youth, Empire and Society: British Youth Movements, 1883–1940*, London: Croom Helm, pp. 37–52; pp. 71–84.

2   Rather than marking a sharp rise in juvenile crime, the growing number of police prosecutions of working-class youngsters during this period was indicative of a general attempt to regulate working youths' leisure pursuits, remove them from uncontrolled environments and channel them into more supervised forms of leisure. See John Gillis, 1975, 'The evolution of delinquency in England, 1890–1914', *Past and Present*, vol. 67, May, pp. 96–126.

3   See John Clarke, 1973, 'The three R's – repression, rescue and rehabilitation: ideologies of control for working class youth', CCCS Occasional Paper no. 41, University of Birmingham; John Clarke, 1985, 'Managing the delinquent: the children's branch of the Home Office, 1913–30', in Mary Langan and Bill Schwarz (eds), *Crises in the British State 1880–1930*, London: Hutchinson, pp. 240–55.

4   This estimate is provided in the National Youth Employment Council, 1957,

Work of the Youth Employment Service 1953–6, London: National Youth Employment Council.

5   See Brighton Education Committee, 1953, *Youth Service Bulletin*, no. 19, January, pp. 10–12.

6   Also indicative of the gravity with which the condition of the youth service was viewed was the publication of UNESCO's comparative survey of developments taking place in youth organizations around the world. See UNESCO, 1960, *New Trends in Youth Organisations: A Comparative Survey*, Educational Studies and Documents no. 35, UNESCO.

7   For an expression of these concerns see J. C. Spencer, 1950–1, 'The unclubbable adolescent', *British Journal of Delinquency*, vol. 1, pp. 113–24.

8   An account of efforts made in this direction by the National Association of Youth Clubs can be found in Mary Morse, 1965, *The Unattached*, Harmondsworth: Pelican.

9   See B. Biven and H. M. Holden, 1966, 'Informal youth work in a café setting', *Howard Journal of Penology and Crime Prevention*, vol. 12, no. 1, pp. 13–25; Cyril S. Smith, 1966, 'The youth service and delinquency prevention', *Howard Journal of Penology and Crime Prevention*, vol. 12, no. 1, pp. 42–51.

10   Committee on Children and Young Persons (Ingleby Committee), 1960, *Report of the Committee on Children and Young Persons*, Cmnd. 1191, London: HMSO. See also A. E. Bottoms, 1974, 'On the decriminalization of the English juvenile courts', in Roger Hood (ed.), *Crime, Criminology and Public Policy*, London: Heinemann, pp. 319–46.

11   Borstals had been created in 1929 as an alternative to imprisonment for youths aged between sixteen and twenty-one.

12   An account of the rise of more visibly authoritarian and punitive ideologies within the juvenile justice system during the late 1970s and early 1980s can be found in John Pitts, 1988, *The Politics of Juvenile Crime*, London: Sage, pp. 40–59.

13   The term 'authoritarian populism' was coined by Stuart Hall to denote a new form of Conservatism that, throughout the 1980s, was able to engender widespread electoral support for a political programme that married a doctrinaire commitment to free market economics with a zealously authoritarian stand on issues of 'law and order'. See Stuart Hall, 1983, 'The great moving right show', in Stuart Hall and Martin Jacques (eds), *The Politics of Thatcherism*, London: Lawrence and Wishart, pp. 19–39.

14   For discussion of these trends see Robert Reiner, 1992, *The Politics of the Police*, 2nd edn, Hemel Hempstead: Harvester Wheatsheaf, pp. 57–106; John Benyon and Colin Bourne (eds), 1986, *The Police: Powers, Procedures and Properties*, Oxford: Pergamon Press.

15   An analysis of these developments can be found in Robert Reiner, 1981, 'Black

and blue: race and the police', *New Society*, vol. 57, no. 983, pp. 466–9; John Benyon, 1986, *A Tale of Failure: Race and Policing*, Policy Papers in Ethnic Relations, no. 3, Centre for Research in Ethnic Relations, University of Warwick.

16   The 'SUS' laws were eventually repealed by the government in 1981. For many, however, the Stop and Search procedures that succeeded 'SUS' were equally pernicious in the way they were used to harass inner-city black youth.

17   See C. F. Willis, 1982, *The Use, Effectiveness and Impact of Police Stop and Search Powers*, Home Office Research and Planning Unit, Paper 15, London: HMSO.

18   An overview of these developments is provided in Nick Jewson, 1990, 'Inner-city riots', *Social Studies Review*, vol. 5, no. 5, pp. 170–4.

19   See Lord Scarman, 1981, *The Brixton Disorders, 10–12 April 1981: Report of an Inquiry*, Cmnd. 8427, London: HMSO, p. 45.

11 'Whatever Happened to the Teenage Dream?': Youth in the 1980s

'One in Ten': The Collapse of the Youth Labour Market

The harsh economic climate of the late seventies and eighties had a profound impact on both young people's lives and media representations of 'youth'. During the fifties and sixties the rise of 'the teenager' as an idealized embodiment of post-war prosperity and affluent consumption had been founded upon a growth in working youngsters' spending power that followed high demand for their labour from the manufacturing and service industries. During the seventies and eighties, however, these trends were undermined. A series of economic recessions led to higher levels of joblessness generally, but young people were especially badly hit by the contraction of those labour markets that had underpinned high levels of youth employment throughout the preceding decades. As a consequence the eighties and early nineties became a period of major transformation and readjustment in the lifestyles and culture of British youngsters.

During the early seventies levels of youth employment had held firm. As Howard Parker found in his study of adolescents living in Liverpool, the buoyancy of the job market even allowed for youngsters to take short 'breaks' between jobs, secure in the knowledge that finding new employment would not be a problem (Parker, 1974, pp. 68–9). Indeed, up until the late seventies the government did not regard youth unemployment as an especially pressing social issue. Largely confined to 'problem' youngsters, such as young offenders or persistent truants, joblessness among the young did not warrant significant anxiety, nor large-scale intervention by the state.[1] Research conducted in 1976 suggested that jobs for youngsters were plentiful, with 32 per cent of school-leavers securing the first jobs they applied for and 86 per cent finding employment within a month of leaving school (West and Newton, 1983). By the end of the following decade, however, industrial decline and market uncertainty had combined to change the position dramatically.

The recession of the eighties saw levels of unemployment in Britain rise across the board, though the contraction of the youth labour market was especially severe. By 1986 the number of unemployed aged between sixteen and twenty-four had reached 727,000, nearly a third of the national total.[2] One of the most striking economic shifts of the eighties was the massive decline in the numbers of youngsters entering full-time employment. In 1972, the year in which the statutory school-leaving age was raised from fifteen to sixteen, nearly two-thirds of young people had left education at the earliest opportunity and all but a few found employment virtually immediately. By the early nineties, in contrast, fewer than one in ten sixteen-year-olds were entering employment directly on leaving school and in 1992 only 13 per cent of sixteen- to seventeen-year-olds possessed full-time jobs (Roberts, 1995, p. 7).

Government responses to the problem of unemployment were heavily geared towards youth, young people being perceived as especially vulnerable to the demoralizing effects of joblessness. Central to government strategy in dealing with youth unemployment was the creation of many new places in education and training. In 1978 the Youth Opportunities Programme (YOP) was launched, giving six months' work experience to otherwise unemployed sixteen- and seventeen-year-olds. In 1981 it was succeeded by the Youth Training Scheme (YTS), intended as a year of 'quality training' between leaving school and starting work. With the duration of its placements extended to a possible two years in 1986, YTS laid great emphasis on vocational training – yet in the context of high youth unemployment it was inevitable that youngsters and employers both would come to regard the scheme as simply a less preferable alternative to a 'real' job. Alongside the launch of youth training schemes the late 1980s also saw a considerable growth in the numbers of young people staying on in education. In the late eighties the number of sixteen- to seventeen-year-olds in full-time education almost doubled, rising from 37 per cent in 1985 to 66 per cent in 1992. The number of youngsters in higher education also underwent significant expansion, with roughly a third of nineteen- to twenty-year-olds entering either full- or part-time education by 1991–2.

This movement of young people out of the labour market and into training schemes and education certainly reduced the scale of youth unemployment statistics, though critics of government policy saw the shift as a poor substitute for permanent, full-time employment. For many commentators the expansion of education and training during the eighties simply represented an attempt to 'warehouse' youngsters – accommodating them until they could secure permanent employment, yet doing little to enhance their access to higher-grade jobs (Roberts, 1995, pp. 65–6). From this perspective the growing provision of youth training and education did very little to address the fundamental problem – the declining number of full-time jobs that were available to young people.

There is no clear agreement as to why youth employment should have been particularly hard hit by the recessions of the eighties and nineties.[3] According to a line of argument forwarded by both Peter Makeham (1980) and David Raffe (1985), young people are especially vulnerable to any increase in levels of unemployment. Under conditions of economic recession employers are likely to cut back on recruitment and training, while young job-seekers face increased competition from adults with greater levels of experience. There is certainly some validity to this account, yet Kenneth Roberts (1995, p. 9) argues that it finds difficulty in explaining the sustained decline in levels of youth employment in Britain. While a period of economic growth during the late eighties saw a decline in levels of joblessness more generally, the youth labour market was not revitalized and levels of youth employment failed to revive. Recent shifts in patterns of youth employment, therefore, are best understood by being placed within the context of a deep-seated restructuring of the British economy.

According to research undertaken by David Ashton and his associates (Ashton and Maguire, 1983; Ashton and Spillsbury, 1989) young workers, especially, have felt the harsh consequences of economic trends that have fundamentally transformed Britain's occupational structures and labour markets. From the 1950s the automation and rationalization of production processes began to reduce the number of jobs within the manufacturing sector, these developments picking up pace from the late seventies onwards. This shift impacted especially on young people since many of the jobs that disappeared were the less skilled manual occupations that had been the bedrock of youth employment during the fifties and sixties. The expansion of the white-collar and service sectors helped offset the decline of manufacturing jobs more generally, though did little to make up for the contraction of youth employment. Many working-class youngsters lacked the skills and qualifications demanded by white-collar jobs, while much of the growth in the service sector was in the form of short-term and part-time employment. This trend offered advantages to some sections of the workforce (for example, opening up new areas of employment to married women and students), but it did little to benefit the section of the youth population that had traditionally left school at the first opportunity to enter permanent, full-time work. For this group of youngsters the restructuring of the British economy offered few opportunities and held little promise.

During the eighties it was anticipated that demographic trends would, to some degree, offset the problem of diminishing levels of youth employment. Throughout the sixties and seventies the birth rate had steadily declined, with the result that fewer young people were set to come into the job market during the late eighties and early nineties. Many commentators, therefore, forecast the explosion of a 'demographic time-bomb', with demand for young workers (especially those who were skilled and possessed qualifications) increasingly outstripping supply, forcing employers to turn to sources of labour that they had hitherto passed over.[4] As a consequence it was predicted that women, minority ethnic groups, the elderly and young workers with few qualifications were all set to benefit from the scarcity of youth labour. However, the much vaunted 'demographic time-bomb' ultimately proved to be something of a damp squib. As the British economy sank further into recession during the early nineties demographic trends were overwhelmed by the scale of the economic downturn. The market for young people's labour remained depressed and the decline of youth employment continued unabated – trends which are set to persist well into the twenty-first century (see table 11.1).

'It Was the Best of Times, It Was the Worst of Times': The Eighties' 'Boom' and the Rise of the Casuals

Not all young people, by any means, lost out in the eighties. The massive expansion of the business and financial sectors, especially in the South, offered high rewards and social mobility to a fortunate minority. Indeed, the figure of the thrusting young entrepreneur, ducking and diving in the fray of the market, became a conspicuous image in both the popular media and political debate. The championing of youthful wheeler-dealers was an especially prominent theme in the New Right's attempts to mobilize popular support via the promise of consumer empowerment in a 'property-owning democracy'. In 1988, for example, the popular press acclaimed 'The Young Revolution' in which 'Britain's youngsters are riding the roller-coaster boom of Mrs. Thatcher's economic recovery. They have seen a new kind of revolution – giving power to the consumer – and they want to join the action before it ends' (*Daily Star*, 11 May 1988). In the eighties' rhetoric of 'enterprise', 'consumption' and 'free market competition', therefore, the stereotypes of 'affluent youth' that had originally been generated in the late 1950s found a new lease of life. Advertisers were especially fond of eulogizing a 'new' brand of youth consumption. In their report *Youth Lifestyle*, for example, market analysts Mintel claimed to have discovered among young people a 'new consumption and success ethic' that had been generated by 'the sustained economic growth of the enterprise culture', while McCann-Erickson's comprehensive survey, *The New Generation*, identified a 'New Wave' of 'post-permissive' youngsters who were committed to a new spirit of possessive individualism and who exhibited 'the most highly developed form of the new multi-profile consumption in our society'.[5]

Table 11.1 Labour force economic activity rates[a] of young people aged 16–24

	Percentages that are part of the labour force	
	Male	*Female*
Estimates		
1984	81.8	69.1
1986	82.6	70.6
1991	81.2	71.3
1992	77.5	67.5
1993	76.1	66.0
1994	75.1	64.6
Projections		
1996	72.4	63.6
2001	70.3	63.3
2006	69.3	63.2

[a] The proportion of the population which is in the labour force.
Source: Central Statistical Office, 1996, *Social Trends No. 26 1996*, London: HMSO, Table 4.4, p. 84.

Developments in subcultural style also seemed to echo the eighties' preoccupation with consumption and acquisitiveness. By the mid-eighties the abrasive skinhead styles that had returned to football terraces at the beginning of the decade had given way to a more narcissistic set of aesthetics. The national press first drew attention to the shift in 1985 after a group of Cambridge football supporters had been convicted of a violent attack on their Chelsea rivals. Reporting the incident, the *Daily Mirror* described the assailants as a 'smartly dressed gang of thugs' wearing 'Pringle jumpers, denims and training shoes to make them look more like the boy next door than hooligans' (20 June 1985). However, rather than a cunning disguise as the *Mirror* suggested, the attire of the Cambridge 'Main Firm' was indicative of a subcultural style that had been crystallizing for several years. Observers noted a degree of variation in this new 'casual' look, with corduroy flares making a comeback in Manchester, while Liverpool saw a vogue for baggy jumpers and sheepskin coats (Redhead and McLauglin, 1985). Yet overall the emphasis was towards a style that was polished and fastidious, a preference for Fred Perry sports shirts and golfing jumpers increasingly giving way to an obsession with more expensive designer labels such as Fila, Lacoste and Ellesse. As the manager of an exclusive menswear shop explained in 1985: 'They come in here in gangs saying, "Where are the Yoosul shirts?"' . . . "Yoosuls? – Oh, *those* Yoosuls", I said as they spotted a rack of Yves St. Laurents' (*New Society*, 30 August 1985). In their attention to detail and fetish for exclusivity the eighties' casuals were redolent of the sixties' mods. The sixties' passion for European panache also found parallels in the casuals' enthusiasm for French and Italian styles. The success of English football in European competitions during the early eighties saw greater numbers of fans travelling to the Continent, where they not only developed a taste for European designer-wear but also encountered the Continental street fashions sported by groups such as the Italian *paninari*.[6] Frequenting the piazzas of Milan and Rome, the *paninari* coupled European sports labels with expensive American designs and under their influence Timberland mountain boots and Chipie jeans began to find a place in the wardrobes of English casuals.

This fascination with style and image was interpreted by some critics as marking a revolution in traditional codes of British masculinity, with young men apparently revelling in pleasures previously branded as taboo or feminine (Mort, 1988). Certainly, the eighties saw a boom in British menswear. Retailing chains such as Top Man, Next and River Island prospered, while a new wave of style magazines, for example *The Face* and *Arena*, established themselves as essential guides to the more exclusive end of the fashion market. These trends, however, were far from unprecedented, both the early sixties and early seventies having witnessed comparable eruptions of style-consciousness among British males. Moreover, in retrospect the idea that eighties' advances in gents' haberdashery translated into a seismic shift in gender relations seems more like a statement of optimism than an observation grounded in social reality.

The spectacle of football terraces full of young men with neatly cut hair, smartly dressed in designer-label clothes and flaunting mobile phones and expensive jewellery created the impression that Britain's soccer hooligans had become more middle class in their social origins. Apparently confirming this perception were the occupations of several young men arrested in 1986 following a series of undercover police operations against hooligan gangs such as the Chelsea Head-hunters. Following the arrests the press made great play of the fact that among those arrested were an executive officer, a dispatch copy manager and a solicitor's clerk.[7] Attracting less attention, however, were the occupations of the rest of the group, all traditionally working class – a labourer, a decorator, a hospital chef and two men who were unemployed. Moreover, while it is quite possible that during the eighties Britain's hooligan armies drew a greater number of recruits from white-collar occupations, this did not necessarily mark an outburst of thuggery among the bourgeoisie. A more likely explanation is that the eighties' explosion in business and finance saw greater numbers of young, working-class men find their way into white-collar jobs, enjoying a more prosperous lifestyle yet retaining the norms and values of working-class masculinity.

In their celebration of conspicuous consumption the casuals appeared to embody the free market ethos of the Thatcher government. Casual style, however, was more complex than a straightforward endorsement of the 'enterprise culture'. In the casuals' strutting exhibitions of affluence there was something flagrant, something transgressive, that gave them an air of challenge and confrontation. Echoing the posture of the Jamaican rude boy, casual style represented a symbolic refusal to conform to dominant expectations (Frith, 1990, p. 179). The casuals' swaggering shows of consumption were, at least partly, two-fingered gestures of defiance to assumptions that members of a subordinate group must necessarily exhibit that subordination through their appearance. Indeed, the determination to set oneself apart from the grim and mundane realities of workaday life through bold and 'flashy' display represents a recurring theme in the history of working-class youth subcultures,[8] stretching from the frantic consumption of the sixties' mods, through the fastidious obsessions of the seventies' skin- and suedeheads, to the label-conscious fixation of the eighties' casuals.

Nor was the casuals' brazen stance lost on authority. The late 1980s saw the return of dominant anxieties that economic empowerment had accrued to an 'undesirable' section of the population – working-class youngsters who lacked the cultural capital and sense of responsibility that befitted such wealth. Originally coined in 1987 by satirical television comedian Harry Enfield,[9] the term 'loadsamoney' passed into public debate, used by both politicians and the media to denote a yobbish style of tawdry affluence that was seen as undermining traditional values and encouraging anti-social behaviour among the young. In 1988 these concerns began to find specific focus around the issue of violent drunkenness among sections of the nation's youth. Following a series of confrontations between the police and drunken youths in towns such as Crowborough, Dorking and Aylesbury the press began to conjure with the idea of a new brand of 'rural' hooliganism, invoking images of violent 'lager louts' running amok through Britain's sleepy market towns and tranquil villages.[10] These incidents allowed the government to turn aside arguments that crime was the result of social deprivation, ministers pointing to the fact that the disturbances involved mostly white, employed youngsters from the South and the Home Counties. Instead, feckless wealth and a lack of respect for authority were posited as causes of the violence, the Home Secretary, Douglas Hurd, contending that the key features of the disorders had been 'too many young people with too much money in their pockets [and] too many pints inside them, but too little self-discipline and too little notion of the care and responsibility which they owe to others' (*Guardian*, 10 June 1988).

Indeed, the post-war decades had seen alcohol come to play a much more pervasive role in the leisure of young people. During the fifties the brewing industry had made few specific attempts to court the youth market. Nor were pubs especially attractive to the young, many youngsters preferring the cosmopolitan vigour of coffee bars to the invariably stuffy and hoary ambience of the local hostelry. From the early sixties, however, brewers began to court young people more vehemently, with advertising campaigns and pub decor that were more noticeably geared to the youth market. In his 1966 study of adolescent life in East London, for example, Peter Wilmott found that several pubs in the area had set out to cater especially for the young, and at the weekends they would be crammed with ebullient youngsters 'shouting to make themselves heard or gyrating to music so loud it makes the floorboards shake' (Wilmott, 1966, p. 38). During the seventies pub culture and alcohol established themselves as the central pillars to young people's leisure and by the eighties the urban pub had become the preserve of the eighteen to twenty-four age group, weekend evenings seeing town and city centres frequented by literally thousands of youngsters.

In the context of what Home Office Minister John Patten termed the 'Saturday night lager cult' (*Guardian*, 19 September 1988) violence was not rare. Given the numbers of young people out drinking and enjoying themselves, however, the number of incidents was not especially high. Nor did the notion of sleepy market towns succumbing to a frightening new breed of 'well-heeled hooligan' accord with the reality of the situation. The image of marauding thugs overrunning England's Green and Pleasant Land was especially emotive yet, as the Home Office report into the incidents observed, all the areas in which the 'rural' disturbances took place were, in fact, quite substantial conurbations with sizeable populations (Tuck, 1989, p. 65). Furthermore, the report cast doubt on any idea that the disorders somehow represented a qualitatively new phenomenon. Rather, as newly populated and prosperous urban centres grew and developed, they inevitably became subject to patterns of behaviour that were long-established features of British urban culture (Tuck, 1989, p. 67).

'Police and Thieves': The Return of Urban Disorder

The eighties' notion of a new phenomenon of 'well-heeled hooliganism' can be seen as, essentially, a spurious mythology that the government manipulated to draw attention away from the continuing problems in British inner cities. Since the explosions of disorder in Brixton and Toxteth in 1981 little had been done to address the chronic problems of urban deprivation and unemployment and in many inner cities conditions had actually deteriorated as a consequence of the eighties' recession. It was, then, only a matter of time before violent confrontation returned to British streets.

Relatively minor disturbances occurred sporadically throughout the early eighties, but in 1985 events of much greater seriousness took place. As in 1981, police operations provided the vital spark that ignited the volatile atmosphere of inner-city anger and resentment. During a police raid on a house in Brixton, the mother of a suspect was accidentally shot and seriously wounded. In the riots that followed the local police station was attacked with petrol bombs and damage estimated at £3 million was caused by looting and arson. In the same year serious disturbances in the Handsworth district of Birmingham saw extensive damage through looting and arson and the death of two Asian brothers who had been unable to escape the fire that gutted many of the shops and businesses in the local area. During September and October the most serious disorders of the year took place on the Broadwater Farm estate in Tottenham, North London. In the course of a police search an innocent woman suffered a fatal heart attack, her death triggering an explosion of pent-up rage and alienation. The Broadwater Farm riots were the most violent Britain had yet witnessed. A maze of walkways and enclosed spaces, the estate was a concrete fortress in which rioters were able to hold police at bay for several hours. In the course of the disturbances a considerable amount of damage was done to property, 200 police officers were injured and, for the first time, some rioters had used firearms against the police. Most shocking of all was the murder of PC Keith Blakelock, stabbed and hacked to death by a crowd of rioters as his unit attempted to withdraw from the blazing estate.

In contrast to Scarman's earlier even-handedness, political responses to the riots of 1985 were markedly more bellicose and hostile. Conservative politicians, in particular, refused to accept social deprivation as a cause of the disorders, instead denouncing them as acts of criminal depravity. As Douglas Hurd put it, the riots were 'not a cry for help but a cry for loot'.[11] Calls for an independent judicial inquiry into the disturbances (similar to that headed by Scarman in 1981) were repudiated by the Home Secretary, Hurd arguing that this would prejudice possible criminal proceedings against some of the 700 people arrested. Moreover, ministers maintained that the government had already gone to great lengths to implement urban regeneration schemes in Britain's inner cities and further aid seemed an inappropriate response to what they saw as the behaviour of a small minority of criminals. The 1985 riots, then, were typecast as acts of criminal violence rather than expressions of frustrated despair and, as such, tougher measures of policing rather than economic assistance were posited as the most appropriate solution. As a response to both the 1985 riots and a spate of violent industrial confrontations, therefore, the government ushered in the 1986 Public Order Act – establishing a well-structured range of offences, with penalties of up to ten years' imprisonment and unlimited fines for those convicted of rioting. Notably, the Labour opposition also took a firm line against the riots, capitalizing on the chance to criticize the government's record on law and order.[12]

Although the late eighties saw no outbreaks of rioting on the scale of Brixton or Broadwater Farm, intermittent disturbances punctuated the end of the decade. In the Chapeltown area of Leeds in 1987, for instance, developing tensions between the police and black youngsters climaxed in two days of disorder in which shops, cars and police vehicles were petrol-bombed. In August 1989, meanwhile, violence returned to London's Notting Hill Carnival, squads of riot police baton-charging groups of stone-throwing youths after officers had been attacked while trying to affect an arrest among the revelling crowd. During the early nineties such confrontations between riotous youth and the police became more frequent. Rather than inner-city black youth, however, it was largely white youngsters from deprived housing estates on the outskirts of relatively affluent towns and cities who were involved in the worst of the violence. Built to rehouse families from inner-city slums, many of these estates had once been models of state housing provision, though the eighties and nineties had seen them fall into steep decline. Possessing few community resources and with levels of youth unemployment that often stood well above 50 per cent, these estates had become desolate environments of deprivation and long-term poverty.

September 1991 saw a spate of violent disorders throughout the country. In the Cardiff suburb of Ely a dispute between local shopkeepers flared into four nights of rioting, while in Birmingham an electricity blackout provided the opportunity for a night of looting. On Oxford's Blackbird Leys housing estate, meanwhile, gangs of local youngsters fought running battles with riot police who had attempted to clamp down on the practice of 'hotting' – the execution of high-speed stunts in stolen high-performance cars. These final disturbances were indicative of the way in which car crime had become a focus for conflict between disenfranchised youth and the police. During the late eighties and nineties the scale of car crime escalated significantly, with over 75 per cent of recorded offences being committed by people under the age of twenty-one.[13] Especially on the run-down housing estates of Yorkshire, Humberside and the East Midlands, there developed a subculture around 'joy-riding' – boredom, frustration and a lack of leisure and job opportunities leading youngsters to seek a sense of status and excitement in car theft and high-speed chases. Priding themselves on their driving abilities, many young car thieves actively sought pursuit, relishing the opportunity to prove their skill against police drivers.

By 1991 legislators had come to view 'joy-riding' as a serious problem. Responding to several well-publicized fatal car accidents the government announced the introduction of a new offence, Aggravated Vehicle Taking (AVT), to cover car thefts that had been compounded by dangerous driving. The police also began to take more assertive action against 'joy-riders'. As in the early eighties, however, such police intervention was often interpreted by youngsters as unjustified harassment and in the early nineties police operations against car crime triggered the worst urban disorders Britain had seen since Broadwater Farm. In September 1991, shortly after the Blackbird Leys disturbances, violence erupted on the Meadow Well estate, one of the most depressed areas of North Tyneside. Enraged by the deaths of two local youths, accidentally killed in a stolen car as they were pursued by the police, a crowd of 400 rioters laid siege to the Meadow Well, chain-sawing trees for barricades, torching local shops and businesses and attacking police with missiles and petrol bombs. Four consecutive nights of violent confrontation ensued, with a wave of arson and looting sweeping through some of Tyneside's most deprived housing estates.

The following year saw a series of similar incidents. In May two nights of rioting and petrol-bombing took place in Coventry's Wood End estate after police confiscated motorcycles they suspected had been stolen. Throughout the summer violent confrontations flared between youths and police around the country. In Huddersfield shops were looted in two nights of disturbances, while in Burnley nearly two hundred youths clashed with riot police. The worst violence, however, occurred in Greater Manchester. Over several months tensions had built up on Salford's Odsall estate where local youths felt policing was unnecessarily brutal. Then, after officers impounded several cars they suspected had been stolen, local resentments finally boiled over and there followed five nights of violence in which local shops and community facilities were burnt down and shots were fired at police vehicles. In Bristol further confrontations erupted on the city's Hartcliffe estate after two local men riding a stolen police motorcycle were killed when they were forced off the road by an unmarked police car.[14] In the three nights of rioting that followed shops were looted and set on fire and local youths fought running skirmishes with the police.

Riots, of course, have not been a feature unique to post-war Britain. Indeed, historically, rioting has been a well-established aspect of the British political process since at least the mid-eighteenth century. Yet in some respects there was something new in the character of the urban disorders of the eighties and nineties. In contrast to earlier episodes of urban disorder these riots were more markedly generational in character, largely the province of disaffected youngsters. The eighties and nineties had witnessed a steady polarization within British youth. While the course of economic change saw some young people prosper, many others faced a bleak future. In Britain's crumbling inner cities and mouldering housing estates there emerged a new under-class of alienated youngsters who faced a life of long-term unemployment and poverty. With little sense of a meaningful future ahead of them, and with no sense of investment in their local communities, they came to represent a volatile constituency. The mid-nineties saw few major explosions of violence in British towns and cities[15] but, while such intense feelings of emptiness and resentment remained among sections of Britain's youth, the potential for more Toxteths and Broadwater Farms would never be far away.

Notes

1 One of the few measures implemented by the government to deal with youth unemployment during this period was the 'Community Industry' scheme. Introduced in 1972, this work scheme was intended to assist youngsters who proved unable to obtain or (more often) maintain permanent employment.

2 These statistics are derived from International Labour Office, 1988, *Year Book of Labour Statistics*, Geneva: International Labour Office, p. 651.

3 An excellent overview of the key shifts in patterns of post-war youth employment and the various interpretations made of these changes is provided in Kenneth Roberts, 1995, *Youth and Employment in Modern Britain*, Oxford: Oxford University Press.

4   See Department of Employment, 1988, *Training for Employment*, Cmnd. 316, London: HMSO; Malcolm Wicks, 1988, 'Demographic dreams', *New Statesman and Society*, vol. 1, no. 11, 19 August, pp. 26–7; John Penycate, 1988, 'The generation game', *The Listener*, vol. 120, no. 3092, 8 December, pp. 28–30.

5   See the *Guardian*, 11 May 1988; McCann-Erickson Worldwide, 1989, *The New Generation: The McCann-Erickson European Youth Study, 1977–87*, London: McCann-Erickson.

6   A snapshot feature on *paninari* style is provided by Peter Martin in 'Piazza posers', *Observer Magazine*, 16 November 1986.

7   In 1987 five of the group received sentences ranging from five to ten years' imprisonment after being convicted of conspiracy and affray. In 1989, however, their sentences were quashed after doubts were raised regarding the accuracy of police evidence. This followed the collapse of a succession of prosecution cases against suspected hooligans after police evidence was deemed unreliable.

8   For explorations of the transgressive dimensions to conspicuous stylistic display see Kobina Mercer, 1987, 'Black hair/style politics', *New Formations*, no. 3, Winter, p. 49; Angela McRobbie, 1989, 'Second-hand dresses and the role of the rag-market', in Angela McRobbie (ed.), *Zoot Suits and Second-Hand Dresses*, London: Macmillan, pp. 46–7.

9   'Loadsamoney' was the name Enfield gave to one of his humorous stage personas – a leery proletarian prone to gratuitous shows of vulgar wealth and voluble exclamations of 'Shut your mouth and look at my wad!'

10 The concerns engendered by the behaviour of so-called 'lager louts' in 1988 were further compounded by the involvement of English football supporters in episodes of drunken violence during the European Football Championships held in Germany. For several months beforehand the drunken behaviour of young British holiday-makers on the Continent had also been a source of outrage both in the press and in Parliament.

11 *Financial Times*, 13 September 1985, cited in Zig Layton-Henry, 1992, *The Politics of Immigration*, Oxford: Blackwell, p. 136.

12 On the Left of the Labour Party, however, there was more sympathy for the rioters. For example, Bernie Grant (then the black prospective parliamentary candidate for Tottenham) became notorious for remarking that at the Broadwater Farm riot 'the police were given a bloody good hiding. They deserved it'. See *The Times*, 9 October 1985.

13 See Brian Webb and Gloria Laycock, 1992, *Tackling Car Crime: The Nature and Extent of the Problem*, Crime Prevention Unit, Paper 32, Home Office.

14 In connection with the incident a detective constable was subsequently found guilty of causing death by reckless driving and was jailed for nine months.

15   Medium-scale disorders continued throughout the mid-nineties. In June
      1995, for example, £1 million worth of damage was sustained after three days
      of disturbances in the Manningham area of Bradford, sparked by Asian
      youths' resentment at what they saw as heavy-handed policing. In the
      following month, meanwhile, two nights of rioting on Luton's Marsh Farm
      housing estate left a shopping centre looted, three schools badly damaged by
      fire and several policemen injured.

12 'Twenty-Four Hour Party People': Dance Culture, Travellers and the Criminal Justice Act

'Madchester Rave On': From Punk to Scallydelia in Greater Manchester

Both academic and popular histories of British youth culture have been marked by a geographic bias, dwelling largely on developments in London and the south-east. Indeed, there is some justification for this focus since trends in and around the capital have been predominant influences on the development of national youth styles and subcultures. The attention of the British media, itself heavily concentrated in the south-east, has invariably focused on shifts in metropolitan youth style – disseminating and popularizing these developments throughout the country. Teddy boys, mods and skinheads, for example, all first emerged in London and through media exposure rose to become the pre-eminent youth styles of particular historical moments. The provinces, however, have also possessed their own, autonomous, histories of youth style and subculture. Confined to their own region and locality, these 'micro-heritages' have usually wielded limited influence over national trends and so have attracted little attention from cultural theorists and historians. On several occasions, however, regionally based styles have captured the imaginations of both the media and the public, emerging as highly visible and influential cultural phenomena. For example, it was the bands and personalities of 'Merseybeat' that led the way in the beat music boom of the early sixties, while the revival of ska and rude boy style during the late seventies was pioneered by young musicians and stylists from the Midlands. Ten years later it was the music and subcultural styles of Manchester that came to the fore, the eighties seeing the city become a centrifugal force within the development of British youth culture.

Although seventies' punk had initially been dominated by bands and entrepreneurs based in London, thriving and energetic punk scenes had quickly developed around the country. The north-west was a case in point. In Manchester venues such as the Lesser Free Trade Hall and the Electric Circus (a crumbling former bingo hall) played host not only to punk bands from London, but also to a growing number of home-grown artists such as the Buzzcocks, Slaughter and the Dogs, the Fall and Joy Division – the latter's stark and severe imagery becoming a seminal influence on the development of the genre.[1] As in London, the Mancunian punk scene inspired a growing infrastructure of artistic and media initiatives that provided the foundation for many subsequent cultural trends. Fanzines such as *Girl Trouble*, *Shy Talk* and *Ghast Up* gave a platform to brash young writers such as Paul Morley who later went on to carve out a prominent space within the national media. In the field of television, whereas national broadcasters were initially suspicious of punk's anti-establishment postures, regional programmers were more willing to embrace the new Young Turks of the music industry. Long jealous of the way in which the BBC's *Top of the Pops* had come to dominate television coverage of pop music, commercial channels experimented with different formats in a bid to challenge the BBC's lead. One such venture was *So It Goes*, launched on Granada Television in 1976. Confined to the backwater of a Sunday evening regional slot, *So It Goes* never came close to deposing its BBC rival. Nevertheless, the programme was a showcase for many emerging punk bands (featuring an early, very memorable, appearance by the Sex Pistols) and also became a proving ground for young media talent. Foremost in this respect was *So It Goes'* charismatic presenter, Tony Wilson. A Cambridge graduate and established local television journalist, Wilson had become captivated by punk's creative verve and after fronting two series of *So It Goes* he became steadily immersed in Manchester's burgeoning music community. Initially manager of local band Durutti Column, Wilson soon began to spread his wings. Working with fellow collaborators Alan Erasmus, Peter Saville and Rob Gretton, Wilson launched the Factory Club in May 1978 as a showcase for Manchester's growing number of

'alternative' bands, the club's success spurring Wilson and his associates to establish Factory Records, a small independent record label intended to promote and publicize the local music scene.

From its modest beginnings Factory prospered. The record label's original flagship, Joy Division, suffered a tragic loss with the suicide of their lead singer, Ian Curtis, but the band re-emerged as New Order and spearheaded Factory's success through the 1980s. Factory became known for its innovative and stylish design aesthetics and, led by Wilson's entrepreneurial drive, the label rapidly expanded and diversified, taking on board an increasingly eclectic range of artists. Further growth came in 1982 with the opening of the Haçienda, a purpose-built club that served as both a disco and one of Manchester's major music venues, followed by the launch of Dry, a fashionable café-bar, and the unveiling of Factory's glamorous new headquarters in Manchester's Charles Street.

The birth and subsequent growth of Factory Records was indicative of a general proliferation of independently owned and controlled record labels in the first half of the eighties. The earlier punk explosion had inspired the launch of a legion of independent labels and during the early eighties the more enduring of these, for example Stiff and Rough Trade, were joined by a new wave of independents. Several of these newcomers stood out as especially innovative and influential. In Glasgow Alan Horne founded Postcard Records in 1980, achieving critical acclaim and commercial success with a roster of local acts that included Orange Juice and Aztec Camera. Equally distinctive was 4AD, formed in early 1980 by Ivo Watts-Russell and Peter Kent, the label coming to prominence with signings the Birthday Party and the Cocteau Twins. Another successful independent was Creation Records, launched by Alan McGee in 1983. Creation first came to the fore in 1984 with the Jesus and Mary Chain, a band whose energy and irreverence brought an avalanche of media interest and inspired an army of imitators, but Creation's prosperity continued throughout the eighties with the Boo Radleys and Primal Scream heading a roll-call of lucrative acts. The growth of independent record labels during the eighties represented a reinvigoration of the British music industry, the growing scale and influence of the independent sector marked by the establishment of new chart lists dedicated to independent releases.[2]

Quickly, however, debate began to surround the question of exactly what constituted an 'independent' record. Initially, the term had been used

to distinguish those labels whose record distribution was independent
from intercession by major record corporations. This distinction, however,
became increasingly difficult to sustain. Without extensive back catalogues
and with limited promotional resources, independent labels began to be
hard hit by a slump in record sales and a narrowing of stocking policy by
big retail outlets.[3] Facing growing financial pressure many of the new
independents were forced to secure distribution deals with major record
companies in order to retain their developing acts or simply to survive. In
the process many independents lost their distinctive identities and came
closely to resemble straightforward subsidiaries of major labels. The term
'independent' or 'indie', therefore, began to shift its meaning. From a
description of the status of a specific record label 'indie' instead came to
denote a particular genre of music and the term 'indie pop' became synonymous with an introspective guitar-based music played by an avant-garde
of wan and earnest young men. The indie scene was especially galvanized
by the release of *C-86*, a compilation tape of leading indie acts that was
given away free with an edition of *New Musical Express*, and during the
mid-eighties indie pop bands sprung up around the country – for example,
the Soup Dragons hailing from Glasgow, the Popguns from Brighton and
Talulah Gosh from Oxford. According to pop journalist Simon Reynolds
Talulah Gosh were, in some ways, the definitive 'indie' band of the mid-
eighties, with their jangling pop guitars and a style that crystallized what
some commentators dubbed the 'shambling' scene – a subcultural milieu
that contrived a child-like sense of asexual innocence and fun.[4] The
'shambling' look was characterized by a quaint jumble-sale chic – for girls
this meant a vogue for floral or polka-dot frocks, dainty white ankle socks
and plimsolls, while for boys it meant washed-out cardigans and pullovers
and short, tousled or pudding-basin haircuts. There was also an abundance
of plain anoraks for both sexes in an affectation of pre-pubescent
androgyny. Once again, Manchester figured prominently in these trends
with local heroes the Smiths representing, for many, one of the finest of
the mid-eighties 'indie' bands, Johnny Marr's spirited guitar melodies
and Steven Morrissey's mournful vocal lilt setting them apart from many
of their more lo-fi peers. During the second half of the eighties, however,
a style was beginning to take shape around Greater Manchester that
was anything but introspective, but was instead brassy and boisterously
hedonistic.

By the mid-eighties the smart, clean-cut look of the casuals had begun to be displaced by baggy, loose-fitting leisure-wear as the sartorial trademark of the north-west's football terraces. Possibly beginning as a humorous riposte to the over-dressed showiness of their southern rivals, northern supporters began turning up to matches wearing flared jeans – some even cutting their own material into the seams to make the widest possible leg. This renaissance of flared denim was accompanied by a fondness for vividly coloured hooded sports tops, trainers and Kicker boots and shoes, the ensemble topped off with a lank, centre-parted page-boy haircut. Fashion magazines such as *I-d*, which had become a chronicle of shifts in the minutiae of subcultural style during the eighties, initially labelled Manchester's new stylists 'Baldricks' (after the cheery scruff in the television comedy series *Blackadder*), but it was the term 'scally' that caught on as an epithet for the look ('scally' being the scouse term for a brazen rogue).[5] The scally image was sometimes misinterpreted as a return to hippy style, but in reality it was avowedly working class. With a laddish, cocksure demeanour, scallies were devoted football supporters and their regional pride made itself felt in a wave of tee-shirts that extolled Manchester's status as the centre of British pop culture – bearing slogans such as 'Manchester – North of England', 'Woodstock 69: Manchester 89' and, most swaggeringly, 'And On the Sixth Day God Created Manchester'. Moreover, as Ted Polhemus (1994, p. 116) observes, for all their good-humoured self-mockery the scallies shared the casuals' aspirational fondness for brand names, in particular the Manchester-based Joe Bloggs label, one of the first companies to cash in on the trend for flares and hooded tops.

Alongside the emergence of the scally the late eighties ushered in a new breed of Mancunian guitar band.[6] Several groups stood out as the vanguard of the 'scallydelic' sound – the Stone Roses, James and the Inspiral Carpets all achieving critical acclaim and commercial success. Above all, however, it was anarchic sextet the Happy Mondays who came to embody the scally scene as it developed in Manchester – or 'Madchester' as it was dubbed in the Mondays' self-mythologizing EP. Lead singer Shaun Ryder and manic percussionist Mark 'Bez' Berry were archetypal scallies in their ribaldrous attitude to life and reputation for alcoholic and pharmaceutical excess, while their high profile in the music press helped popularize Manchester as the hub of British youth culture in the late eighties.[7] Musically, the Happy Mondays were also significant. Rather than the guitar-oriented sound of their peers, the Mondays' records were layered with funkier dance rhythms, a feature indicative of the growing impact of dance music within Manchester club life.

During the early eighties Manchester had been a parochial satellite of a club culture that was heavily focused on London night-life. By 1985, however, this was beginning to change. Increasingly, the capital was eclipsed by the north-west as the centre for innovation in the British club scene. At the epicentre of this shift in fortunes stood the Haçienda. According to Mick Middles' (1996) history of Factory Records, when it first opened the Haçienda had seemed to be the company's cavernous folly. Without a clear cultural niche the venue proved to be an expensive drain on Factory's financial resources and more than once Tony Wilson had considered closing it down. The end of 1985, however, saw new booking policies at the Haçienda, with a trend towards nights without any band performing, simply a DJ mixing and blending together different records (Middles, 1996, p. 229). This shifting axis marked a return to the heritage of northern soul and the vibrancy of the Wigan Casino and the Twisted Wheel – and it proved to be an unqualified success. Club nights such as Nude and Temperance saw the Haçienda's sweating, pounding dance floor packed solid and the venue established itself as a focal point of British club life. The key contributions of the Haçienda were twofold. Firstly, the club was one of the first British venues to cultivate the cult of the club DJ as celebrity, figures such as Dave Hasslam and Mike Pickering becoming renowned for the way they could creatively twist and layer different tracks. Secondly, the Haçienda was one of the first clubs to introduce Chicago house and Detroit techno dance music to British dance floors. As such the venue stood as an archetype for the acid house dance movement that began to emerge in the late eighties. ▬

Rave New World: The Acid House and Rave Phenomenon

Dispute surrounds the precise origins of the term 'acid house'. Rather than being derived from the slang term for the hallucinogenic drug LSD, it has been argued that the term 'acid' came from the argot of Chicago street subculture where the phrase 'acid burn' meant to steal – 'acid house' music taking its name from the practice of poaching samples of music from various sources and then mixing them together to produce a new recording.[8] This explanation, however, has been contested by acid house party activist Paul Staines. According to Staines it is based on an account he fabricated at a series of press conferences in the late eighties in an attempt to play down the drug associations of the music at a time when the acid party scene was subject to mounting negative coverage in the media and greater measures of official control were looming.[9] Whatever the exact derivations of the terminology it seems clear that the origins of the music that dominated the British dance scene during the late eighties and nineties are to be found in American club culture.

According to Chris Kempster (1996, pp. 11–13), the foundations of house music first took shape in New York's club underground in the early seventies. At clubs such as the Sanctuary and, later, the Loft and the Gallery many of the mixing techniques that later came to characterize house first began to appear. The segueing together of records into one seamless groove brought out the rhythmic dimension of the tracks while the simultaneous playing of two records to create a unique composite began to transform the DJ into the creative hero of dance culture.[10] The distinctive sound of house, however, emerged in recognizable form during the early eighties in predominantly gay clubs in Chicago – for example the Future, the Playground and, especially, the Warehouse Club where DJ Frankie Knuckles became famous for his innovative role in crafting the house sound of Chicago by taking disco records, extending certain sections and giving the whole a mix with a deeper and more uplifting rhythmic beat (Kempster, 1996, p. 14). In the clubs of Detroit, meanwhile, another force was beginning to cohere. Here, the grip of disco had been less strong and instead the rhythmic traditions of funk came together with the influence of European synthesizer bands such as Kraftwerk to form techno – a hypnotic blending of electronic instrumentation that later became an important influence on the development of the dance scene throughout Europe.

These new forms of dance music filtered into British youth culture during the mid-eighties via several routes. In Manchester the Haçienda took up the torch the north had held for black American dance music throughout the sixties and seventies and the vibrancy of the city's music scene was maintained by new house-based projects such as 808 State. In London a growing number of clubs also began to champion the new music, for example Raid on Tottenham Court Road and the Project in Streatham. The capital's gay club scene also proved an important influence. Disco, house and techno had all largely been born in the gay club life of American cities and in Britain the embryonic house music scene found a receptive atmosphere at gay venues such as Heaven. Heaven played host to some of London's best-known early house clubs, for instance Spectrum and Noel Watson's Delirium, and by 1988 London had a firmly established and rapidly expanding dance scene (Kempster, 1996, pp. 85–7). A proliferation of pirate radio stations also promoted house music and the sound was subsequently taken up with fervid enthusiasm at a further wave of new clubs – Trip at the Astoria, Shoom, and a series of clubs such as Future and Land of Oz that were run by DJ Paul Oakenfold. Oakenfold was significant in that he, along with DJs such as Danny Rampling, Andy Weatherall, Trevor Fung and Terry Farley, drew inspiration not only from the gay club scene but also from the dance floors of Ibiza.[11] A fashionable and lively Balearic resort, Ibiza became a centre for club culture during 1987 and early 1988, its night-clubs exuding a carnivalesque party atmosphere and its DJs experimenting with house beats to produce continuous mixes of music that kept dance floors packed throughout the night. In Britain the Ibizian atmosphere was recreated not only in clubs such as Spectrum and Shoom but also in a circuit of one-off, often illegal, 'warehouse' parties. Held in factories and warehouses left empty and disused by the economic downturn, these impromptu parties were advertised through word of mouth and attracted hundreds of exuberant, young party-goers in scenes that were reminiscent of the all-dayer and weekender events of northern soul.

As warehouse parties became larger in scale they attracted greater police attention. Having established the location of a party the police would mount a raid on the illicit gathering – though if the event was already in full swing, rather than closing it down, officers would usually simply turn away newcomers to avoid engendering a confrontation with the assembled crowd (Staines, cited in Saunders, 1995, p. 20). In an attempt both to sidestep the increasing police controls and profit from the growing enthusiasm for dance culture, a group of associates headed by young entrepreneur Tony Colston-Hayter sought to organize parties on an even grander scale. Operating under the name 'Sunrise Productions' the group calculated that if a big enough party could be assembled quickly enough then the event would be virtually unstoppable. According to Paul Staines (cited in Saunders, 1995, pp. 18–21), their schemes were meticulously planned and executed. Having set up generators, sound systems and all manner of facilities and amenities in a given location, a computer system linked to thousands of phone lines was used to release spoken directions to a specific meeting point, invariably on the M25 orbital motorway that encircles London.[12] Prospective party-goers got access to the appropriate telephone number by buying a ticket on which it had been printed and once a crowd of sufficient size (usually several thousand) had gathered, Colston-Hayter and his colleagues would then use mobile phones to record and release details of the party venue – reasoning that the police would be unable to halt such an enormous convoy of party-goers.[13]

The scheme was a success, though the police quickly became familiar with the strategies employed by the party entrepreneurs. In an attempt to keep ahead of police operations, party organizers began to turn their attentions to rural settings on the outskirts of the capital. The so-called 'orbital raves', organized around the M25 by promoters such as Sunrise, Biology and Eclipse, were huge events. Attracting thousands of party-goers, these open-air raves were equipped with gargantuan sound systems, strobe and laser light shows, dry ice and, at the largest events, even fairground attractions such as bouncy castles and dodgems. The phantasmagoria of the rave experience prompted many ravers to hail 1988 as the second 'Summer of Love', rave's use of psychedelic imagery echoing the hippy 'acid test' parties of California in 1967.[14] Nor did the similarities with the sixties' counter-culture stop with rave's use of psychedelic designs and aesthetics. The earlier counter-culture's association with hallucinogenic drugs also seemed to be paralleled by the close relationship that developed between the rave scene and the drug MDMA, or ecstasy as it became more commonly known.

Ecstasy quickly emerged as the drug of choice among ravers. Outlawed by the Misuse of Drugs Act 1971, the use of ecstasy among British clubbers had begun on the fringes of the gay club scene during the early eighties and in Ibiza during the summer of 1986. As British raves grew in popularity, the drug began to reach a much wider group of youngsters. The drug's appeal lay in the way its effects resonated with the new trends in dance music. Originally developed as an appetite suppressant, ecstasy's powerful psychoactive effects offered users both a stimulating 'rush' of energy and a relaxed sense of well-being and empathy, a combination which heightened the pleasures of the rave experience by enhancing the rhythmic sensations of the music's loud, repetitive beat and intensifying feelings of collectivity and open-hearted communication.

Ecstasy arrived in Britain at a time when the association between heroin use and AIDS had led illicit drugs to be regarded with a greater sense of alarm, a large-scale state sponsored advertising campaign warning of the dangers of hard drugs and discouraging their use among the young. The anti-drugs campaign, however, had minimal impact on the spread of ecstasy usage. As Steve Redhead (1993a, p. 10) observes, patterns of the drug's use seemed to set it apart from the rituals and relationships characteristic of harder and more potentially addictive drugs such as heroin.[15] Instead, ecstasy established around itself a recreational reputation, youngsters invariably taking it at weekends and in conjunction with club-going and dancing, the drug becoming regarded by many young people as a valid and enjoyable component of their leisure time.[16] This greater use and acceptance of illegal drugs among the young represents one of the most profound transformations to take place within British youth culture since 1945. Previous chapters have shown that illicit drug use has been a feature of a range of subcultural groups throughout the post-war decades, though the practice was always confined to a comparatively narrow section of the youth population. By the early nineties, however, the situation had changed dramatically. In 1992 statistics published by the Home Office showed that, within two years, Customs' seizures of ecstasy had increased eightfold, the figures testifying to the wider availability and greater use of the drug. In the same year the Institute for the Study of Drug Dependence, in its annual national audit of drug misuse, reported that a 'new age' of drug use was dawning among youngsters, studies suggesting that one in four fourteen-year-olds had tried cannabis and one in five had used ecstasy. In 1996 these findings were further supported by one of the biggest ever studies carried out among young people in Britain. Research based on a study of over 7,700 youngsters in Scotland found that nearly half of all fifteen- and sixteen-year-olds had tried illegal drugs, their use becoming an increasingly normalized feature of young people's lives.[17]

The increased profile of illicit drugs in the leisure of young people was pioneered within rave culture. Rave organizers employed an array of new media technologies to create a total experience of sound, light and image – and amid this intoxicating atmosphere ecstasy played an important role in generating a sense of pleasure, physical abandonment and harmonious unity. Sexuality, however, was downplayed. While the effects of ecstasy heightened a sense of sociability and affability among its users, sexual drive tended to be depressed. Dancing rather than romance provided the rationale for rave and, as a whole, rave culture revelled in the iconography of innocent and pre-sexual childhood. The anthems of acid house self-consciously lifted melodies and phrases from children's television programmes like *The Magic Roundabout* and *Sesame Street*, while rave playfully appropriated simple, child-like symbols such as the vivid yellow 'smiley' logo. Dance-wear was always loose and baggy, typically in bright, primary colours, and (although brand labels such as Naf Naf and Mau Mau soon commanded prestige within dance culture) the look was always understated and simplistic. As such, rave style could be read as a gesture of avoidance, its symbols signifying a shirking of adulthood's burdens of responsibility in favour of a universe of pleasure and play.[18] Yet elements of disaffection could also be detected in the postures of young ravers. The simplicity and practicality of rave style seemed to renounce the ethos of acquisitive individualism that had come to the fore during the eighties, while rave's bonhomie stood in marked contrast to the sense of exclusivity that had pervaded club culture at the beginning of the decade. Rave, then, represented an escape into hedonism (Melechi, 1993) – it both rejected a dominant culture that prioritized competition and individual success and it refused to succumb to the economic depression and political severity of the late eighties.

For all rave culture's rhetoric of boundless harmony, however, as a phenomenon it was always defined by a distinct set of demographics – for the most part being the province of white, heterosexual, working-class youngsters (Thornton, 1995, p. 25). Moreover, though the acid house and rave scenes may have negated dominant values and aspirations through their style and attitude, in other respects they were founded on very traditional business principles. Like the counter-culture of the sixties, rave was led by a coterie of entrepreneurs whose quest was as much for profit as for a fraternity of peaceful party-goers. For example, acid house parties such as those organized by Colston-Hayter were thriving business enterprises. A party attended by 10,000 people could have a total turnover of as much as £250,000 and, since possible fines for licensing offences amounted to a maximum of £2,000, likely profits for one event could be in excess of £50,000 (Staines, cited in Saunders, 1995, p. 21). By the end of the eighties several commentators had picked up on the business dimension to rave culture. For writers such as Stuart Cosgrove (1989) and Hillegonda Rietveld (1991, pp. 24–6; 1993, pp. 55–6) what had begun as a meaningful creative expression had become 'recuperated' by an exploitative commercial culture and had been reduced to a 'stylized look' predominantly driven by market forces. As earlier chapters have shown, however, narratives which depict 'authentic' youth subcultures as being absorbed and 'incorporated' by a commercial apparatus tend to misinterpret the nature of relationships between youth culture and the commercial market. In the case of rave, profit played a part in even the earliest warehouse parties and, during the mid-eighties, the booking policies of clubs such as the Haçienda and Heaven were financially as much as creatively driven. However, although the market and commerce were integral to the mediation of rave culture, participants in the party scene often conceived of themselves as part of an outlaw underground, taking pride in a culture which they saw as existing beyond the grip of the corporate media. This romantic self-image, moreover, seemed to be confirmed by the negative media comment and stigmatization that increasingly cohered around the acid party scene.[19]

Initially the popular press had eagerly embraced acid house, greeting it as the latest exciting dance craze. During the summer of 1988, however, as the links between acid house and the use of ecstasy became more widely known, media coverage rapidly turned against the developing rave scene. The *Sun* and the *Daily Mirror*, in particular, seemed to be competing to publish the most lurid headlines and stories on what they now reviled as 'the evil Acid House cult'. This stigmatisation continued into the following year, climaxing with the *Sun*'s exposé of a huge acid house party held in a disused aircraft hangar near Maidenhead. Under the banner headline 'Spaced Out!', the account was calculated to shock, the tabloid regaling how 11,000 'drug-crazed kids' had descended on a deserted airfield in an eight-hour party orchestrated by 'evil drug dealers' (26 June 1989).

In response to reportage that was exaggerated, and often spurious, the acid house scene was subject to increasing measures of control and regulation. In October 1988 controversy surrounded the first acid track to enter the Top Twenty – D-Mob's 'We Call It Acieeed'. Although the BBC maintained that it was not banning acid house music, the single was not given a place on Radio One playlists and to many it seemed as though the music was being officially censored.[20] At the same time legally run venues and clubs were more closely monitored by the police and faced stricter regulation from local magistrates. The introduction of the 1988 Licensing Act increased the frequency of licensing sessions, empowered magistrates to revoke a club's licence at any time during its currency and gave the police greater discretionary powers to object to the granting of licences. In some parts of the country magistrates were liberal in the way the law was enforced. In London, for example, much of the appeal of illicit events was undermined in 1990 when several night-clubs had their licenses extended, allowing them to remain open virtually until dawn. Elsewhere, however, the law was more sternly implemented. In Manchester several established clubs were forced to close and the police objected to the renewal of the Haçienda's licence on the grounds that the venue had become a centre for drug-dealers. The Haçienda was ultimately granted a reprieve,[21] but the episode was indicative of the increasing alarm with which the authorities regarded the developing rave scene.

Unlicensed acid house parties also faced a police clamp-down. In the autumn of 1988 police in the Home Counties mounted a series of raids against illicit warehouse parties and outdoor raves. Operations continued throughout 1989, police raiding events across the country and confiscating equipment in an effort to confound the activities of party organizers. Legally, the situation was complex. Although the Public Entertainment Act required a licence to be granted for the staging of any public entertainment, several court cases saw acid party organizers successfully contend that they were not bound by this requirement since their raves were 'private' functions. Instead, local authorities began to turn to the 1967 Private Places of Entertainments Act, a seldom invoked piece of legislation which required the licensing of any private entertainment staged for financial gain (Redhead, 1993a, pp. 20–1). This move certainly strengthened the hand of the authorities, but pressure was mounting on the government to introduce much tougher measures to control the acid house party phenomenon. As a consequence the Entertainments (Increased Penalties) Act was piloted through Parliament in 1990. Dubbed 'the Acid House Bill', the new legislation significantly increased penalties for holding an unlicensed public entertainment, giving the courts the power to impose a fine of up to £20,000, a prison sentence of up to six months, or both, for each proven offence.

In many respects the anxieties that surrounded the acid house movement were similar to moral panics that had attended many earlier shifts within British youth culture. The behaviour of the young people involved was distorted by sensational media coverage, the press exaggerating dimensions of lawlessness and presenting the acid house subculture as a barometer of wider social ills and cultural decline. Yet there were also some relatively new features to the media furore of the late eighties and early nineties. Young women were especially visible in media representations of the 'evil acid house cult', girls portrayed as particularly vulnerable to predatory drug-dealers and the 'morally corrupting' influences of ecstasy – which itself was caricatured as a 'mind-bending sex drug'.[22] In 1995 the 'sexualization' of the moral panic became especially pronounced following the death of Leah Betts, an Essex teenager who had lapsed into a coma after taking an ecstasy tablet at her eighteenth birthday party.[23] Earlier ecstasy-related deaths had attracted a degree of publicity, but nothing compared with that which followed the Betts tragedy, the media mobilizing her death as a potent image of innocence corrupted by a dangerous and malevolent subculture.

The acid house moral panic was also marked out by the greater presence of groups willing to contest the stereotypes and misconceptions generated within media discourse. A greater range of agencies and experts, for example, were prepared to step forward and challenge the media's demon-ization of youth, countering the vocality of the traditional moral crusaders (McRobbie, 1994b, p. 217). Moreover, the 'folk devils' themselves began to form self-help and pressure groups to defend their interests, fighting the increasingly tough legislation introduced by the government. In October 1989, timed to coincide with the Conservative Party Conference, Tony Colston-Hayter launched the Freedom to Party Campaign, a body intended to organize opposition to legislation that would effectively outlaw acid house parties. In many respects, of course, this campaign was simply an attempt by Colston-Hayter and other party organizers to defend their business concerns. At the same time, nevertheless, the Freedom to Party movement was able to attract the support of thousands of young rave fans and at the beginning of 1990 a rally in Trafalgar Square saw over 10,000 demonstrators gather to protest against the introduction of anti-party legislation (see figure 12.1). The campaign, furthermore, led to a growing convergence between the interests of the rave contingent and another subcultural group facing similar stigmatization and punitive legislation – the 'New Age travellers'.

Tribal Gatherings: The Free Festival Movement and New Age Travellers

According to one line of argument, the political subversion and cultural dissent of the sixties' counter-culture had all but disappeared by the early

FREEDOM TO PARTY
CAMPAIGN

RALLY, SATURDAY, MARCH 3, 1990, 2.00ᴘᴍ, HYDE PARK, LONDON

SUPPORTED BY : ASSOCIATION OF DANCE PARTY PROMOTERS (ADPPro), RAVERS, RADIO STATIONS, RECORD COMPANIES AND MAGAZINES

On Saturday, January 27ᵗʰ, 10,000 ravers gathered to dance at Trafalgar Square in a peaceful protest against the new anti-party laws being introduced. One week later 2,000 ravers gathered in Manchester to fight for the right to party - around the country, in city after city, the protests continue....

Saturday, March 3ʳᵈ sees the climax of the campaign - parliament debates the new law on March 9ᵗʰ. Untold thousands of ravers from around the country will gather for a national day of protest. If the new law goes through there won't be another "Summer of Love" and there won't be any more raves, so stand up for your right to party. Show the media and the government our strength.

ARE YOU GOING TO LET THEM TAKE AWAY YOUR RIGHT TO PARTY ?

CAMPAIGN INFORMATION : 0836 405411

Freedom to Party Campaign, 27 Old Gloucester Street, London, WC1N 3XX.

Figure 12.1   Leaflet for the 'Freedom to Party' Campaign, February 1990

seventies. For Daniel Foss and Ralph Larkin (1976) the oppositional ener-
gies of the counter-culture retreated into mysticism and New Age cultism,
while for Elizabeth Nelson (1989) the sixties' movement had simply 'faded
away' after it had 'failed to achieve its objectives'. Writers such as George
McKay (1996), however, have more accurately shown that the counter-
culture remained a potent force throughout the seventies and eighties,
continually reinvigorated by a succession of subcultural movements.

During the early seventies a loose nexus of 'alternative' printing
presses, bookshops, music venues and cafés maintained the political
idealism that had grown up during the sixties (McKay, 1996). The urban
squatting movement, meanwhile, provided a new focus for direct political action, seasoned veterans of sixties' activism joining forces with a new
generation of counter-cultural radicals to seize possession of, and live in,
buildings left empty or derelict by their owners. Above all, however, it was
a circuit of free festivals and fairs that sustained the British counter-
culture through the seventies and eighties. Outside the security fences of
sixties' pop festivals there had often developed a rival scene of free entertainments and shows and during the early seventies the utopian ethos that
underpinned these pageants had begun to develop into distinct occasions
and events. In 1971, for example, farmer Michael Eavis organized the first
Glastonbury Fayre on his land at Worthy Farm in Somerset. Originally
to be a one-off festival of free music, the Glastonbury event subsequently
established itself as an important annual fixture on the counter-cultural
calendar. In 1972, meanwhile, the first Windsor Free Festival attracted a
crowd of 15,000 and the following year saw the event held with equal success. In 1973 the third and final Windsor Festival was broken up by
police, but by then a whole network of convocations had begun to take
shape.

Among the wide variety of counter-cultural festivals staged during the
seventies it was the Stonehenge People's Free Festival, held in celebration
of the summer solstice, that proved to be the most important and long-
lasting. Held at the site of prehistoric standing stones in Wiltshire, the
festival had originally been the brainchild of an anarchist hippy known as
'Wally' Hope. Inspired by gatherings such as those held at Windsor, Hope
had envisioned a larger-scale event where like-minded people could carve
out a communal space of utopian pleasure and freedom of expression. First
held in 1974, the Stonehenge Festival became a regular event, with thousands of people thronging a hippy encampment of tipis and tents that

surrounded the monument for much of June every year. By the mid-seventies a full programme of free festivals stretched across the south and south-west of England during the summer months, encouraging a growing number of festival-goers to weave their way between sites in convoys of tatty-looking vans, lorries, buses and caravans. For some, these journeys between summer festivals extended into a year-round nomadic lifestyle, and by the beginning of the eighties the New Age travellers had emerged as a distinct cultural movement.[24]

In many ways the new travellers were a group more socially hetero-geneous than had been the counter-culture of the sixties. Certainly, their ranks included many veterans of sixties' radicalism whose origins were distinctly middle class and bourgeois. On the other hand, there was also a younger, more working-class constituency. The latter had been hard hit by the harsh economic climate of the eighties and had found themselves on the road as a result of unemployment, homelessness and the withdrawal of social security and housing benefits for young people. In their 1994 study *Out of Site, Out of Mind*, for example, the Children's Society found that two-thirds of New Age travellers had been forced into their lifestyle through socio-economic circumstances that included homelessness, finan-cial hardship, abuse, family or relationship breakdown, or inability to find permanent accommodation after leaving a children's home, the army or prison. Among these young travellers and their allies a distinct form of dress began to take form during the early eighties. In what became known as the 'crusty' look, elements of hippy and punk style coalesced. The basic uniform consisted of baggy army fatigues, oversize combat boots and matted or dreadlocked hair, often shaved at the sides. On badges and jackets the anarchists' circled 'A' symbol proliferated, while body piercings and tattoos of Celtic and other 'mystic' symbols became popular. Sometimes scrawny mongrels also featured as 'crusty' fashion accessories, the scruffy-looking mutts setting off an image of the worldly traveller with his or her trusty companion.

As we saw in chapter 8, although seventies' punks had reviled the hippy scene of the sixties, in many respects punk itself had marked a progression of counter-cultural concerns and attitudes. Indeed, in the late seventies and early eighties the rise of punk led to a reinvigoration of the counter-culture's political activity and radicalism. Central here were Crass, an anarcho-pacifist collective who had been influenced by the sense of incen-diary idealism that had initially surrounded punk.[25] Crass sought to develop punk's political edge much more keenly. Determinedly guarding their artistic and political autonomy, they nevertheless thrived as a radical underground organization throughout the early eighties, establishing their own record company, producing their own music and establishing links with other radical groups through the organization of an alternative concert circuit. Many of the Situationist ideas that had influenced the first wave of punk artists and entrepreneurs also surfaced in Crass's use of the visual arts, especially the striking photomontage style that became a trademark of their outpouring of record covers, books, posters and magazines. Crass's records also sold remarkably well and in 1983 the group enjoyed a measure of national notoriety, prompting questions in Parliament after Conservative MPs had been outraged by the release of the band's single, 'How Does It Feel (To Be the Mother of a Thousand Dead)?' – a virulent attack on Margaret Thatcher's belligerent jingoism during the Falklands War.

Crass's radical endeavours laid the way for a revival of counter-cultural activism during the eighties, much of which centred on the free festival scene and the traveller movement. During the early eighties an especially close relationship developed between travellers' convoys and peace groups campaigning against the stationing of American nuclear weapons at British air bases. In 1981 protesters had established a 'peace camp' outside the US Air Force base at Greenham Common and the following year (shortly before the camp became a women-only venture) they were joined by a large contingent of travellers who showed solidarity by identifying themselves as the 'Peace Convoy'. A smaller group of travellers joined a similar peace camp at Molesworth RAF base, a traveller community known as 'Rainbow Village' surviving until 1985 when it was forcibly evicted by the Ministry of Defence. Interaction with the peace camps was indicative of a growing politicization within the traveller movement and the second half of the eighties saw many travellers play an active and highly visible role in episodes of political protest and direct action. Travellers, for example, were especially active in the widespread campaign against the introduction of the poll tax (Community Charge) and had a high profile in the rioting in Trafalgar Square that followed a huge anti-poll tax demonstration in March 1990. In the early nineties the success of the anti-poll tax movement gave way to a profusion of direct action campaigns based around ecological and environmental issues and, once again, travellers played a prominent part. One of the most famous protests centred on the extension to the M3 motorway at Twyford Down in Hampshire. The campaign against the extension had been active for many years but in 1992, as construction work was about to commence, local protesters were joined by an army of traveller activists calling themselves the Dongas Tribe (after the name given to the medieval pathways that crossed the local downland). The Dongas eschewed the lobbying tactics of mainstream environmental pressure groups in favour of direct confrontation with the building contractors – squatting on the proposed site of the extension, staging mass trespasses to disrupt the building work and sabotaging bulldozers and excavating equipment. Although the Twyford Down protest ultimately failed the actions of the Dongas acted as a major spur to direct action campaigns throughout the nineties – for example, protests against the extension of the M11 motorway in London and the M77 in Glasgow, and volatile demonstrations against the export of live animals from the ports of Brightlingsea and Shoreham.

The New Age travellers' unorthodox lifestyle and political activism won them vilification in the popular media and opprobrium from the authorities. As a consequence, the mid-eighties saw the escalation of police operations against free festivals and the 'Peace Convoy', measures that were constituent in a more general heightening of political tensions during the period. The miners' strike of 1984–5 had signified a wider intensification of social and political conflict in Britain, the state coming to rely more heavily on authoritarian strategies of surveillance and control. In many respects the travellers represented, for the government, one more aspect of a pervasive 'enemy within' and as such the full force of the social control apparatus began to be directed against them. In 1985 matters came to a violent climax in what became known as the 'Battle of the Beanfield'.

By the mid-eighties the Stonehenge Free Festival had grown markedly in scale, attracting some 50,000 people at its peak. In 1985 English Heritage and the National Trust, the monument's custodians, became uneasy at the prospect of the influx of thousands of festival-goers and, arguing that the festival would be detrimental to land of archaeological significance, obtained an injunction to stop it from taking place. Enforcing the court's ruling, the police established an 'exclusion zone' preventing travellers from getting within four miles of the site. The travellers, however, were equally determined that their solstice celebrations should take place and by the beginning of June hundreds of their vehicles were snaking towards Stonehenge. One traveller convoy, halted at a police roadblock, was forced to turn into surrounding fields where it was attacked by squads of riot police with a degree of ferocity that shocked many onlookers. Officers assaulted the assembled travellers indiscriminately, using their truncheons to smash vehicles' windscreens, dragging their occupants through the debris and making over 500 arrests.[26] The 'Battle of the Beanfield' effectively broke up the traveller convoy, some members retreating northwards, to festivals held in Cumbria, Norfolk, Yorkshire and Wales, while others sought refuge on farmland owned by a Christian community near Glastonbury. Official action against the travellers, however, continued throughout the following years. Every June saw an elaborate police operation to cordon off Stonehenge and prevent the staging of a festival, while in 1986 the passage of a new Public Order Act increased police powers to evict travellers from unofficial sites and changes in Social Security regulations made it more difficult for travellers to claim welfare benefits.

Despite such measures the late eighties saw small groups of travellers continue to play 'cat and mouse' with police forces across the south of England. Most travellers were deterred from gathering at Stonehenge but the event was reconvened at Glastonbury, where the annual pop festival had grown rapidly from a small free gathering to a huge commercial enterprise attracting crowds of 50,000 music fans. The travellers, however, enjoyed an uneasy relationship with the official festival organizers and friction between the groups led to the cancellation of the event in 1988. In its place several free festivals were staged throughout Wiltshire and on the night of the solstice 5,000 travellers attempted to walk to Stonehenge where, once again, violence flared as they were blocked by teams of riot police. Nor were the New Age travellers the only group to experience a tightening of authoritarian control during this period. The moves against raves and warehouse parties that had begun in the late eighties grew in severity during the early nineties. The spring and summer of 1990 saw a spate of police raids on unlicensed parties, with numerous arrests and the confiscation of sound equipment. Police forces in the north of England took an especially hard line, with several high-profile operations against parties. In June 1990, for example, 230 arrests were made as police broke up a party under a motorway viaduct near Wakefield. The following month, meanwhile, one of the largest mass arrests for decades occurred when police took 836 party-goers into custody after raiding a party at a disused warehouse on the M62 near Leeds. In both instances officers were accused of using undue force against the young party-goers and nearly all of those arrested were subsequently released without charge.

Increasingly repressive control brought a siege mentality to both the traveller and rave communities, the bonds of their cultures actually tightening as a consequence. During the early nineties links between the two groups also steadily grew. Traveller-influenced sound systems such as Spiral Tribe, Circus Normal and Bedlam toured a circuit of raves and free festivals, the events serving as a meeting-ground where diverse youth subcultures encountered and interacted with one another. Processes of cross-fertilization steadily brought a fusion of the rave and traveller scenes, the cross-over culminating in May 1992 at Castlemorton Common in Hereford. Here, up to 40,000 travellers and ravers joined force, camping out for over a week and enjoying the biggest free festival in six years. Although the rave broke up peacefully after the landowners issued an eviction order, the police faced criticism from the media and politicians for failing to evict the gathering. Once again, the government promised even tougher measures to curb raves and festivals and the groundwork was laid for one of the most controversial pieces of legislation to reach the post-war statute books – the Criminal Justice Act.

Revelry and Repression: The 1994 Criminal Justice Act and Its Impact

The 1994 Criminal Justice and Public Order Act – or Criminal Justice Act as it became more generally known – was an exceedingly comprehensive piece of legislation. The new measures it introduced embraced a wide range of areas, including the prevention of terrorism, the juvenile justice system, police powers to stop and search, and the control of pornography. Part V of the Act, however, was particularly significant in that it created a series of new criminal offences that were expressly designed to deal with the problems thrown up by the acid house party and New Age traveller movements of the late eighties.

The lifestyle of New Age travellers was especially hard hit by the terms of the Act. In provisions clearly aimed at the solstice gatherings at Stonehenge, chief constables were empowered to apply for an order prohibiting 'trespassory assemblies' that might cause either 'serious disruption to the life of the community' or 'significant damage' to land, buildings, or monuments of 'historical, architectural, archaeological or scientific importance' To organize such a prohibited assembly became a criminal offence with a maximum penalty of three months' imprisonment and participation was punishable with a fine. The Act also effectively criminalized the travellers' nomadic way of life by strengthening police powers to evict people they believed to be trespassing on land with the purpose of 'residing there for any period'. Failure to leave the area, or to return to it within three months, became an offence with a maximum penalty of three months' imprisonment, police being given additional powers to seize, remove and dispose of any vehicle left behind. New Age protesters such as the Dongas Tribe were also hit by the creation of the new offence of 'aggravated trespass' – a maximum sentence of three months' imprisonment being introduced for those found guilty of trespass that disrupted, obstructed or intimidated people engaged in lawful activity. These measures could also be used against acid party organizers and revellers, though the Act included additional provisions that were specifically geared towards outlawing the outdoor rave scene.

The 1994 Act greatly augmented the ability of the police to deal with unlicensed raves. Under its terms officers were empowered to order people to leave an area if they believed there was about to take place an unlicensed entertainment event with the playing of amplified music that would 'cause serious distress to the inhabitants of the locality'. Failure to comply with police directions became a criminal offence with a maximum penalty of three months' imprisonment and, once again, police were empowered to seize vehicles and sound equipment which had not been removed from the land. Additionally, within a radius of five miles of the site, the police were empowered to stop people they believed to be going to the event and direct them to turn back – failure to comply representing an offence punishable with a fine. Even the Act's definition of music as 'sounds wholly or predominantly characterized by the emission of a succession of repetitive beats' seemed specifically designed to prohibit acid house parties and rave events.

Implemented in October 1994, the Criminal Justice Act had a mixed impact on the field of British youth culture. Fearful of falling prey to the strict, new measures, many of the smaller rave organizers were either pushed out of business or went abroad, organizing raves in a party scene which now stretched from Goa to San Francisco. Ironically, however, the Act was a gift to the biggest promoters. With ample experience and resources at their disposal, major rave organizations like Joy, Live the Dream and Sunrise were able to meet strict licensing regulations and stage legitimate, fully licensed and very profitable events. In May 1995, for example, rave promoters Universe joined forces with the Mean Fiddler entertainments group to host Tribal Gathering '95 – a vast open-air rave on 60 acres of Oxfordshire farmland which attracted 25,000 revellers. At the same time, the declining number of unlicensed outdoor parties brought an upsurge of urban club culture. Clubs such as the Ministry of Sound in south-east London became major money-spinners, with an annual turnover approaching £2.3 million and all over Britain a new crop of night-clubs began to prosper – for example the Sanctuary in Milton Keynes and Wandsworth's Club UK.

Before the 1994 Act came into force its critics were pessimistic about its consequences. The implementation of the Act, it was argued, depended too heavily on the discretion of the police and local authorities and offered potential for a marked erosion of freedoms and civil liberties. New offences such as 'aggravated trespass' were especially criticized for delivering to the police a battery of powers that could be used to curtail fundamental rights while, if vigorously applied, the Act seemed likely to criminalize a whole section of the youth population by banning their raves and parties. In prac-tice, however, the police and local authorities were circumspect in the way they implemented the new laws. In many areas guidelines and procedures were drawn up to ensure that the terms of the Act were applied with discre-tion and restraint. Some police forces, in fact, seemed reluctant to use the new measures at all, often turning a blind eye to the small-scale, unlicensed parties that continued all over the country. When officers did crack down they invariably avoided inflaming tense situations by opting to make arrests and confiscate equipment using older, public order laws rather than resorting to the more sweeping provisions of the new legislation. At least initially, therefore, the full vigour of the Criminal Justice Act was rarely felt.

Indeed, by the time the Criminal Justice Act was implemented many of the problems it sought to address had ceased to be major issues. Well before 1994 a host of legislation and policing measures had taken their toll on the ranks of New Age travellers. Changes in Social Security laws, combined with court injunctions, eviction orders and exclusion zones, made life on the road much harder. The days of the large-scale 'Peace Convoy' were over and travellers were more commonly found in much smaller encampments and park-ups. Significant changes had also already taken place in the rave scene. The Criminal Justice legislation undoubtedly accelerated a move from huge outdoor parties towards indoor, urban club-life, but the beginnings of this shift had preceded the 1994 Act. Dance music of the late eighties had always been an amalgam of myriad influences and by the early nineties the scene had begun to fracture into an array of different sub-genres. Garage and handbag house, for example, reclaimed house's gay disco heritage by focusing on slower vocals and melody, contrasting markedly with the more frenetic and accelerated pace of techno – which itself had begun to rupture into a range of different variants and idioms. By the beginning of the nineties a distinctive 'ambient' scene had also emerged. A languid layering of hypnotic chord arrangements, the roots of ambient house lay in Brian Eno's experiments in electronic music during the seventies, the music coming of age in the 'chill-out' zones of nineties' dance events, where ravers acclimatized to their post-ecstasy come-down (Kempster, 1996, p. 89). During the early nineties a whole subculture began to cohere around the ambient sounds of performers such as the Aphex Twin and the Orb, inspiring clubs exclusively geared to ambient timbres and providing a framework for further developments such as trip hop and lounge core (a heavily ironic appropriation of the 'easy listening' music of the fifties and sixties). Large-scale outdoor raves continued into the late nineties, but the 'fragmentation' of the dance movement led to the rise of a multiplicity of subcultural scenes that found a more natural home in smaller, more distinctive club environments.

Although the police and courts did not rigorously apply Part V of the Criminal Justice Act, hostility to the legislation remained pronounced and the 'right to party' campaign continued through the mid-nineties. Indeed, the passage of the new laws led to a further 'politicization' of some sections of the party movement. Groups such as the Brixton-based Freedom Network and the Brighton-based Justice? collective were formed to fight the Act, voicing their objections and forging links with other social groups affected by legislation that seemed to pose a significant threat to civil liberties and the right to protest. In other respects a greater 'political' dimension also began to register within factions of the rave scene. In Luton, for example, the Exodus collective was formed in 1992, staging some of the area's biggest raves and using the profits to fund community projects such as the renovation of derelict buildings to rehouse homeless youngsters. The rise of the 'right to party' movement and projects such as Exodus were, in some respects, indicative of a wider move towards 'micro-politics' that began to feature in British society. Alongside the 'traditional' battle-lines of orthodox party politics, the nineties saw an upsurge of issue-based campaigns and movements operating outside the constitutional frame-work. New agendas were set by a proliferation of campaigns related to ecological, environmental and ethical issues, a wide constituency of people being mobilized in an unlikely set of alliances that drew together young, radical activists and sections of the middle-aged, respectable middle class. At the same time an array of new pressure groups working on behalf of various minority interests (in terms of gender, sexuality, ethnicity and disability) also seemed to confirm a shift away from the class-bound polit-ical struggles of the past towards a new era of political hybridity. Here, political conflict could no longer be reduced simply to the dynamics of social class, but instead embraced wider and more complex dimensions of identity and interest.

This sense of a greater plurality and 'fluidity' to contemporary cultural life also registered in attempts to make sense of youth culture and subcul-ture. For theorists affiliated to the Manchester Institute of Popular Culture, for example, the form and texture of post-punk youth subcultures were qualitatively different from their predecessors.[27] The multitude of nineties' dance cultures, in particular, seemed to defy attempts at uncov-ering any concrete sense of 'meaning' behind their styles. Instead, these cultures appeared to be 'free-floating' sets of images and signifiers that were not locked into any specific historical moment or location. In the nineties, therefore, many writers sought fresh ideas and theories in order to make sense of the new 'postmodern' social, economic and cultural condi-tions facing young people at the end of the twentieth century.

Notes

1   An excellent overview of the rise of the Manchester punk scene is provided in Mick Middles, 1996, *From Joy Division to New Order: The Factory Story*, London: Virgin, pp. 11–73.

2   One of the first and most influential independent charts was launched by *New Musical Express* in 1981, the paper championing independent labels and 'indie' music throughout the 1980s.

3   Even relatively long-established independents with sizeable financial turnovers were hard hit by declining record sales and general economic reces-sion. Factory Records, for example, managed to weather a series of economic

crises during the eighties but finally succumbed to receivership in late 1992.

4 In 1986 Simon Reynolds produced an insightful etymology of the 'shambling' scene. See Simon Reynolds, 'Ladybirds and Start-rite kids', *Melody Maker*, 27 September 1986.

5 By the beginning of 1990 fashion magazines and the national press were both widely using the term 'scally' to designate trends in style and fashion in Manchester. See, for example, Mike Noon, 1990, 'Freaky dancing – scallies on the march', *I-d*, No. 77, February; Stuart Maconie, 'The Manchester guardians', *Guardian*, 21 April 1990.

6 For an overview of the development of the music scene in Manchester during the late eighties see Sarah Champion, 1990, *And God Created Manchester*, Manchester: Wordsmith.

7 The Manchester scene even attracted global attention, with a cover feature in *Newsweek* in July 1990 celebrating 'Madchester – Britain's Feel-Good Music Movement'.

8 This account has won support from several notable commentators. See, for example, Simon Reynolds and Paul Oldfield, 1990, 'Acid over', in Simon Reynolds (ed.), *Blissed Out: The Raptures of Rock*, London: Serpent's Tail, p. 177.

9 Cited in Nicholas Saunders, 1995, *Ecstasy and the Dance Culture*, London: Saunders, p. 18.

10 For an account of the early development of house music and its subsequent entry into British youth culture see Chris Kempster (ed.), 1996, *History of House*, London: Sanctuary.

11 An extensive account of the biographies of Britain's leading DJs of the late eighties and nineties can be found in Jonathan Fleming, 1995, *What Kind of a House Party Is This? The History of a Music Revolution*, Slough: MIY.

12 In the North similar parties were organized on the outskirts of Blackpool, Huddersfield, Preston and Blackburn.

13 These details of the acid party organizers' strategy are elaborated by Paul Staines in Saunders, *Ecstasy and the Dance Culture*, pp. 20–1.

14 For an exploration of the links and similarities between the rave phenomenon of the late eighties and the psychedelic counter-culture of the late sixties see Kristian Russell, 1993, 'Lysergia suburbia', in Steve Redhead (ed.), *Rave Off: Politics and Deviance in Contemporary Youth Culture*, Aldershot: Avebury, pp. 91–174.

15 Controversy surrounds the risks of addiction and physical harm associated with ecstasy. Deaths associated with the use of the drug have been rare but are certainly not unknown. For example, the Christmas 1996 period alone saw three ecstasy-related deaths. The drug's champions, on the other hand, maintain that its associated risks are minimal. For an unembellished and objective

account of the drug's effects and possible risks to health see Andrew Tyler, 1995, *Street Drugs*, rev. edn, London: Hodder and Stoughton, pp. 247–52; 263–8. For a compelling history of the relationship between ecstasy and the various dance subcultures of the late eighties and early nineties see Matthew Collin, 1997, *Altered State: The Story of Ecstasy Culture and Acid House*, London: Serpent's Tail.

16 See Steve Redhead, 1993, 'The politics of ecstasy', in Redhead (ed.), *Rave Off*, pp. 10–12.

17 See Patrick Miller and Martin Plant, 1996, 'Drinking, smoking, and illicit drug use among 15 and 16 year olds in the United Kingdom', *British Medical Journal*, vol. 313, no. 7054, pp. 394–7.

18 For a more detailed analysis of these child-like dimensions of rave style see Angela McRobbie, 1994, 'Shut up and dance: youth culture and changing modes of femininity', in Angela McRobbie, *Postmodernism and Popular Culture*, London: Routledge, pp. 168–9.

19 According to Sarah Thornton, members of the rave scene actually greeted media condemnation with a degree of relish since this censure seemed to preserve rave's underground status and confirmed their self-image as transgressive rebels. See Sarah Thornton, 1994, 'Moral panic, the media and British rave culture', in Andrew Ross and Tricia Rose (eds), *Microphone Fiends: Youth Music and Youth Culture*, London: Routledge, pp. 176–92; Sarah Thornton, 1995, *Club Cultures: Music, Media and Subcultural Capital*, London: Polity Press.

20 Stories that 'We Call It Acieeed' had been banned outright by the BBC originated, in fact, as a marketing strategy developed by D-Mob's record company.

21 In February 1991 the Haçienda voluntarily closed for a temporary period in response to an escalation in violence between Manchester's rival drug gangs.

22 See Steve Redhead and Antonio Melechi, 1988, 'The fall of the acid reign', *New Statesman and Society*, vol. 1, nos. 29/30, 23–30 December, pp. 21–3.

23 Rather than dying from the effects of the ecstasy itself, Leah Betts had died from liver failure caused by drinking too much water in an effort to stave off the dehydrating effects of the drug.

24 For an account of the history and lifestyle of the traveller movement see Fiona Earle, Alan Dearling, Helen Whillte and Roddy Glasse, 1994, *A Time to Travel? An Introduction to Britain's Newer Travellers*, Lyme Regis: Enabler Publications. A revealing collection of autobiographical essays written by travellers can also be found in Richard Lowe and William Shaw (eds), 1993, *Travellers: Voices of the New Age Nomads*, London: Fourth Estate.

25 A history of the Crass organization, together with an assessment of the group's contribution to subsequent developments in direct action politics is provided

in George McKay, 1996, 'CRASS 621984 ANOK4U2', in George McKay, *Senseless Acts of Beauty: Cultures of Resistance Since the Sixties*, London: Verso, pp. 73–102.

26 Following the 'Battle of the Beanfield' a group of twenty-four travellers fought for compensation at Winchester High Court in one of the longest-running civil actions ever brought against the police. The case ended with awards of damages totalling more than £23,000 to the plaintiffs for assault, damage to their vehicles and property, and not being given adequate reasons for their arrest.

27 For one of the leading expositions of the line of argument see Steve Redhead, 1990, *The End-of-the-Century Party: Youth and Pop Towards 2000*, Manchester: Manchester University Press.

13 'Welcome to the Jungle': Youth at the End of the Century

'Everything Changes': Youth Culture, Postmodernism and the New Hybridity

The late twentieth century was a time of rapid change and uncertainty. Generally, the eighties and nineties were marked by the transformation of world political orders, major industrial restructuring and economic realignment, rapid developments in technology and the media, and significant shifts in family and community relationships. Taken together, these developments began to be interpreted as representing a fundamental sea-change in contemporary life – the beginning of a new, 'postmodern' era. For its proponents the new 'postmodern condition' was defined by a steady collapse of traditional securities, all overarching claims to knowledge and truth being subjected to growing scepticism and doubt (Lyotard, 1984). Mirroring this crisis in the status of knowledge, it was argued, were a distinctive set of cultural changes in which a proliferation of media and information technologies had altered traditional senses of time and space, the difference between representation and reality collapsing until nothing remained but a surfeit of endlessly circulating images. This 'ecstasy of communication' (Baudrillard, 1985) was seen as erasing boundaries between formerly discrete areas of social and cultural life, producing a wealth of interconnections and fluid exchanges. Although a thoroughgoing analysis and appraisal of postmodern theory is beyond the scope of the present study,[1] some of the key shifts identified by postmodern theorists seemed to be especially reflected in the lives and culture of young people at the end of the twentieth century. It is, therefore, worth briefly reflecting on the nature of some of these developments.

Newly emergent media forms seemed to embody the elements of pastiche, intertextuality and a collapsing of boundaries that many theorists identified as characteristic features of postmodernity. Pop videos, in particular, came into their own during the eighties and were hailed by some critics as emblematic of a new postmodern culture (Jameson, 1984; Kaplan, 1987). Those featuring artists like Madonna or the Pet Shop Boys were seen as unequivocally postmodern in the way they plundered a spectrum of cinematic genres, deploying a visual style that collapsed the boundary between commercial promotion and 'high' art.[2] Television programmes oriented around pop music and youth culture also seemed to reflect post-modern traits, with a growing emphasis on style, surface and a stream of information. In Britain the work of television producer Janet Street-Porter was especially influential. First with Network 7 for Channel 4 in 1987, and then with Def II for BBC 2 in 1988, Street-Porter pioneered a style of tele-vision production that employed a welter of different communication styles, bringing together a collage-like blend of sound, image and bites of information. As Street-Porter herself explained in 1988: 'I'm making programmes for a generation who have grown up with TV, with visual images all around them, who are very familiar with computers and video technology . . . my shows have set out to arrest audiences, to hold them, to play all sorts of tricks to keep them from turning over.'[3]

The rise of the pop video was accompanied by the launch of MTV (Music Television) in 1981. A twenty-four-hour, commercial cable televi-sion channel with a staple content of pop music videos, MTV was American in origin but quickly established a legion of national franchises across the world. In this respect MTV seemed indicative of postmodern claims that the eighties and nineties had seen a trend towards processes of 'globalization'. Here, rapid developments in communications technology were seen as producing an intensification of cultural flows and economic links between different countries. As economic and cultural boundaries steadily dissolved it seemed as though nations, communities and organi-zations were becoming integrated as never before (McGrew, 1992). Indeed, developments in youth culture seemed to support these claims. The rise of satellite and cable television channels, together with the trans-global marketing of pop artists by multinational corporations such as Sony, Warner and Geffen, meant that groups of young people far removed from one another in terms of time and space became audiences for the same sets of messages and images and, in many respects, came to share the same cultural vocabulary. By the early nineties, therefore, it was possible for the first time to speak of a 'global' dimension to many youth styles and cultures.

In the field of pop music the 'postmodern' use of intertextual references and the blurring of cultural boundaries became a defining aesthetic during the late eighties and nineties. The period saw a proliferation of 'cover-versions' and the remixing of existing material, as well as an increasing intersection between popular music and other media forms, especially the cinema. By the late eighties, for example, pop soundtracks had become a prominent feature within many new film releases, each promoting the sales of the other. Moreover, the self-conscious mixing of different genres and styles became common practice among pop artists, together with the 'sampling' of various instruments, music and media. These practices were first associated with the rise of rap music in the early eighties and the records of African-American artists such as Grandmaster Flash and Afrika Bambaataa, though by the nineties they had become established features across the field of popular music. The playfulness and love of irony often associated with postmodern cultural forms also registered markedly in contemporary pop. The early eighties saw a marked sense of 'knowingness' among artists who revelled in the artifice of their medium, 'new pop' bands such as ABC and Frankie Goes to Hollywood delighting in an ironic play of images which parodied the established sensibilities and iconography of the pop industry. Irony and pastiche remained key features in nineties' pop, taken to new limits by the mischief-making antics of the KLF[4] and by the more subtle disco chic of the Pet Shop Boys. Nineties' pop also seemed to efface the boundary between high and popular culture. Written about and discussed by a variety of commentators and academics, pop music seemed to defy traditional cultural categories in the way it was increasingly treated as a 'serious' artistic form.[5]

To some commentators the 'postmodern' traits of fragmentation and heterogeneity became especially visible within the youth fashions of the nineties. For some observers of youth style a former, more straightforward, polarity between a 'mainstream' style and a more dramatic subculture had given way to a much more complex and diverse universe of cultural options available in a new, postmodern 'supermarket of style' (Polhemus, 1994). Certainly, the proliferation of media forms in the nineties enlarged the range of texts and artefacts available to young people as they carved out their cultural identities, the period seeing a wealth of stylistic options rubbing shoulders with one another. However, the novelty of this phenomenon should not be exaggerated. The tendency to celebrate a multiplicity of 'styletribes' during the nineties has exaggerated the degree to which stylistic choice was circumscribed in earlier periods. Indeed, throughout the post-war era British youngsters have always faced a relatively open and flexible range of stylistic options rather than a simple choice between being 'cool' or 'square'.

The speed with which the dance and rave scenes came to dominate youth culture in the late eighties and nineties was remarkable. In response several commentators were tempted to interpret this rapidity in 'postmodern' terms, suggesting that it represented a collapse of boundaries between subcultural 'authenticity' and commercial 'fabrication'. Steven Connor, for instance, contended that in the closing decades of the twentieth century the cycle of 'innovation' and 'incorporation' within youth style had speeded up 'to the point where authentic "originality" and commercial "exploitation" are hard to distinguish' (Connor, 1989, p. 185). Steve Redhead concurred, arguing that post-punk subcultures had 'been characterized by a speeding up of the time between points of "authenticity" and "manufacture"' (Redhead, 1991, p. 94). However, as we saw in chapter 6, notions of a divide ever having clearly separated subcultural expressions from the commercial market and the media are intrinsically flawed. Rather than processes of 'recuperation' having been 'accelerated' during the eighties and nineties, youth subcultures have *always* been entwined with the institutions of the market in an *ongoing* relationship of exchange. While young people have undoubtedly been involved in practices of stylistic innovation, it has largely been the media and other commercial industries that have shaped these practices into coherent and identifiable subcultural formations. A symbiotic relationship between youth subcultures and the commercial market, then, is not a quality unique to some new 'postmodern condition', but has been a defining characteristic of young people's cultural expressions since at least 1945.

If any fundamentally novel features existed in the form and texture of youth culture during the late twentieth century they were to be found in the greater dimensions of hybridity and heterogeneity that featured in the subcultural scenes emerging during the late eighties and early nineties. Distinctive in this respect was a musical genre variously known as jungle, breakbeat or drum'n'bass – a form of dance music distinguished by its crossing of cultural boundaries and its poaching and blending of musical forms and cultural signifiers. From the fracturing of the warehouse party and dance/rave scenes in the late eighties jungle emerged as a pre-eminently black dance music that amalgamated elements of reggae, hip-hop, hard-core and house music styles. Exploiting cutting-edge computer and sound recording technologies, jungle promiscuously sampled from an ever-expanding array of sources. The intricate sonic land-scapes that resulted were dominated by a preponderant reggae bass line, though the composite whole rattled along at a break-neck speed of 160 beats per minute. In many respects jungle harked back to the sound system days of the early sixties, with a scene that was originally focused on club sessions at London's Astoria and the Paradise Club and which was spear-headed by a small coterie of DJs such as Fabio and Grooverider. In sartorial terms jungle also recalled elements of sixties' black style, the rude boy's displays of conspicuous wealth and sombre menace finding echoes in jungle's taste for gangster posturing, expensive gold jewellery and ex-clusive designer labels. Around jungle there developed a network of underground clubs which, together with record labels such as Moving Shadow and Juice Box and pirate radio stations such as Kool FM and Eruption FM, increasingly drew together a fusion of black, Asian and white youngsters. By the mid-nineties jungle had gained national exposure in releases by artists such as Kemet Crew, a Guy Called Gerald and especially Goldie – a former graffiti artist who became the face of jungle through the success of his debut album *Timeless* in 1995 and the popularity of his Sunday night Metalheadz club which quickly established itself as the place to be seen on London's jungle scene.[6]

Jungle was undoubtedly one of the most fertile and creative areas of dance music to emerge in the early nineties, yet in cultural terms it can also be interpreted as significant. Jungle drew together diverse elements of Jamaican, American and British subcultural life, redrawing young people's maps of national identity in the way it fused a deeply felt sense of local iden-tification (rooted specifically in London) with a transcendence of both national and cultural boundaries. As such, jungle could be seen as elabo-rating (albeit temporarily) a range of identity positions that were relatively more inclusive and less rigidly determined by the divisions of race, class and gender than many identity options found elsewhere in the field of youth culture (Back, 1996, pp. 232–5). Here, a parallel can be drawn between the new identities offered in jungle and what some theorists have seen as a more general growth of cultural hybridity in contemporary societies.

According to this line of argument processes of globalization have had profound ramifications for modern identity positions. On the one hand a polarization of ethnic identities has taken place in which some sections of minority ethnic groups (in response to cultural racism and exclusion) have embarked on a reidentification with their cultures of origin or a reassertion of religious orthodoxy. Here, examples from the field of youth culture might include the impact of Rastafarianism in Britain during the 1970s, or many Asian youths' reaffirmation of their Muslim identities in the wake of the controversy that surrounded the publication of Salman Rushdie's *The Satanic Verses* in 1988. However, alongside this dimension of polarization (and much more typical of trends within British youth culture) has been the simultaneous widening of potential identity positions. Under the impact of processes of social, economic and cultural globalization identities have become less fixed and more fluid, with the emergence of new forms of cultural identification (Hall, 1992b, pp. 310–14). This can be seen as a state of what Homi Bhabha (1990) terms 'translation' – a condition in which a complex of cultural cross-currents and cross-fertilizations produce a wealth of hybrid identities that simultaneously blend together a diversity of cultural traditions. Jungle, then, could be taken as an embodiment of these processes of 'translation'. A peculiarly British musical genre, jungle was also a bearer of strong links with specifically black cultural traditions, a cultural hybrid generated as black youngsters negotiated and translated their way through the different cultural contexts created by post-colonial migration.

'Hybrid subcultural identities', however, are not a uniquely contemporary phenomenon. Rather than being perfectly formed cultural entities, subcultures have always been fluid and fragmented 'hybrids' in which cultural allegiances have been mutable and transient. Instead of making a firm set of stylistic commitments most youngsters have instead cruised across a range of affiliations, constantly forming and reforming their identities according to social context. In this respect the open-ended, fragmented identities many theorists see as common to the late twentieth century were, perhaps, anticipated by tendencies already present within the youth cultural formations of the 1950s and 1960s.

Nevertheless, this embrace of hybridity represents a markedly more optimistic interpretation of contemporary cultural trends than that offered by the first wave of postmodern theorists. Writers such as Jean Baudrillard (1983; 1985) and Frederic Jameson (1984) had viewed cultural trends with differing degrees of despair and resignation, interpreting the media-saturated age of postmodernity as marking the rise of a uniquely 'depthless' form of cultural existence. In contrast, rather than lamenting the demise of modernity's certainties, authors such as Stuart Hall (1990; 1992a; 1992b) and Angela McRobbie (1994a) have welcomed what they see as the potentially liberating dislocation of identity positions that has accompanied the profound uncertainties of the 'postmodern' environment. For these writers, inscribed within modernity's claims to order and progress there had always been an oppressive apparatus of subordination and control which worked to marginalize, suppress and silence a range of dissenting voices. Amid the instability and uncertainty of postmodernity, on the other hand, there have opened up a greater range of spaces through which these formerly subjugated positions can make themselves heard. In a context where traditional assumptions have been steadily destabilized, a new range of fragmented identities have come into view, promising greater prominence and empowerment to groups once confined to the periphery of cultural systems. Theorists of gender, ethnicity and sexuality, therefore, have all been keen to explore the new dimensions of cultural hybridity that have sprouted through the fissures and disjunctions of postmodernity. However, perhaps it is in youth subcultures such as jungle, with its unstable fusion of fragmented and contradictory reference points, that this 'decentring' (Hall, 1987) of identity has been most readily apparent.

A Lost Generation? Youth in the Age of Uncertainty

The notion that the late eighties and early nineties marked the birth of a new postmodern (even post-historical) epoch can be seen, in some respects, as unduly premature and grandiose. Few of the trends identified as 'postmodern' were entirely unprecedented or unique to the late twentieth century, while any change in the form and fabric of contemporary life was inevitably uneven and incomplete rather than uniform and universal. Nevertheless, although postmodern perspectives may overstate and embroider the character of societal change, they can still be helpful in highlighting the general trajectory of trends and developments. Postmodern approaches have, for example, been especially productive in illuminating processes such as the impact of a rapidly expanding mass media, the erosion of traditional boundaries between different areas of social, economic and cultural life, and the declining confidence in traditionally accepted belief systems. In some respects the trends highlighted by post-modern theorists hold promise and are occasion for optimism. The crumbling of established cultural hierarchies and the 'dislocation' of identity positions may have 'loosened' social frontiers, allowing a range of previously marginalized and excluded voices to come to the fore. Yet the greater measure of instability and cultural fluidity that characterized the closing decades of the century was not without cost. A cost, moreover, which weighed especially heavily on the lives of the young.

For many commentators the philosophical and cultural instabilities of postmodernism were matched by a new economic insecurity in which 'traditional' economies based on large-scale manufacturing for mass markets had gradually disappeared. In their place new, 'post-Fordist' economies were seen as emerging (Murray, 1989). Here, processes of consumption became more central to economic life, bringing a growth of employment in the service and technology sectors and the rise of more specialized markets. In turn, these shifts demanded more flexible relationships to production, the term 'McJobs' (from the McDonald's chain of hamburger restaurants) being coined to denote the growth of employment that was often part-time or temporary and generally low-paid. In these terms, therefore, labour markets were characterized by a growing polarization between professional and multi-skilled workers on one hand and, on the other, an army of low-paid service workers in much less assured part-time and casual employment.[7]

Again, the scope of this study does not allow for a thorough analysis of how far the economic changes of the eighties and nineties amounted to the rise of a new 'post-Fordist' era.[8] Yet the trends outlined above were especially tangible in the lives of young people. In chapter 11 we saw how, since the seventies, industrial restructuring and automation brought a major decline in youth employment and an increase in numbers of young people in education and training schemes. Many also found themselves in the burgeoning number of 'McJobs' as economic shifts brought a postponement of transition into full-time, permanent employment. Overall, young people's futures began to look much less secure. By the mid-nineties the pace of technological change and greater economic instability had made it more difficult to predict young people's occupational biographies with any certainty (Evans and Heinz, 1994). Even youngsters in possession of skills and qualifications felt less confident about their future, academic credentials no longer representing a reliable passport to a permanent career and material rewards. With traditional certainties disrupted and undermined, youngsters' life choices seemed to carry a much greater degree of risk.[9]

During the eighties the downward drift in youngsters' earnings that followed the collapse of the youth labour market was compounded by government moves towards the deregulation of youth employment. In 1986, in the belief that youngsters were being priced out of jobs, the government removed young people from the protection of Wages Councils that had set minimum rates of pay in industries where trade union organization was traditionally weak. Three years later this was followed by the repeal of much of the protective legislation that had restricted young people's hours and conditions of work. To a degree these measures may have prevented further rises in the level of youth unemployment, yet this was at the expense of further undermining young people's rates of pay. During the eighties, therefore, a combination of factors conspired to significantly reduce young workers' earnings, both in real terms and as a proportion of adult pay.[10] As a result many youngsters became increasingly dependent on both the welfare state and (especially after most sixteen- and seventeen-year-olds lost their entitlement to Social Security benefits in 1988)[11] their parents. Even those in higher education were affected by these shifts, students increasingly drawn into casual work by reductions in the value of other sources of their income and the withdrawal of their entitlement to most Social Security and housing benefits during the early nineties (see table 13.1).

As a consequence of these developments retailers' and manufacturers' obsession with youth gradually faded. In Britain during the eighties and nineties youth subcultures were as visible as they had been in the early sixties, yet the commercial youth market had begun to be eclipsed by new growth areas – the fashion, film and music industries all beginning to realign to the consumer appetites of 'empty-nesters' and the 'thirty-something' generation. Rather than the 'swinging teenager', then, it was the image of the more mature and cosmopolitan 'yuppie' that captured the mood of the eighties' and nineties' 'good times'. This shift also registered in the modes of address of media forms that had formerly been geared to a youth audience. By the late eighties the television, film, music and adver-

Table 13.1 Average real annual income of students in higher education[a]

Source of income	£ adjusted to 1992/93 prices		
	1986/87	*1988/89*	*1992/93*
Grants/awards	1,604	1,592	1,715
Parental contributions	1,757	1,573	1,277
Earnings	138	240	230
Loans/overdrafts	141	139	147
Other income	372	527	293
All sources	4,010	4,071	3,662

[a] Students aged under twenty-six at the start of their course.
Source: Central Statistical Office, 1995, *Social Trends No. 25 1995*, London: HMSO, Table 3.30, p. 60.

tising industries were gearing themselves less to specific generational categories than to particular 'mind-sets' and attitudes. In its approach to programming the satellite music channel MTV, for example, used 'youth' less to denote a particular age-group than as a description of a distinctive set of attitudes and styles of viewing behaviour (Frith, 1993). In these terms definitions of 'youth' were coming to be distinguished not by generational age, but by a particular set of lifestyle choices and consumption practices – taste rather than age coming to be the defining feature of 'youth' culture.

By the eighties and nineties, therefore, the very term 'teenager' had come to sound strangely dated and anachronistic. Always more than a simple descriptive noun, the 'teenager' had been an ideological terrain on which particular definitions of post-war change – embracing notions of growth, consensus and classlessness – had been constructed. As these definitions collapsed, the 'teenager' began to disappear from view. In its place a more ambiguous, even bleak, set of representations began to come to the fore, emblematic of an age which seemed to be marked by a general mood of instability and doubt.

From *Generation X* to *Generation X*: Shifting Representations of Youth

In 1945 British society had entered peacetime full of hope and expectation for the future. In media coverage and political debate the imagery of youth figured as a torchbearer of this optimism, young people seen as a vibrant and invigorating social force that would boldly lead the way into a new age of prosperity and dynamic growth. This optimism seemed to be justified by the economic and social trends that characterized the lives of British youngsters during the fifties and much of the sixties. Buoyant levels of youth employment provided for a high measure of disposable income among the young and a new 'teenage' lifestyle dominated by consumption and pleasure seemed to come into view. Doubts were certainly raised by the series of moral panics about young people's behaviour that punctuated the period. Overall, however, the mood was upbeat, the character of the times captured by social researchers Charles Hamblett and Jane Deverson in their book *Generation X* (1964). From their interviews with an array of sixties' youngsters Hamblett and Deverson detected feelings of vulnerability and diffidence, yet on the whole they were impressed by what they found. Young people, they argued, were bravely facing the problems thrown up by a period of rapid change and development. Sixties' youth, the authors concluded, was a generation that could be trusted with the future and would rise to the challenge of their allotted task – 'to guide the human race through the final and crucial decades of this explosive century' (Hamblett and Deverson, 1964, p. 8).

By the closing years of the century, however, the clear-eyed confidence of the early sixties had dissolved into a sense of hesitant uncertainty. Although young people were still occasionally championed in media and political comment, this enthusiasm sounded distinctly forced compared with that of earlier decades. Images of 'affluent youth' were, for example, clearly evident amid the eighties' discourses of 'enterprise' and 'consumer empowerment' (see chapter 11), yet even here 'youth' really made no more than a cameo appearance. Compared with the ubiquitous presence that images of 'youth as fun' had held within the ideas of dynamism and prosperity which dominated during the fifties and sixties, representations of youth were relatively marginal to the rhetoric of the eighties' 'boom'. Indeed, by the early nineties any concept of the teenager as the embodiment of hedonistic consumption had become untenable. The commercial market that had provided the motor for the post-war 'teenage revolution' had been undercut by a combination of the demographic contraction of the youth population, growing levels of youth unemployment and a widening gap between youth and adult rates of pay.

The growing sense of uncertainty and malaise in young people's lives found stylistic expression in the 'grunge' look that took shape in the late eighties. In 1987 white rock music in America was revitalized by the loud and distorted guitars of several bands associated with the Seattle-based record label Sub Pop. The angstful rock of groups like Mudhoney, Soundgarden, Pearl Jam and Nirvana seemed to articulate the sensibilities of young, college-educated, white men who had become disillusioned with traditional goals and career aspirations. This disaffection took material form in a vogue for long, unkempt hair, limp flannel shirts and grubby-looking jeans – a style that began in America but which quickly found resonance in youth subcultures across the globe. The grunge style, then, seemed to testify to a sense of indifference among many youngsters, their detachment born of a social and economic insecurity that had come to define the life experiences of many young people.

From Richard Linklater's (1991) film of the same name the term 'slackers' was coined to denote post-baby-boom youngsters who were over-educated for the employment opportunities available to them and who had retreated into a listless lifestyle of casual jobs and capricious leisure.[12] The narrative of *Slackers* proceeded through a series of accidental encounters between young characters in Austin, Texas, the film creating the vision of youngsters leading aimless, disconnected lives saturated by the images and products of the mass media.[13] In this respect the film not only captured the plight of an American youth that had become alienated from traditional norms and values, but also tapped into the feelings of young people around the world, striking a chord with audiences who saw the film as articulating their own experiences and feelings of estrangement from any guiding purpose or set of long-term objectives.[14] Therefore, although grunge and slacker style were originally American phenomena, they were taken up by many British youngsters who saw in them a meaningful response to the social and economic situations with which they were confronted.

Alongside the slacker and grunge scenes the term 'Generation X' was resurrected in the title of Douglas Coupland's (1992) novel dealing with a new generation of anomic and nihilistic youngsters. Coupland's 'Generation X' were quirky characters and, born in the early to mid-sixties, they were actually quite mature. Nevertheless the phrase 'Generation X' caught the public imagination and the name was increasingly used to denote a younger cohort of underemployed juveniles leading an apathetic and dispirited existence (Acland, 1995, pp. 145–6). Films such as *River's*

Edge (dir. Tim Hunter, 1986) and *Kids* (dir. Larry Clark, 1995) developed the motif, painting a picture of an adolescence that, while not necessarily depraved, was desolate and alienated. Though these texts were American they found their equivalent in British novels such as Irvine Welsh's *Trainspotting* (1993, released as a film directed by Danny Boyle in 1995) and John King's *The Football Factory* (1996), both books foregrounding a theme of bleak and meaningless young lives. These depictions, then, contrasted markedly with Hamblett and Deverson's original, more optimistic, caricature of Generation X. Thirty years later the term had acquired much more ambivalent, even pessimistic, connotations – reflecting both the changed social situation facing young people and the rise of official and public perceptions of youth that were palpably more negative than those of earlier decades.

'Something Wicked This Way Comes'? Authoritarianism Revisited

During the late eighties and early nineties a vague sense of national decline steadily cohered around unease at levels of juvenile crime and a belief that the morality of young people was somehow less principled than that of earlier generations. The period saw a succession of moral panics around the youth spectacle – with illicit drug use, urban violence, deviant sub-cultures, and the influence of violent media all being cited as chilling testimony to the moral bankruptcy of a large section of British youth (see figure 13.1). Indeed, according to Angela McRobbie (1994b, p. 211), during the closing decades of the twentieth century the turnover of such moral panics rapidly accelerated, these episodes becoming a non-stop procession on which the media projected the political issues of the day.

In the early nineties concerns about the behaviour and morality of young people were given added impetus by two horrific murders. In 1993 four people, all in their teens and twenties, were convicted of the murder of Suzanne Capper, a sixteen-year-old girl who had been doused in petrol and set on fire after being held captive and tortured for six days in a house in north Manchester. In the same year, two-year-old James Bulger was found dead on a railway line after being abducted and beaten by two ten-year-olds from Merseyside. In both cases suggestions were made that the violent content of certain videos had been an important influence on the behaviour of the killers. There was, however, little proof to substantiate these claims. Indeed, evidence that violent or pornographic media can incite young people to commit crime remains inconsistent and contradictory. Nevertheless, in 1994 the government chose to introduce greater restrictions on the availability of violent videos. This further strengthened controls that had already become some of the toughest in Europe after the introduction of the 1984 Video Recordings Act in the wake of an earlier moral panic around the links between video violence and juvenile crime.[15]

The shocking features of the Capper and Bulger murders, coupled with the youth of the killers, seemed to testify to a new immorality among the young, fears that were compounded by a growing apprehension that Britain was falling victim to a crime-wave perpetrated by a hard-core of persistent young offenders. In 1993 a chorus of calls for a shake-up of the

Figure 13.1 The growing array of moral panics surrounding delinquent youth, *Daily Mirror*, 13 July 1988

juvenile justice system followed reports that a large proportion of crime (especially car crime and burglary) was perpetrated by a small group of youngsters who repeatedly offended. In February the Association of Metropolitan Authorities reported that juvenile crime rates were being boosted by the criminal records of a hard-core of young offenders, a picture seemingly substantiated by the police publication of the criminal records of children dubbed 'Ratboy' and 'Spiderboy' – these young teenagers apparently representing 'one-boy crime waves'. The Home Secretary, Kenneth Clarke, responded with a resolute pledge to deal with the problem of 'nasty, persistent juvenile little offenders' (*Guardian*, 22 February 1993). In this stand, which marked a reaffirmation of punitive approaches to youth crime, Clarke was following the lead of Prime Minister John Major who, in an earlier interview with the *Mail on Sunday*, had announced a new 'crusade against crime' and had called upon society 'to condemn a little more and understand a little less' (21 February 1993). Nor was the government alone in this crusade. The Labour Party also began to abandon its usual emphasis on the social causes of crime. Tony Blair (then Shadow Home Secretary) spoke of a 'moral vacuum' in Britain and laid stress on the need for a greater sense of individual duty and responsibility, which his successor, Jack Straw, maintained in Labour's new appeal to 'traditional' moral values.[16] Indeed, by the mid-nineties Straw seemed to be locked into a struggle with his opposite number, Michael Howard, each vying to take the toughest stand against juvenile crime.

These calls for more determined measures to deal with youth crime followed a period of relative liberalization in the juvenile justice system during the late eighties. William Whitelaw's 'short, sharp shock' experiment of 1981 had proved an embarrassing penal failure. Home Office research found that the disciplinarian detention regimes had done nothing to reduce offending on release and had registered no discernible deterrent effect on rates of youth crime generally.[17] As a consequence these regimes were quietly phased out in 1986. Magistrates also seemed to have lost confidence in Detention Centres, with the number of Detention Centre Orders falling from 13,000 in 1980 to 8,000 in 1987, the sentence finally being abolished in the 1988 Criminal Justice Act. During the late eighties and early nineties more effort went into diverting juveniles away from both custody and the court process. The period saw a large increase in the use of police cautioning, together with a greater use of community penalties by the courts. As a result 1990 saw just 1,700 custodial sentences passed on juveniles in England and Wales, the lowest figure since 1965. The 1991 Criminal Justice Act (implemented in 1992) made further significant changes to the treatment of juvenile offenders, including a new sentencing framework in which it was envisaged that the practice of remanding fifteen- and sixteen-year-olds to prison institutions would end by the middle of the decade, replaced by the provision of local authority secure accommodation.

However, amid 1993's concerns about persistent juvenile offenders, the 1991 Act became subject to criticism. Judges and police officers argued that the Act had limited the court's power to pronounce custodial sentences on the small number of school-age children who were thought to be responsible for a high proportion of urban crime. The Home Secretary's response came with the proposal of a new 'Secure Training Order', to be passed by the court on twelve- to fifteen-year-old seriously persistent offenders. The extensive Criminal Justice and Public Order Act followed in 1994. As well as introducing measures to control acid house parties and New Age travellers, the 1994 Act provided for a new kind of privately run residential institution, a 'Secure Training Centre', to which the court could sentence persistent young offenders for periods of between six months and two years. Additionally, the Act extended the powers of the court to detain youngsters aged between ten and thirteen and increased the maximum sentence in a young offender institution for fifteen- to seventeen-year-olds from one to two years. Furthermore, the 1994 Act enabled the imposition of curfew orders accompanied by electronic monitoring (known as 'tagging'), to be introduced area by area following pilot trials.

Progress at implementing the terms of the 1994 Act, however, was slow. Two years later the Home Office confirmed that building had still not commenced on the five promised Secure Training Centres. Nevertheless, the Home Secretary's commitment to firm remedies to juvenile crime remained unshaken, with discussion of further measures that included a curfew order enforced by electronic tagging for children as young as ten (*Guardian*, 12 November 1996). This 'new punitivism' also made itself felt in relation to older age groups. In December 1995 Home Office and Ministry of Defence officials agreed on arrangements whereby selected young offenders would complete the last six months of their sentence at the Colchester Military Corrective Training Centre in Essex, an idea inspired by the 'high impact incarceration programmes' – more commonly referred to as 'boot camps' – which began operation in many American states during the early eighties. The introduction of the Colchester scheme was delayed by legal regulations that prevented the military from running a civilian prison, yet a 'boot camp' run along less overtly military lines was established at Thorn Cross Young Offenders' Institution in Cheshire.

In their highly structured regimen of physical exercise, drill and manual labour the nineties' 'boot camps' bore an uncanny resemblance to the 'short, sharp shock' institutions that had been an ignominious failure during the early eighties. Indeed, at the time of writing (1997) it seems highly unlikely that any expansion of the 'boot camp' programme will be any more successful in dealing with the problem of youth crime. In fact, rather than a genuine attempt to reduce levels of delinquency, the turn to more punitive systems of juvenile justice may have been a cynical ploy by politicians of both major parties who, in the run-up to the 1997 general election, were anxious to court the electorate by demonstrating their tough stand on issues of law and order. Experience shows, however, that all forms of institutional custody or care for young offenders have limited deterrent effect and result in high rates of recidivism. For example, research into the effectiveness of Approved Schools (renamed Community Homes with Education in 1969) and Secure Units during the seventies indicated that they often increased rather than reduced the likelihood of reoffending.[18] To their critics, then, both Secure Training Centres and 'boot camps' looked like misguided, ineffective and very costly measures that would simply repeat the mistakes of the sixties, seventies and early eighties.

Throughout the early nineties disagreement and confusion surrounded the scale of youth crime in Britain. Contrary to the popular impression that the country faced an explosion in juvenile delinquency many indices actually pointed to a fall in levels of juvenile crime during the late eighties and early nineties. This period, for example, saw a sharp fall in the number of juveniles known to be committing offences. After reaching a peak in 1985, the number of offenders aged under eighteen convicted or formally cautioned began to decline markedly. Between 1980 and 1990 the number of youngsters found guilty or cautioned for indictable offences fell by 37 per cent, from 175,000 to 110,900, a decline that far outstripped the 25 per cent fall in the number of juveniles in the general population. Moreover, the proportion of crime known to be committed by juveniles fell from 32 per cent in 1980 to 22 per cent in 1990 (Prison Reform Trust, 1993, pp. 1–2).[19] Furthermore, the kind of offences committed by youngsters were, for the most part, not especially serious – with over half of all crimes committed by juveniles in 1990 being offences of theft or the handling of stolen goods.

Of course, crime statistics should always be treated with a high measure of caution. By themselves these figures did not disprove anecdotal evidence from police officers and judges that levels of youth crime were at an unprecedented high. It is theoretically possible, for example, that juvenile offenders were responsible for a large number of the many crimes that went unreported, together with many of those that the police were unable to clear up. However, it is difficult to explain why crime committed by juveniles should have been disproportionately prone to under-reporting, or especially difficult for the police to solve. Overall, then, it seems the statistical evidence pointed to a genuine fall in the numbers of juvenile offenders in Britain in the late eighties and early nineties. Contrary to media comment and the perceptions of the public, therefore, the juvenile justice policies of this period may have actually enjoyed a significant measure of success – the policy of diversion from prosecution and custody coinciding with a substantial reduction both in the rate of juvenile offending and in expenditure on juvenile custody (Prison Reform Trust, 1993, p. 7).

These statistics also stood as an important, though seldom cited, counterweight to claims that British society was teetering on the edge of social disintegration. If media comment and political discussion during the mid-nineties were to be believed, an epidemic of depravity and wickedness had broken out among British youngsters. In 1996 this pessimism cohered around events at the Ridings school in Halifax. Near anarchy seemed to reign at the Ridings, the school being forced to close temporarily after teachers refused to teach sixty pupils they considered to be unmanageably rowdy and disruptive. In public debate the Ridings was cited as symptomatic of a more general collapse of morality among young people, a shocking testament to Britain's steady social and cultural decline over the post-war period.

Certainly, post-war delinquency and crime have not been spurious media inventions. In Britain's declining inner cities and deprived housing estates juvenile crime has undoubtedly represented a genuine problem throughout the post-war period. Yet media coverage of, and political responses to, delinquency have invariably both exaggerated its scale and distorted the nature of its causes. Rather than marking a descent into moral turpitude, empirical evidence suggests that levels of juvenile crime have always been closely entwined with economic and social disadvantage in terms of family background, unemployment and housing (Stewart and Stewart, 1993). Moreover, the nineties' alarm about the morality of youth should be contextualized as the latest cycle in a long history of moral panics in which, since the nineteenth century, levels of delinquency and crime have been misrepresented as a new and radical departure from the stable traditions of the 'British way of life'.[20] These recurring appeals to a mythical golden age of peace and rectitude are best seen as a bewildered response to periods of intense social and cultural transformation – a quest for certainty and order at times of rapid change and development. As interpretations of historical shifts in the social and cultural climate, however, such responses are misleading and dangerously retrograde. In their tendency to evoke 'permissiveness' and moral laxity as explanations of the behaviour of young offenders these accounts draw attention away from the fundamental roots of juvenile crime and delinquency – the material circumstances of social deprivation that have remained pronounced features of life in contemporary Britain.

Moreover, while it is impossible to quantify or measure the nature of morality, there were indications that in the late twentieth century Britain had, in some respects at least, actually become a much more principled and tolerant society. For example, by the mid-nineties moves towards greater equality in gender relations were evident and problems such as racism, homophobia and child abuse were increasingly being confronted.[21] Environmental and ecological issues had also become firmly established on the political agenda and, especially among young people, groups opposing all kinds of discrimination and prejudice had proliferated. At the end of the twentieth century, therefore, the morality of British youth should be occasion for optimism rather than pessimism. Indeed, the degree of many young people's moral integrity was remarkable given that, by the end of the nineties, they were faced by an economic situation of unprecedented insecurity and, in the 1994 Criminal Justice Act, a set of social and cultural controls that were the most comprehensive and authoritarian since 1945.

Notes

1   Accessible and authoritative introductions to postmodern theory and its associated debates can be found in E. Ann Kaplan (ed.), 1988, *Postmodernism and its Discontents*, London: Verso; Stephen Best and Douglas Kellner, 1993, *Postmodern Theory: Critical Interrogations*, Basingstoke: Macmillan; Madan Sarup, 1993, *An Introductory Guide to Post-Structuralism and Postmodernism*,

London: Harvester Wheatsheaf; Dominic Strinati, 1995, *An Introduction to Theories of Popular Culture*, London: Routledge, pp. 221–46.

2 Other theorists, however, have judged the 'postmodern' traits of pop videos more cautiously. Andrew Goodwin, for example, argues that although many pop videos have clearly evidenced prominent elements of eclecticism, inter-textuality and pastiche, this does not, of itself, distinguish them as intrinsically postmodern. See Andrew Goodwin, 1991, 'Popular music and postmodern theory', *Cultural Studies*, vol. 5, no. 2, pp. 174–90.

3 See Andy Medhurst, 'Def sentences', *The Listener*, 29 September 1988, pp. 16–17.

4 During the early nineties KLF duo Bill Drummond and Jimmy Cauty became notorious for their increasingly bizarre attempts to satirize and subvert the pop music industry. In 1992, for example, after being adjudged Best British Group in the industry's prestigious Brit Awards, the pair responded by dumping a dead sheep outside the reception. They had originally intended to disembowel the carcass on stage as they accepted their trophy.

5 In the late eighties and early nineties pop music seemed to achieve a new respectability, becoming the topic not only for well-received novels such as Nick Hornby's 1995 *High Fidelity*, London: Victor Gollancz, and Giles Smith, 1995, *Lost in Music*, London: Piccolo, but also the subject-matter of a growing number of courses in universities and other institutions of higher education.

6 For an account of the early development of jungle, and Goldie's rise to the forefront of the genre, see Tim Barr, 1996, 'Concrete Jungle', in Chris Kempster (ed.), *History of House*, London: Sanctuary, pp. 145–54.

7 For an influential interpretation of these labour market transformations see André Gorz, 1982, *Farewell to the Working Class: An Essay on Post-Industrial Socialism*, London: Pluto Press.

8 A detailed overview of debates related to the nature of industrial and economic change in the late twentieth century can be found in John Allen, 1992, 'Post industrialism and post-Fordism', in Stuart Hall and Tony McGrew (eds), *Modernity and Its Futures*, Cambridge: Polity Press, pp. 169–220.

9 Some theorists have seen a lack of certainty and a greater measure of risk as features endemic to life in contemporary western societies. For one of the leading expositions of this position see Ulrich Beck, 1992, *Risk Society: Towards a New Modernity*, London: Sage. For a survey of how these developments may have impacted on the lives of the young see Kenneth Roberts, 1995, *Youth and Employment in Modern Britain*, Oxford: Blackwell, pp. 110–26; Andy Furlong and Fred Cartmel, 1997, *Young People and Social Change: Individualization and Risk in Late Modernity*, Buckingham: Open University Press.

10   See Chris Pond, 1984, 'The generation gap', *New Statesman*, vol. 107, no. 2755, p. 11; D. Byrne, 1987, 'A disposable work force: the youth labour market after the 1986 Wages Act', *Youth and Policy*, no. 20; Kenneth Roberts, 1995, *Youth and Employment in Modern Britain*, Oxford: Oxford University Press, p. 17.

11   Under the terms of the 1988 Social Security Act the government withdrew Income Support for unemployed sixteen- to seventeen-year-olds in an effort to encourage them to be less dependent on state benefits. In return, young-sters were guaranteed a place on youth training schemes, though allowances granted on these programmes were grudging – beginning at £28 for sixteen-year-olds and rising to £35 in the subsequent year.

12   For accounts and discussion of the Generation X/slacker phenomenon see Neil Howe and Bill Straus, 1993, *13th Gen: Abort, Retry, Ignore, Fail?*, New York: Vintage; Douglas Rushkoff, 1994, *The GenX Reader*, New York: Ballantine.

13   An analysis of the film *Slackers* that is both penetrating and engaging can be found in Douglas Kellner, 1995, *Media Culture: Cultural Studies, Identity and Politics Between the Modern and the Postmodern*, London: Routledge, pp. 139–43.

14   This sense of distrust and scepticism among the young brought about a marked change in advertising strategy during the nineties. In the belief that young consumers had become less easily impressed by the hard-sell of tradi-tional campaigns, advertisers increasingly sought to make an impact on young audiences through the use of dark, even shocking, imagery. In 1995, for example, the Leagas Delaney campaign for Pépé jeans deployed jarring images of alienated youth and teenage suicide in an attempt to 'speak the language' of their target audience.

15   For analysis of the moral panic around 'video nasties' during the 1980s see Martin Barker (ed.), 1984, *The Video Nasties: Freedom and Censorship in the Media*, London: Pluto Press.

16   Indicative of the Labour Party's growing attempts to commandeer the rhetoric of the 'law and order' debate was the authoritarian tone taken in their discussion paper *Tackling Youth Crime: Reforming Youth Justice*, published in 1996.

17   See Home Office Young Offender Psychology Unit, 1984, *Tougher Regimes in Detention Centres*, London: HMSO.

18   See New Approaches to Juvenile Crime, 1996, *Creating More Criminals: The Case Against a New 'Secure Training Order' for Juvenile Offenders*, London: New Approaches to Juvenile Crime.

19   In August 1994 figures collated by the Central Statistical Office also suggested that fewer juveniles in England and Wales were committing offences.

According to their statistics the number of youngsters aged between ten and sixteen found guilty of offences or cautioned fell by almost 35 per cent between 1981 and 1992. See Central Statistical Office, 1994, *Social Focus on Children*, London: HMSO.

20   The work of historian Geoffrey Pearson provides the most thorough and insightful analyses of the recurring social anxieties around the issues of juvenile crime and delinquency. See Geoffrey Pearson, 1983, *Hooligan: A History of Respectable Fears*, London: Macmillan; Geoffrey Pearson, 1984, 'Falling standards: a short, sharp history of moral decline', in Martin Barker (ed.), *The Video Nasties*, London: Pluto Press, pp. 88–104; Geoffrey Pearson, 1987, 'Short memories: street violence in the past and in the present', in Eric Moonman (ed.), *The Violent Society*, London: Frank Cass, pp. 13–46.

21   Amid the public debate that cohered around the issue of young people's morality throughout autumn 1996, Martin Jacques was one of the few commentators prepared to question the widely held assumption that a significant decline in moral standards had taken place during the nineties. See his essay 'Decline and fallacy' in the *Guardian*, 9 November 1996.

14 Conclusion: 'Things Can Only Get Better'?

In the second half of the twentieth century the life experiences of British youngsters have been subject to profound transformation. The character of change has, to a large part, been a direct consequence of fundamental shifts in the structure of the labour market. In the three decades after the Second World War buoyant demand for working youngsters' semi- and unskilled labour underpinned an expansion of the commercial youth market and a heightening of young people's profile as a distinct cultural group. Although a degree of anxiety always figured in social responses to young people's patterns of leisure, the apparent affluence of many youngsters allowed representations of youth to become emblematic of economic growth and consumer prosperity. From the mid-seventies, however, this situation was dramatically reconfigured. The series of recessions during the 1980s and early 1990s, combined with the steady decline of manufacturing and the rise of the service sector within western economies, brought wholesale change to the nature of youth employment. Demand for young people's labour – especially that of relatively unqualified school-leavers – declined, as employers reduced labour costs through the downsizing of their workforce and the use of more 'flexible' employment practices (such as the increased use of part-time and temporary workers). The collapse of the youth labour market brought with it not only higher levels of youth unemployment but also a huge increase in the numbers of young people either inducted into government-sponsored training schemes or remaining in full-time education beyond the age of sixteen. It was, however, questionable how far the move towards training and education made a meaningful impact on the employment prospects of most youngsters while the overall economic climate remained depressed and the availability of permanent, full-time employment steadily diminished. Media representations of young people, meanwhile, became tangibly more negative during the eighties and nineties – images of youth becoming more deeply associated with notions of urban decay, rising crime rates and a general decline in national morality.

For many the election, in May 1997, of Tony Blair's Labour government seemed to herald a revival in the nation's social and economic fortunes. Commanding the largest Commons majority since the war, the new administration announced a political programme that embraced a 'mixture of idealism and realism necessary to modernize Britain in the name of economic efficiency and social justice' (*Guardian*, 15 May 1997). Young people, in particular, seemed set to benefit from the new government's intended changes. One of Labour's key election pledges had been the use of a windfall levy on the privatized utilities to finance the release of 250,000 under-twenty-five-year-olds from dependency on welfare benefits. In the Queen's Speech that followed the Labour victory it was announced that youngsters who had been unemployed for over six months were to be presented with four options – a job with a private sector employer (who would receive a financial incentive of £60 a week in return for hiring them); work with a voluntary group for a wage slightly above the level of benefits; full-time study on an approved training course for those without qualifications; or a job with a new 'environmental task force'. Refusal to take up any of these options would, it was anticipated, result in a heavy reduction of welfare benefits.

Labour's plans were welcomed by many commentators, yet there was room to doubt how far the new schemes would make a genuine impact on the plight of many unemployed youngsters. Certainly, some young people would benefit from the new opportunities to move into the world of work. It seemed likely, however, that firms (eager to capitalize on government subsidies) would snap up those youngsters with most employment potential, leaving the remainder to languish in a government 'task force' that made dubious contribution to their long-term employment prospects. Moreover, faced with the choice between benefit sanctions and low-paid work in government employment programmes, it was possible that a hard-core of disenchanted youngsters would opt out of the system altogether – their livelihood instead coming to depend on the informal economy and crime. Overall, therefore, it is unlikely that the early twenty-first century will see a major change in the patterns of youth employment established during the 1980s and 1990s. While youngsters in possession of qualifications and sought-after skills will continue to enjoy access to job opportunities and their material rewards, their less qualified peers are likely to struggle on the margins of the labour market – consigned to government training schemes of questionable value and vulnerable to periods of unemployment.

Trends towards the 'criminalization' of young offenders are also likely to continue. Evidence for rising crime rates during the eighties and nineties was contradictory and inconclusive and there was certainly no real evidence for a wholesale breakdown in social values. Nevertheless, in its 1997 election campaign the Labour Party made a prominent feature of its tough stand on crime. Promising a 'zero tolerance' of delinquency, the new Labour government announced a Crime and Disorder Bill that would introduce a battery of measures to deal with the problem of juvenile crime. A system of 'fast-track punishment' for persistent young offenders would halve the time between arrest and sentencing, while repeat police cautions would be replaced with a single warning that would trigger intervention by a multi-agency Youth Offender Team. Courts were also set to receive new powers of sentencing for juveniles, including the introduction of parental responsibility orders that would require parents of young offenders to attend 'guidance sessions' where they would be held responsible for their children's behaviour. Most controversially, legislation would also abolish the presumption that children aged between ten and thirteen are incapable of telling right from wrong, so moving the burden of proof on criminal responsibility from the prosecution to the defence. The punitive ethos that characterized responses to juvenile crime under the Conservative administrations of the eighties and nineties, therefore, is set to remain a guiding philosophy of the juvenile justice system of the next century.

Existing trends in the fields of youth style and culture are also likely to continue into the next millennium. Dimensions of hybridity and globalization, for example, are certain to remain integral features of the universe of youth style. For example, British dance music during the late nineties continues to be influenced and informed by the practices of quotation and sampling pioneered by the first wave of techno DJs in Detroit during the 1980s. The dance and house music scenes, meanwhile, have steadily fragmented into an ever-widening range of hybrid music genres. The growing linkages between international youth communities and subcultures also looks set to continue apace as developments in media and communications technology, combined with the growth of global marketing, disseminate music, images and fashions around the world with increasing rapidity. In the face of these globalizing influences, however, indigenous musical forms and cultural traditions have been tenacious and will remain a resource in the way young people elaborate their cultural identities. Indeed, in the field of pop music some theorists have recently identified the beginnings of a shift away from Anglo–American music and towards local or regional popular styles (Laing, 1997). Although inroads into the hegemony of Anglo–American pop have been most discernible in the countries of Asia and Europe, it is possible that this trend may become more widely established – European dance music already having made a huge impact on British and American record markets during the 1990s.

For some commentators an upsurge of support for single-issue political movements focused on environmental issues or questions of personal freedom represents one of the most significant recent developments in British youth culture. These movements, many of which lay claim to a 'New Age' world view that presents itself as separate and distinct from orthodox rationalism (Ross, 1992), have been taken as representative of a disintegration of traditional political loyalties and a growing scepticism towards conventional political movements. However, it is doubtful that the rise of groups such as road protesters and animal rights activists represents a qualitative transformation in the political attitudes and beliefs of British youngsters. The single-issue and direct-action movements of the nineties were, for example, prefigured by groups such as CND during the 1950s, the anti-Vietnam War movement in the 1960s and the anti-racist campaigns of the 1970s. Moreover, as Andy Furlong and Fred Cartmel (1997, p. 98) argue, where young people voice support for a political grouping it still tends to be for one of the mainstream political parties and there is little evidence to show any fundamental shift is taking place in patterns of political affiliation among British youth.

In youngsters' lifestyles and leisure practices it is possible that more profound changes are beginning to take shape. During the 1970s and 1980s the bulk of sociological research testified to the important role played by social class as a determinant of young people's tastes in pop music and fashion. Although strong links still exist between social class and young people's styles and social identities, it is possible that a convergence of cultural preferences will gradually occur as young people from all social strata share the experience of an extended period of transition between the world of school and that of work. Nevertheless, while some youth styles may increasingly cut across class boundaries it is unlikely that class divisions will be evacuated from British youth culture in the twenty-first century. Indeed, in some respects social inequalities may become even more pronounced in the realm of young people's lifestyles. Access to leisure will still be determined by the possession of material resources and youngsters on the margins of the job market – either unemployed or channelled into government training schemes – will find themselves less able to participate in a youth culture which has come to revolve around the consumption of commercial goods and entertainments. In short, while Britain remains a society characterized by structural inequalities in the distribution of life chances and material resources these inequalities will continue to be central to our understanding of young people's social and economic experiences.

Outline Chronology

1933 Children and Young Persons Act – reform of juvenile justice system.

1944 Education Act – introduction of tripartite system of universal secondary education.

1947 School-leaving age raised to fifteen.

1948 Criminal Justice Act – introduction of Attendance and Detention Centres. National Service Act – introduction of conscription.

1952 Derek Bentley convicted of murder. *New Musical Express* introduces first singles' chart.

1953 Michael Davies convicted of murder.

1954 Teddy boys identified by the national press.

1955 Mary Quant opens her first boutique. Bill Haley and the Comets reach number one with 'Rock Around the Clock'.

1956 Screenings of *Rock Around the Clock* accompanied by cinema 'riots'. Elvis Presley first enters the charts with 'Heartbreak Hotel'.

1958 'Race riots' in Notting Hill and Nottingham. Harsher regimes introduced to Detention Centres. CND formed.

1959 First 'Mardi Gras' held at Paddington (later reinstituted as the Notting Hill Carnival).

1960 End of conscription. Albermarle Report on the condition of the Youth Service.

1962 The Beatles first enter the charts with 'Love Me Do'.

1963 Robbins Report – recommends expansion of

higher education. Children and Young Persons Act – age of criminal responsibility raised to ten. *Ready, Steady, Go!* launched on ITV. 'Biba' fashion chain established.

1964   Mod 'invasions' of seaside resorts. *Top of the Pops* first screened on the BBC.

1965   The Beatles awarded MBEs.

1966   Twiggy promoted as 'The Face of '66'. *International Times* launched. Radical Students Alliance formed.

1967   Pirate radio outlawed, BBC Radio 1 begins broadcasting. *Oz* launched. LSE sit-in. 'The 14 Hour Technicolour Dream' held at Alexandra Palace. First Grosvenor Square demonstration against the Vietnam War. Rolling Stones drug trial. Skinhead style begins to coalesce. Growing concerns about football violence.

1968   May – student occupation of the Sorbonne in Paris. Student unrest at Essex, Hornsey, Hull and Birmingham.

1969   Children and Young Persons Act – aiming to minimize the criminalization of the young. The Rolling Stones play in Hyde Park. First Isle of Wight Festival.

1970   Jimi Hendrix appears at the Isle of Wight Festival. *Sounds* launched. Garden House trial.

1971   The voting age lowered from twenty-one to eighteen. First Glastonbury Fayre held. Misuse of Drugs Act. *Oz* trial. *A Clockwork Orange* released.

1972   School-leaving age raised to sixteen. Windsor Free Festival.

1974   Red Lion Square demonstration. Spiked fences introduced to Old Trafford football ground. First Stonehenge People's Free Festival.

1975   The Bay City Rollers reach number one with 'Bye, Bye Baby'. Bob

Marley first enters British charts with 'No Woman No Cry'.

1976   Rock Against Racism established. Sex Pistols appear on Thames TV's *Today* programme.

1977   Sex Pistols' single 'God Save the Queen' reaches number two in the year of the Queen's Jubilee. Anti-Nazi League launched.

1978   *Saturday Night Fever* released. Sex Pistols split up in America. Two-Tone Records formed by Jerry Dammers. Anti-Nazi League carnival in Victoria Park. Youth Opportunities Programme introduced.

1979   'The First Futurama Science Fiction Festival'. Factory Records founded. New romantics emerge in London club scene. Southall riot.

1980   'Short, sharp, shock' regimes introduced to Detention Centres. St Paul's riot, Bristol.

1981   'Oi' emerges as a more proletarian version of punk. Riots in Brixton and Toxteth. 'SUS' laws repealed. Bob Marley dies. Peace camp established at Greenham Common. MTV launched. Youth Training Scheme introduced.

1982   The Haçienda opened in Manchester. Criminal Justice Act – greater powers delivered to juvenile court magistrates.

1983   Crass release 'How Does It Feel (To Be the Mother of a Thousand Dead)?' ZTT records founded.

1984   Frankie Goes to Hollywood score three number one hits. Video Recordings Act follows concerns about the influence of 'video nasties' on young people.

1985   Heysel Stadium disaster at European Cup Final held in Brussels. Football casuals come to the fore. 'Madchester' and the scally scene. Live Aid. Peace Convoy and 'Battle of the Beanfield'. Riots in Brixton, Handsworth and Broadwater Farm.

1986   Levi's 501 'Launderette' advertising campaign. Public Order Act.. Undercover police operations against football hooliganism. Young people removed from the protection of Wages Councils. 'Short, sharp shock' regimes in Detention Centres phased out. Youth Training Scheme extended into a two-year programme.

1987   Ibiza emerges as the hub of a dance culture soon recreated in British clubs such as Shoom and Spectrum.

1988   Series of 'rural disorders' involving 'lager louts'. 'Orbital' parties and the second 'Summer of Love'. Most sixteen- to seventeen-year-olds lose their entitlement to Social Security benefits.

1989   Freedom to Party campaign launched.

1990   Entertainments (Increased Penalties) Act – the 'Acid House Bill'. 'Poll tax riot' in Trafalgar Square. Students lose their entitlement to housing benefit. Student loans introduced and value of maintenance grants is frozen.

1991   Disorders in Cardiff, Birmingham, Oxford, Tyneside and Greater Manchester. Legislation introduced to deal with 'joy-riding'.

1992   Dongas Tribe campaign against M3 extension at Twyford Down. Exodus Collective formed in Luton. Free festival at Castlemorton Common.

1993   James Bulger murdered.

1994   Criminal Justice and Public Order Act.

1995   Leah Betts dies after taking ecstasy. Tribal Gathering '95. Headmaster Philip Lawrence murdered.

1996   The Spice Girls reach number one with 'Wannabe'. The Ridings school in Halifax temporarily closes.

Bibliography

There exists an ever-growing wealth of material dealing with the issues of youth and youth culture in Britain since 1945 and only a brief summary of the available texts can be provided here. For further reading related to more specific topics readers should consult the notes provided in the relevant chapters of this book.

Geoffrey Pearson offers an excellent account of youth culture in Britain prior to 1945 and the social responses it elicited in *Hooligan: A History of Respectable Fears* (Macmillan, London, 1983). The growth of the commercial youth market between the wars is considered in some detail in David Fowler's *The First Teenagers: The Lifestyle of Young Wage-Earners in Interwar Britain* (Woburn, London, 1995). Informed and very readable overviews of developments in the decades immediately following the Second World War are provided by both John Springhall's *Coming of Age: Adolescence in Britain, 1860–1960* (Gill and Macmillan, Dublin, 1980) and John Davis's *Youth and the Condition of Britain: Images of Adolescent Conflict* (Athlone, London, 1990).

Mike Brake's *Comparative Youth Culture* (Routledge and Kegan Paul, London, 1985) remains an excellent account of the development of youth subcultures in modern Britain and also provides a thorough critique of various sociological interpretations of their significance. Brake's survey is nicely complemented by Iain Chambers' cultural history of British pop music, *Urban Rhythms: Pop Music and Popular Culture* (Macmillan, Basingstoke, 1985). Alternatively, Simon Frith's *Sound Effects: Youth, Leisure and the Politics of Rock'n'Roll* (Constable, London, 1983) also offers an insightful exploration of the area. Stanley Cohen's *Folk Devils and Moral Panics: The Creation of the Mods and Rockers* (Paladin, St Albans, 1973) is an enduring classic of sociological analysis, while the revised (1980) edition includes a new introduction which gives an effective critique of developments in the sociological analysis of youth during the 1970s.

A visually attractive, if necessarily simplified, survey of post-war subcultural style is provided by Ted Polhemus in *Streetstyle: From Sidewalk to Catwalk* (Thames and Hudson, London, 1994) while an extensive anthology of theoretical writings on the nature and significance of youth subcultures can be found in Ken Gelder and Sarah Thornton (eds), *The Subcultures Reader* (Routledge, London, 1997).

A thorough history of the counter-culture in the sixties exists in Elizabeth Nelson's *The British Counter-Culture, 1966–73: A Study of the Underground Press* (Macmillan, London, 1989), while developments since the early seventies are covered in depth by George McKay in *Senseless Acts of Beauty: Cultures of Resistance Since the Sixties* (London, Verso, 1996). The most meticulous history of black popular music and youth culture can be found in Dick Hebdige's *Cut'n'Mix: Culture, Identity and Caribbean Music* (Methuen, London 1987), while Paul Gilroy provides a penetrating analysis of the politics of 'race' during the post-war period in *'There Ain't No Black in the Union Jack': The Cultural Politics of Race and Nation* (Hutchinson, London, 1987). Angela McRobbie's output on young women and contemporary cultural politics has been prolific and the recent anthologies of her writing (*Feminism and Youth Culture: From Jackie to Just Seventeen*, Macmillan, London, 1991; *Postmodernism and Popular Culture*, Routledge, London, 1994) map out the field with perception and clarity.

In *The Politics of Juvenile Crime* (Sage, London, 1988) John Pitts offers a solid history of the post-war changes taking place in the juvenile justice system, while Kenneth Roberts's (1996) survey of developments in patterns of youth employment is both accessible and invaluable.

Texts dealing with shifts in the nature of youth culture and the representation of youth during the late 1980s and 1990s are appearing with increasing rapidity. To date the best analyses are provided in Steve Redhead's *The End of the Century Party: Youth and Pop Towards 2000* (Manchester University Press, Manchester, 1990), his edited collection *Rave Off: Politics and Deviance in Contemporary Youth Culture* (Avebury, Aldershot, 1993) and Sarah Thornton's *Club Cultures: Music, Media and Subcultural Capital* (Polity Press, London, 1995).

References

The following list includes sources cited in the text and in the Bibliography.

Abrams, M., 1959. *The Teenage Consumer*, London: Press Exchange.
—— 1961. *Teenage Consumer Spending in 1959*, London: Press Exchange.
—— 1964. *The Newspaper Reading Public of Tomorrow*, London: Odhams.
Abrams, Philip and Alan Little, 1965. 'The young activist in British politics', *British Journal of Sociology*, vol. 16, pp. 315–33.
Acland, Charles R., 1995. *Youth, Murder, Spectacle: The Cultural Politics of 'Youth in Crisis'*, Oxford: Westview.
Ashton, D. N. and M. Maguire, 1983. *The Vanishing Youth Labour Market*, Occasional Paper 3, London: Youthaid.
—— and M. Spillsbury, 1989. *Restructuring the Labour Market: The Implications for Youth*, London: Macmillan.
Back, Les, 1994. 'The "White Negro" revisited: race and masculinities in South London', in A. Cornwall and N. Lindisfarne (eds), *Dislocating Masculinity: Comparative Ethnographies*, London: Routledge, pp. 172–83.
—— 1996. *New Ethnicities and Urban Culture: Racisms and Multiculture in Young Lives*, London: UCL.
Baudrillard, Jean, 1983. *Simulations*, New York: Semiotext.
—— 1985. 'The ecstasy of communication', in Hal Foster (ed.), *Post-Modern Culture*, London: Pluto Press, pp. 126–35.
Bhabha, Homi (ed.), 1990. *Narrating the Nation*, London: Routledge.
Blackstone, Tessa, Kathleen Gales, Roger Hadley and Wyn Lewis, 1970. *Students in Conflict: LSE in 1967*, London: Weidenfeld and Nicolson.
Bogdanor, Vernon and Robert Skidelsky (eds), 1970. *The Age of Affluence, 1951–64*, London: Macmillan.
Bourdieu, Pierre, 1984. *Distinction*, London: Routledge and Kegan Paul.
Brake, Mike, 1980. *The Sociology of Youth Culture and Subcultures*, London: Routledge and Kegan Paul.
—— 1985. *Comparative Youth Culture*, London: Routledge and Kegan Paul.

British Medical Association, 1961. *The Adolescent: Observations Arising from Discussion Among Members of the British Medical Association*, London: BMA.

Cashmore, Ernest, 1984. *No Future*, London: Heinemann.

Chambers, Iain, 1985. *Urban Rhythms: Pop Music and Popular Culture*, Basingstoke: Macmillan.

Children's Society, 1994. *Out of Site, Out of Mind*, London: Children's Society.

Clarke, John, 1973. 'The three R's – repression, rescue and rehabilitation: ideologies of control for working class youth', CCCS Occasional Paper no. 41, University of Birmingham.

—— and Tony Jefferson, 1976. 'Working class youth cultures', in Geoff Mungham and Geoff Pearson (eds), *Working Class Youth Culture*, London: Routledge and Kegan Paul, pp. 138–58.

——, Stuart Hall, Tony Jefferson and Brian Roberts, 1976. 'Subcultures, cultures and class: a theoretical overview', in Stuart Hall and Tony Jefferson (eds), *Resistance Through Rituals: Youth Subcultures in Post-War Britain*, London: Hutchinson, pp. 9–74.

Cochraine, Raymond and Michael Billig, 1984. 'I'm not National Front myself but . . .', *New Society*, vol. 68, no. 1121, 17 May, pp. 255–8.

Cohen, Phil, 1972. 'Subcultural conflict and working class community', *Working Papers in Cultural Studies*, no. 2, pp. 4–51.

—— 1981. 'Policing the working class city', in Mike Fitzgerald, Gregor McLennan and Jennie Pawson (eds), *Crime and Society: History and Theory*, London: Routledge and Kegan Paul.

Cohen, Stanley, 1973. *Folk Devils and Moral Panics: The Creation of the Mods and Rockers*, St Albans: Paladin.

—— and Alan Waton, 1971. 'The typical student?', *New Society*, vol. 18, no. 475, 4 November, pp. 873–5.

Connor, Steven, 1989. *Postmodernist Culture: An Introduction to Theories of the Contemporary*, Oxford: Blackwell.

Cosgrove, Stuart, 1989. 'Acid enterprise', *New Statesman and Society*, vol. 2, no. 71, pp. 38–9.

Coupland, Douglas, 1992. *Generation X: Tales for an Accelerated Culture*, London: Abacus.

Daniel, Susie and Pete McGuire, (eds), 1972. *The Paint House: Words from an East End Gang*, Harmondsworth: Penguin.

Davis, John, 1990. *Youth and the Condition of Britain: Images of Adolescent Conflict*, London: Athlone.

Douglas, J. W. B., 1964. *The Home and the School: A Study of Ability and Attainment in the Classroom*, London: Macgibbon.

Downes, David, 1966. *The Delinquent Solution*, London: Routledge and Kegan Paul.

Ehrenreich, Barbara, Elizabeth Hess and Gloria Jacobs, 1987. 'Beatlemania: girls just want to have fun', in Barbara Ehrenreich, Elizabeth Hess and Gloria Jacobs (eds), *Re-Making Love: The Feminization of Sex*, London: Virago, pp. 10–38.

Evans, Karen and Walter Heinz (eds), 1994. *Becoming Adults in England and Germany*, London: Anglo-German Foundation.

Ferguson, Ken and Sylvia Ferguson, 1965. *Television Show Book*, London: Purnell.

Fergusson, T. and J. Cunnison, 1956. *In Their Early Twenties: A Study of Glasgow Youth*, London: Oxford University Press.

Foss, Daniel and Ralph Larkin, 1976. 'From "The Gates of Eden" to "Day of the Locust": an analysis of the dissident youth movement of the 1960s and its heirs of the early 1970s – the post-movement groups', *Theory and Society*, vol. 3, no. 1.

Fowler, David, 1995. *The First Teenagers: The Lifestyle of Young Wage-Earners in Interwar Britain*, London: Woburn.

Frith, Simon, 1978. *The Sociology of Rock*, London: Constable.

—— 1983. *Sound Effects: Youth, Leisure and the Politics of Rock'n'Roll*, London: Constable.

—— 1990. 'Frankie said: but what did they mean?', in Alan Tomlinson (ed.), *Consumption, Identity and Style: Marketing, Meanings and the Packaging of Pleasure*, London: Routledge, pp. 172–85.

—— 1993. 'Youth/music/television', in Simon Frith, Andrew Goodwin and Lawrence Grossberg (eds), *Sound and Vision: The Music Video Reader*, London: Routledge, pp. 67–84.

Fryer, Peter, 1984. *Staying Power: The History of Black People in Britain*, London: Pluto Press.

Furlong, Andy and Fred Cartmel, 1997. *Young People and Social Change: Individualization and Risk in Late Modernity*, Buckingham: Open University Press.

Fyvel, T. R., 1963. *The Insecure Offenders: Rebellious Youth in the Welfare State*, Harmondsworth: Pelican.

Garratt, Sheryl, 1984. 'All of us loves all of you', in Sue Steward and Sheryl Garratt (eds) *Signed, Sealed and Delivered: True Stories of Women in Pop*, London: Pluto Press, pp. 140–51.

Garside, W. R., 1977. 'Juvenile unemployment and public policy between the wars', *Economic History Review*, vol. 30, pp. 322–39.

Gelder, Ken and Sarah Thornton (eds), 1997. *The Subcultures Reader*, London: Routledge.

Gillis, John, 1974. *Youth and History*, New York: Academic Press.

—— 1975. 'The evolution of juvenile delinquency in England 1890–1914', *Past and Present*, vol. 67, pp. 96–126.

Gilroy, Paul, 1987. *'There Ain't No Black in the Union Jack'*: *The Cultural Politics of Race and Nation*, London: Hutchinson.

—— and Errol Lawrence, 1988. 'Two-tone Britain: white and black youth and the politics of anti-racism', in P. Cohen and H. S. Bains (eds), *Multi-Racist Britain*, London: Pluto Press, pp. 121–55.

Guthrie, Robin, 1963. 'The biggest years in a boy's life', *New Society*, vol. 1, no. 16, 17 January, pp. 19–21.

Hall, G. Stanley, 1904. *Adolescence: Its Psychology and Its Relation to Physiology, Anthropology, Sociology, Sex, Crime, Religion and Education*, New York: Appleton.

Hall, Stuart, 1987. 'Minimal selves', in Lisa Appignanesi (ed.), *Identity*, ICA Documents 6, London: Institute of Contemporary Arts.

—— 1990. 'Cultural identity and diaspora', in Jonathan Rutherford (ed.), *Identity*, London: Lawrence and Wishart.

—— 1992a. 'New ethnicities', in James Donald and Ali Rattansi (eds), *'Race', Culture and Difference*, London: Sage, pp. 252–60.

—— 1992b. 'The question of cultural identity', in Stuart Hall, David Held and Tony McGrew (eds), *Modernity and its Futures*, Oxford: Polity Press, pp. 273–327.

Halsey, A. H., 1988, 'Higher education', in A. H. Halsey (ed.), *British Social Trends Since 1900: A Guide to the Changing Social Structure of Britain*, 2nd edn, Basingstoke: Macmillan.

Hamblett, Charles and Jane Deverson, 1964. *Generation X*, London: Tandem.

Hargreaves, David, 1967. *Social Relations in a Secondary School*, London: Routledge and Kegan Paul.

Hawes, Derek, 1966. *Young People Today: An Account of Young People in Voluntary Youth Organisations*, London: National Council of Social Service.

Hebdige, Dick, 1976. 'The meaning of mod', in Stuart Hall and Tony Jefferson (eds) *Resistance Through Rituals: Youth Subcultures in Post-War Britain*, London: Hutchinson, pp. 87–98.

—— 1979. *Subculture: The Meaning of Style*, London: Methuen.

—— 1987. *Cut'n'Mix: Culture, Identity and Caribbean Music*, London: Methuen.

—— 1988a. 'Towards a cartography of taste, 1935–1962', in Dick Hebdige, *Hiding in the Light: On Images and Things*, London: Routledge, pp. 45–76.

—— 1988b. 'Hiding in the light: youth surveillance and display', in Dick Hebdige, *Hiding in the Light: On Images and Things*, London: Routledge, pp. 17–36.

—— 1989. 'After the masses', in Stuart Hall and Martin Jacques (eds), *New Times: The Changing Face of Politics in the 1990s*, London: Lawrence and Wishart, pp. 76–93.

Hill, John, 1991. 'Television and pop: the case of the 1950s', in John Corner (ed.),

Popular Television in Britain: Studies in Cultural History, London: BFI, pp. 90–107.

Hoggart, Richard, 1958. *The Uses of Literacy*, Harmondsworth: Penguin.

Hopkins, Harry, 1963. *The New Look: A Social History of the Forties and Fifties*, London: Secker and Warburg.

Jameson, Frederic, 1984. 'Postmodernism or the cultural logic of late capitalism', *New Left Review*, vol. 146, pp. 53–92.

Jephcott, Pearl, 1954. *Some Young People*, London: Allen and Unwin.

—— 1967. *A Time of One's Own*, Edinburgh: Oliver and Boyd.

Kaplan, E. Ann, 1987. *Rocking Around the Clock: Music Television, Postmodernism and Consumer Culture*, London: Routledge.

Kempster, Chris (ed.), 1996. *History of House*, London: Sanctuary.

Labour Party Youth Commission, 1959. *The Younger Generation*, London: Labour Party.

Laing, Dave, 1997. 'Rock anxieties and new music networks', in Angela McRobbie (ed.), *Back to Reality? Social Experience and Cultural Studies*, London: Routledge, pp. 116–32.

Laurie, Peter, 1965. *The Teenage Revolution*, London: Anthony Blond.

Lewis, Peter, 1978. *The Fifties*, London: Heinemann.

Lewis, Peter M., 1991. 'Mummy, matron and the maids: feminine presence and absence in male institutions, 1934–63', in Michael Roper and John Tosh (eds), *Manful Assertions: Masculinities in Britain Since 1800*, London: Routledge, pp. 168–89.

Lydon, John, 1994. *No Irish, No Blacks, No Dogs*, Coronet: London.

Lyotard, Jean François, 1984. *The Postmodern Condition: A Report on Knowledge*, Manchester: Manchester University Press.

Makeham, Peter, 1980. *Youth Unemployment*, Research Paper 11, London: Department of Employment.

Marcuse, Herbert, 1972. *Counterrevolution and Revolt*, Boston: Beacon.

Marks, Anthony, 1990. 'Young gifted and black: Afro-American and Afro-Caribbean music in Britain 1963–88', in Paul Oliver (ed.), *Black Music in Britain: Essays on the Afro-Asian Contribution to Popular Music*, Milton Keynes: Open University Press, pp. 102–17.

Marsh, Peter, 1977. 'Dole-queue rock', *New Society*, vol. 39, no. 746, 20 January, pp. 112–14.

McKay, George, 1996. 'The free festivals and fairs of Albion', in George McKay, *Senseless Acts of Beauty: Cultures of Resistance Since the Sixties*, London: Verso, pp. 11–44.

McGrew, Anthony, 1992. 'A global society?', in Stuart Hall, David Held and Tony McGrew (eds), *Modernity and Its Futures*, Cambridge: Polity Press, pp. 61–116.

McRobbie, Angela, 1991. *Feminism and Youth Culture: From 'Jackie' to 'Just Seventeen'*, London: Macmillan.

—— 1994a. 'Postmodernism and popular culture', in Angela McRobbie, *Postmodernism and Popular Culture*, London: Routledge, pp. 13–23.

—— 1994b. 'The moral panic in the age of the postmodern mass media', in Angela McRobbie, *Postmodernism and Popular Culture*, London: Routledge, pp. 198–219.

—— and Jenny Garber, 1976. 'Girls and subcultures: an exploration', in Stuart Hall and Tony Jefferson (eds), *Resistance Through Rituals: Youth Subcultures in Post-War Britain*, London: Hutchinson, pp. 209–21.

Melechi, Antonio, 1993. 'The ecstasy of disappearance', in Steve Redhead (ed.), *Rave Off: Politics and Deviance in Contemporary Youth Culture*, Aldershot: Avebury, pp. 29–40.

Melly, George, 1972. *Revolt into Style: The Pop Arts in Britain*, Harmondsworth: Penguin.

Middles, Mick, 1996. *From Joy Division to New Order: The Factory Story*, London: Virgin.

Ministry of Education, 1947. *School Life: A First Enquiry into the Transition from School to Independent Life* (Clarke Report), London: HMSO.

—— 1960. *The Youth Service in England and Wales* (Albermarle Report), London: HMSO.

Morgan, A. E., 1939. *The Needs of Youth*, London: Oxford University Press.

Mort, Frank, 1988. 'Boys own? Masculinity, style and popular culture', in Rowena Chapman and Jonathan Rutherford (eds), *Male Order: Unwrapping Masculinity*, London: Lawrence and Wishart, pp. 193–224.

Murdock, Graham and Robin McCron, 1973. 'Scoobies, skins and contemporary pop', *New Society*, no. 547 pp. 690–2.

—— and —— 1976. 'Youth and class: the career of a confusion', in Geoff Mungham and Geoff Pearson (eds), *Working Class Youth Culture*, London: Routledge and Kegan Paul, pp. 10–26.

Murray, Robin, 1989. 'Fordism and post-Fordism', in Stuart Hall and Martin Jacques (eds), *New Times: The Changing Face of Politics in the 1990s*, London: Lawrence and Wishart, pp. 38–53.

Musgrove, Frank, 1974. *Ecstasy and Holiness: Counter Culture and the Open Society*, London: Methuen.

Nava, Mica, 1984. 'Youth service provision, social order and the question of girls', in Angela McRobbie and Mica Nava (eds), *Gender and Generation*, London: Macmillan, pp. 1–30.

Nelson, Elizabeth, 1989. *The British Counter-Culture, 1966–73: A Study of the Underground Press*, London: Macmillan.

Newsom, John, 1948. *The Education of Girls*, London: Faber and Faber.

Parker, Howard, 1974. *A View From the Boys*, Newton Abbot: David and Charles.

Pearson, Geoffrey, 1983. *Hooligan: A History of Respectable Fears*, London: Macmillan.

Phizacklea, Annie and Robert Miles, 1979. 'Working class racist beliefs in the inner-city', in Robert Miles and Annie Phizacklea (eds), *Racism and Political Action in Britain*, London: Routledge, pp. 93–123.

Pitts, John, 1988. *The Politics of Juvenile Crime*, London: Sage.

Polhemus, Ted, 1994. *Streetstyle: From Sidewalk to Catwalk*, London: Thames and Hudson.

Polsky, Ned, 1971. *Hustlers, Beats and Others*, Harmondsworth: Pelican.

Prison Reform Trust, 1993. *Trends in Juvenile Crime and Punishment*, Juvenile Justice Paper 4, London: Prison Reform Trust.

Raffe, David, 1985. *Youth Unemployment in the UK 1979–84*, Edinburgh: Centre for Educational Sociology.

Redhead, Steve, 1990. *The End of the Century Party: Youth and Pop Towards 2000*, Manchester: Manchester University Press.

—— 1991. 'Rave off: youth, subcultures and the law', *Social Studies Review*, vol. 6, no. 3, pp. 92–4.

—— 1993a. 'The politics of ecstasy', in Steve Redhead (ed.), *Rave Off: Politics and Deviance in Contemporary Youth Culture*, Aldershot: Avebury, pp. 7–28.

—— (ed.), 1993b. *Rave Off: Politics and Deviance in Contemporary Youth Culture*, Aldershot: Avebury.

—— and Eugene McLauglin, 1985. 'Soccer's style wars', *New Society*, vol. 73, no. 1181, 16 August, pp. 225–8.

Reich, Charles, 1972. *The Greening of America*, Harmondsworth: Penguin.

Rietveld, Hillegonda, 1991. *Living the Dream: Analysis of the Rave-Phenomenon in Terms of Ideology, Consumerism and Subculture*, Manchester: Unit for Law and Popular Culture, Manchester Polytechnic.

—— 1993. 'Living the dream', in Steve Redhead (ed.), *Rave Off: Politics and Deviance in Contemporary Youth Culture*, Aldershot: Avebury, pp. 41–78.

Roberts, Kenneth, 1995. *Youth and Employment in Modern Britain*, Oxford: Oxford University Press.

Roberts, Robert, 1973. *The Classic Slum*, Harmondsworth: Pelican.

Rock, Paul and Stanley Cohen, 1970. 'The Teddy boy', in Vernon Bogdanor and Robert Skidelsky (eds), *The Age of Affluence, 1951–64*, London: Macmillan, pp. 288–320.

Ross, Andrew, 1992. 'New Age technoculture', in Lawrence Grossberg, Cary Nelson and Paula Treichler (eds), *Cultural Studies*, London: Routledge.

Roszak, Theodore, 1970. *The Making of a Counter-Culture: Reflections on the Technocratic Society and Its Youthful Opposition*, London: Doubleday.

Rowbotham, Sheila, 1985. 'Revolt in Roundhay', in Liz Heron (ed.), *Truth, Dare or Promise: Girls Growing Up in the Fifties*, London: Virago, pp. 189–212.

Rutter, M., P. Graham, O. F. D. Chadwick and W. Yule, 1976. 'Adolescent turmoil: fact or fiction?', *Journal of Child Psychology and Psychiatry*, vol. 17, pp. 35–56.

Saunders, Nicholas, 1995. *Ecstasy and the Dance Culture*, London: Saunders.

Smith, Cyril, 1966. *Young People: A Report on Bury*, Manchester: University of Manchester.

Springhall, John, 1980. *Coming of Age: Adolescence in Britain, 1860–1960*, Dublin: Gill and Macmillan.

Stewart, Gill and John Stewart, 1993. *Social Circumstances of Young Offenders Under Supervision*, London: ACOP.

Storch, Robert, 1975. 'The plague of blue locusts: police reform and popular resistance in northern England, 1840–57', *International Review of Social History*, no. 20, pp. 61–90.

Sugarman, Barry, 1967. 'Improvement in youth culture: academic achievement and conformity in school', *British Journal of Sociology*, vol. 18, pp. 151–64.

Taylor, Derek, 1987. *It Was Twenty Years Ago Today*, London: Bantam.

Thompson, Paul, 1975. *The Edwardians: The Remaking of British Society*, London: Weidenfeld.

Thornton, Sarah, 1995. *Club Cultures: Music, Media and Subcultural Capital*, London: Polity Press.

Tuck, Mary, 1989. *Drinking and Disorder: A Study of Non-Metropolitan Violence*, Home Office Research Study 108, London: HMSO.

Tutt, Norman, 1980. 'Reforming the juvenile justice system', *Journal of Adolescence*, vol. 3, no. 1, pp. 11–16.

Weir, Stuart, 1978. 'Youngsters in the frontline', *New Society*, vol. 44, no. 812, 27 April, pp. 189–93.

West, M. and P. Newton, 1983. *The Transition from Work to School*, London: Croom Helm.

Wilkins, L. T., 1960. *Delinquent Generations*, London: HMSO.

Willcock, H. D., 1949. *Report on Juvenile Delinquency: A Mass Observation Report*, London: Falcon Press.

Willis, Paul, 1977. *Learning to Labour: How Working Class Kids Get Working Class Jobs*, London: Gower.

Willis, Paul, 1978. *Profane Culture*, London: Routledge and Kegan Paul.

Willmott, Peter, 1966. *Adolescent Boys of East London*, Harmondsworth: Pelican.

York, Peter, 1980. *Style Wars*, London: Sidgwick and Jackson.

Young, Jock, 1971. *The Drugtakers: The Social Meaning of Drug Use*, London: Paladin.

Youth Service Development Council, 1969. *Youth and Community Work in the Seventies*, London: HMSO.

Zweig, Ferdynand, 1963. *The Student in the Age of Anxiety: A Survey of Oxford and Manchester Students*, London: Heinemann.

Index

254   *Index*